Carl Nicolai Starcke

The primitive family in its origin and development

Carl Nicolai Starcke

The primitive family in its origin and development

ISBN/EAN: 9783337414436

Printed in Europe, USA, Canada, Australia, Japan

Cover: Foto ©ninafisch / pixelio.de

More available books at **www.hansebooks.com**

THE INTERNATIONAL SCIENTIFIC SERIES

THE

PRIMITIVE FAMILY

IN ITS ORIGIN AND DEVELOPMENT

BY

C. N. STARCKE, Ph. D.

OF THE UNIVERSITY OF COPENHAGEN

NEW YORK

D. APPLETON AND COMPANY

1889

PREFACE.

IT has been my aim in this work to ascertain the nature of the primitive family, and to point out the ideas on which it is based, as well as the germ of moral growth which it contains. The family, however, exists within a larger community, by which it is influenced, so that such a task impels us at every turn to exceed its narrow limits. The difficulty of resisting this impulse is increased by the fact that it has been necessary to give a mainly critical character to this work. The theories previously set forth, to which we are opposed, have, generally speaking, neither admitted nor defined the border-line between the clan and the family, so that we were compelled to adapt our criticism to these theories. Since, however, we had no desire to increase the size of our work, and the number of the problems on which it touches, beyond measure, we decided only to enter into these questions so far as criticism demands, and to restrict ourselves within narrower limits whenever it was possible. Hence there may be a certain want of proportion in the course taken in these inquiries, and we ask our readers' forgiveness, wherever this is the case.

C. N. STARCKE.

COPENHAGEN,
January, 1888.

CONTENTS.

—◆◇◆—

INTRODUCTION.

SECTION I.

DEFINITION OF KINSHIP.

CHAPTER I.

AUSTRALIA.

CHAPTER II.

AMERICA.

SECTION II.

THE PRIMITIVE FAMILY.

CHAPTER I.

FATHER AND CHILD.

CHAPTER II.

POLYANDRY.

CHAPTER III.

THE LEVIRATE AND NIYOGA.

CHAPTER IV.

INHERITANCE BY BROTHERS, AND OTHER SUPPOSED PROOFS OF POLYANDRY.

2

CHAPTER V.

NOMENCLATURES.

CHAPTER VI.

EXOGAMY AND ENDOGAMY.

CHAPTER VII.

MARRIAGE AND ITS DEVELOPMENT.

CHAPTER VIII.

THE FAMILY, THE CLAN, AND THE TRIBE—CONCLUSION.

THE PRIMITIVE FAMILY.

INTRODUCTION.

The comparative method—The materials for inquiry—The hypotheses of evolution and degradation—Question of uniformity of primitive state —Anthropology and philology—Plan of inquiry—Border-line between institutions originally fluctuating—Groups of kinship—The primitive tie of blood.

THE researches which we propose to make in the present work lead us into paths which have of late years been trodden by many men of more or less importance. In earlier times an attempt was often made to construct the process of man's physical development in accordance with the conceptions of abstract speculation. The worthlessness of this process is now established, and it is only through the analytical method of comparative history that we can hope to understand the historical facts of this development. The importance of the comparative method is well known to philologists. In his valuable work on *Comparative Politics*, Freeman asserts that the discovery of this method is an event of sufficient importance to distinguish our century as one of the great eras in the history of mankind. Even if this estimate is exaggerated, it must be admitted that the comparative method has diffused light over many things which previously lay in the deepest darkness. The relationship between different races has been ascertained by the method in question, and it has taught us how to form a conception of the stage of culture attained by the primitive race.

The fitness of this method is explained by the special character of the subject. The sound-symbols which designate given objects were for the most part quite arbitrarily chosen, and it is therefore improbable that two distinct peoples should ever have chosen the same symbol for the same object. Whenever, therefore, we find such agreement, we may almost certainly infer, either that one people has borrowed the word from the other, or that both peoples are derived from one and the same primitive stock. A careful analysis will establish the store of words which were used by this primitive stock. By means of these words we learn what ideas were common to the race, or, in other words, what was their state of civilization.

When we have to do with matters which do not involve such an arbitrary choice, the use of this method cannot afford equally good results. Similar legends and myths, similar social institutions, usages, and customs cannot be taken as a proof of common origin, since these resemblances may result from causes which occur quite independently in different places and at different periods. The comparative method here serves another purpose, by making it possible to discover the definite causes from which given myths and institutions necessarily result. In this case the comparative method only serves for the application of the ordinary methods of experimental inquiry to a field which is withdrawn from direct experimental control. When, for example, races which we have reason to believe are uninfluenced by each other, possess any institution in common, it may be surmised that the cause must be sought in the relative conditions which are common to all races. As soon as this preliminary assumption has been made, we must inquire whether there is any race in which the institution is found without these relative conditions, or if the conditions occur without the institution. And, finally, we must inquire whether, during the development of a race, the institution and the relative conditions can vary, independently of each other. The results which may be obtained in this way will be almost of equal value with those of the exact sciences. The conditions of social development are generally so complex that the possibility of error must be admitted, and it is well to remember this. Yet I believe that too great allowance has been made for such error, since, although we have to do with forces which cannot be included within the range of experience already mentioned, yet it is most probable that these forces are so insignificant that they need not be taken into account.

We have already said that many scientific men have made use of the comparative method in the study of the primitive forms of the social life of man, and of its modes of development, as well as of its limits and stages. Yet we find a wide difference of opinion among them, both with respect to the more important points of view, and to smaller questions of detail. In such cases it may be supposed that facts which are interpreted by competent inquirers in quite opposite ways are absolutely useless for the purposes of science. This would, however, be an error, since it is the common fate of every dawning science to advance gradually from daring hypothesis to truth. I propose in this work to attempt to make a slight step in advance, and if errors should occur, the fault is not to be found in the material, but in the use I make of it.

The material may be divided into several sections: (1) We have direct historical accounts of the development of a single community during a long period; (2) the narratives of travellers, who have described an isolated phase of the life, as it existed at the time, of a race either now extinct or still living; (3) ancient laws and customs, recorded in writing; (4) ancient myths and legends, and archæological remains, by means of which we may reconstruct periods of which we have no direct observation. It is also absolutely necessary to be acquainted with psychology, in order not to be misled by deceptive appearance. It must be taken for granted that we are not, in this case, bound to prove the trustworthiness of our material. Such proof, which is very difficult, must be assumed to have been given elsewhere. We must now subjoin the following fundamental considerations.

In order to become acquainted with the development of a given community, we can desire no better material than the reports of its condition at different times, as they have come down to us. In fact, however, this mode of establishing laws, or general rules of development, is only possible to a limited extent. For the most part we are without the means of constructing such abstractions as are necessary to establish laws, since the material is far from being sufficient to entitle us to draw conclusions with respect to the non-existence of negative instances. There are comparatively few communities of which we possess sufficient records, and these moreover only include a limited portion of the life of the community in question; we must remain absolutely ignorant of the long pre-historic period. We may indeed admit the possibility of discovering an apparent solidarity in the social development. For we may become acquainted with the primitive condition and earliest development of a community by means of the report of another community of higher civilization, which goes back to the period in which the former had its origin. Yet this solidarity is only apparent. No primitive community can be carefully observed for any length of time by a civilized community without being placed in such relations to the latter as to modify it in many ways, so as to affect its actual development in a way which will not permit us to draw general conclusions with respect to the spontaneous development of any given community. Hence it becomes necessary to form our ideas of the primitive conditions of given historical peoples in accordance with the conditions of primitive races still in existence.

But in order to adopt this course, two conditions are necessary, neither of which will stand alone. We have first to assume the rude primitive origin of such a community; and secondly, that the original conditions of races have so much in common, that their development usually passes through the same general phases. I take the first of these assumptions to be now indisputable, and indeed it is generally accepted. But I only conditionally admit the second assumption to be correct in a very general sense.

It is an admitted fact, that when men first became aware that the earth is not the centre of the universe, and that the sun does not really move above our heads, they for a long while found it impossible to reconcile this new view with the Bible history of creation. Subsequently they became resigned to the inevitable, and found it possible to bring the Bible and natural science into agreement by defining their conception of the biblical narrative in accordance with the results of science. Whenever one of these old narratives is corrected by a scientific man, the same conflict arises, and it is always decided in the same way. That the Darwinian theory should have effected a metamorphosis of the old conception of the biblical story,[1] affords the strongest proof of the deep roots which this theory has taken in common opinion. And the difficulty of reconciling such theories with biblical history is shown by the tardy manner in which concessions are made. While the theory of the origin of the arts is for the most part accepted, the first consequence of this theory is obsti-

---

[1] Fabro d'Envieu, *Les Origines de la Terre et de l'Homme.*

nately opposed: namely, the progressive development of civilization. It is, even now, affirmed that our forefather Adam was very superior to the rude men whom we still find in various parts of the world. From Adam's relatively high position, men are supposed to have developed on the one hand, under the Divine guidance, into even higher civilization, and on the other, their sins have subjected them to the wrath of God, and have degraded them into the hopelessly backward races which we call Bushmans or Negritos. It appears to me unnecessary to show how far this theory is from agreeing with the facts of archæology, and I am content to show that the degradation theory is now beginning to appear unsatisfactory under the pressure of the time. Mr. Fison, an Australian missionary, frankly declares that he does not see why the degradation theory should be regarded as an orthodox necessity.[1] Adam appears to him to have resembled the Australians. I need therefore only offer a few objections to the theory in question.

The degradation theory is worthless, unless it can be founded on certain knowledge; this is so far from being the case that it implies an absolute breach with all that we know of the development of mankind. All scientific knowledge is founded on the connection of phenomena in that series of natural causes and effects which is accounted to be possible. If we are compelled to leave the problem of the first cause unsolved, the breach which occurs in our knowledge must be assigned to the sphere of metaphysics, by which men are not directly affected. But we can only admit a similar breach in our knowledge of concrete empirical phenomena, when the reasons for doing so are irresistible. We admit that psychical forces cannot be referred to physical causes, so that their occurrence in the empirical world is still an unexplained phenomenon; but it is quite another matter to admit that a psychical being can come into the world in posses-

---

[1] Fison and Howitt, p. 161.

sion of such a perfect psychical organization that it cannot be explained by a prior existence of other psychical beings. The degradation theory can therefore only be accepted if it is possible to adduce undoubted and direct proofs of its truth; it is by no means to be accepted until another which is completely satisfactory can be substituted for it. The theory of progression is in agreement with the organization of our thinking faculty, while the theory of degradation imposes upon us a complete abnegation of knowledge.

The second assumption which must be established, if we are with undoubting confidence to make use of the material afforded by the descriptions of primitive communities, is that the primitive condition of all human communities is virtually the same. We find distinct varieties of a given animal species, living under very distinct social forms, and we have no reason to suppose that these forms have not been distinct, as long as the varieties themselves have been distinct. So likewise we may perhaps assume that distinct social forms date from the time when men were scattered into several communities. The question as to a uniform primitive state involves the question: What is meant by a primitive state?

If it is assumed that mankind sprang from a single ancestral pair, it follows as a matter of course that all peoples have passed through the same primitive state. I doubt, however, whether such a statement will satisfy those who maintain that mankind had a uniform origin: such an assumption would have no weight with them. That the primitive community with which we are now concerned should have been of such a nature as to affect its subsequent modifications, can neither be affirmed nor denied: the primitive community must ever be an hypothetical construction, designed to explain the existent forms, and it cannot become the subject of practical experience. So long as we are within the sphere of experience, we cannot begin by assuming that there was at any time only a single human community. Experience begins with a plurality of communities, and the single community of which we are in search must be found on the indeterminate boundary between man and animals. If this boundary were sharply defined, it would be comparatively easy to show what is meant by primitive man; but the sharp line which now divides the highest type of animal from the lowest type of man can only be explained by the fact that the intermediate forms have become extinct. The assumption of an indeterminate boundary between man and animals only means that it is impossible, throughout the long series of intermediate forms, to point to two in succession, of which the one is undoubtedly a lower animal, and the other undoubtedly a man. We can no more discover the first primitive community than we can discover the first man; the history of mankind begins with a plurality of distinct groups, and hence the fact of a uniform beginning is at any rate doubtful.

Another consequence of the assumption of an indeterminate line between man and animals may here be adduced. We have no reason to regard the social life of man as a recent form. Not only do the same psychical forces which influence gregarious man also influence the gregarious animal; probability also leads us to infer that the primitive communities of mankind are derived from those of animals. Since man in so many respects only goes on to develop the previous achievements of animal experience, it may be supposed that he made use of the social experience of animals as the firm foundation of his higher advancement. An inquiry into the primitive human community merely implies a research into the solidarity between man and animals in their social relations; the inquiry is not concerned with a rude state which possesses none of the social faculties, since these faculties are exercised by the lowest human communities with which we are acquainted.

The distinction between the animal and the human community does not appear to me to depend on the larger or smaller number of useful acts performed by the individuals comprised in the community, since there are human communities which are far less firmly established than those of animals. It may even be asserted that the social faculty is positive in animals and negative in man. The social instinct of animals attaches them to their community, while man is generally restrained from breaking social bonds by fear of the dangers which threaten the race from without. Man is less subservient to his instincts than animals are, and although he is also influenced by inclination and inherited impulses, at any rate the underlying motive assumes the form of reason. The reasons which affect him may be insufficient, yet he finds them convincing, and they show that he is impelled to assign an explanation for his impulse. The different forms which the explanation may take depends on all sorts of accidental circumstances. We cannot refrain from ascribing to this explanation an influence on the development of given instincts, but it is a more probable assumption that it is due to a certain unlikeness in the earliest human communities. Yet when we estimate the importance of this possible unlikeness, we have no reason to regard it as considerable. We may lay down this principle to guide our judgment: that in the same proportion in which a given way of life can be explained by the natural conditions of primitive life, it must be held to be common to all. Nothing but the apparent influence of special ideas will compel us to decide on the distinction between several races. We shall presently show that the most important features of the life of a community are due to forces at once simple and universal; we do not hesitate to renounce the possible reconstruction of special characteristics, since we are only concerned with general causes.

We may now consider both the distinction and the

3

connection which exist between our present undertaking and that of the philologist.

The philologist is concerned with the relationship between peoples which are historically distinct, and to this we are indifferent. We are, however, agreed in taking an interest in the state of civilization of the ancestral race; yet here also there is an essential difference between us. The philologist wishes to introduce as many details as possible into his description of the primitive state, while we desire to define its general character. It is not always possible to infer the general character of the whole from these details, and the philologist often finds that the use of definite words proves nothing, since several ideas and conceptions may be comprised in one and the same word. Hehn has pointed out that the existence of the word "horse," for example, does not entitle us to infer that the horse was used as a domestic animal. The difficulty is still greater when we come to the organization of family life and of the race. It is wholly impossible to infer from words alone what were the opinions held by communities, and, as we shall presently show, they do not even reveal to us the external organization. The nomenclature of the degrees of kinship presents many difficulties, and the functions imposed upon a "king" may differ widely. In order to form a picture of the primitive life of our forefathers, we must have learned how to estimate the general effect of social forces by means of our observation of the primitive peoples still in existence.

As far as the scheme of the following inquiries is concerned, it seems to present no difficulty. We propose to study the origin and primitive development of the family; and nothing can be more simple than the description of family life in different communities. It is, however, impossible to keep the different institutions distinct, since the differentiation which occurred was gradual, and the characteristic features by which we now distinguish the family and the state are valueless from the primitive standpoint. We have therefore no choice, but must decide to give a general description of the typical character of the primitive community, and to go on from this to discover the way in which differentiation took place. Some remarks which may serve as a cursory definition of our point of view will not be out of place.

It is not necessary to observe the primitive communities very closely in order to become aware that each human community consists of smaller groups, which are held together by ideas of kinship. This would imply that the family was a primitive institution; yet it does not mean that the original organization of the family was the same as that of later times, or that our ideas and conceptions prevailed in the family in its beginning. ✗The word "family" may be used in different senses. It is sometimes applied only to parents and to the unmarried children who remain at home; the family sometimes includes all the descendants of a living pair, including sons' wives and daughters' husbands; sometimes again we mean by a family all the blood relations, both by direct and collateral descent, exclusive of cases in which the relationship is so remote that it cannot be taken into account. None of these meanings can be disregarded, since under certain conditions each may come into play. The feature common to whatever is now termed a family is, that the kinship becomes more remote in proportion to its distance from the connection between parent and child : brothers and sisters are not so closely related to each other as each of them is to the parents.

In the primitive races this is by no means the case. Some of their ideas of kinship appear to us to be quite unintelligible. The primitive man often makes no distinction between degrees of kinship which are carefully distinguished by us, and which imply very different degrees of kinship in blood. Each of these groups is a

family, because it is believed to spring from a common
ancestor, either male or female; but the degrees in collateral lines, which play such an important part with us,
find no place with them. Where the "family group"
predominates, the family, in its narrower sense of parents
and children, may still be found; but it is by no means
of the same strength and importance as it is with us;
indeed, it is so little apparent that it has sometimes been
supposed that the family in this sense had originally no
existence.

In order to avoid confusion in what follows, we will
distinctly state the terms by which we propose to represent the different forms of the family. The word *family*
will only be used for the small group of parents and
children. We shall designate by the name of *family group*
the group which includes different generations, taking
into account their more or less remote kinship. The
group in which the different degrees of kinship are not
taken into account belongs to the category of a *clan*.
We shall only use the word *race* for a collection of individuals who live together and possess the bond of a
common habitation, language, etc. A race may include
a number of clans, of family groups, and of families, and
the same clan may be dispersed among several races. It
will be asked whether there was any original distinction
between the race and the clan. The race must be taken
as the primitive form of development into a state, but
the clan must be classified under those forms which are
founded on the idea of kinship. Yet I have reason to
think that the modern state was developed out of the
clan, and that the organization of our families is only to
a limited extent derived from the organization of the
clan. The following remark must, however, be made.

A family is founded by marriage, and in this respect
our circumstances do not differ from those of primitive
times. It is evident that we cannot suppose marriage
to have been in all times such a sacred institution as it

has now become. In its widest sense, marriage is only a connection between man and woman which is of more than momentary duration, and as long as it endures they seek for subsistence in common. A family group, and still more a clan, is compacted by blood kinship, that is, each individual is born a member of the group. Thus we have two distinct and apparently incompatible foundations for the associated family. The family becomes more closely compacted in proportion to the sacred character of the marriage tie between the parents; on the other hand, there is a character of stability in the family group and clan, which is neither founded nor dissolved, but merely present and living. These groups resemble glaciers; they appear to be always the same, always stationary, yet in reality they are always in motion, and ever renewing their youth. Generation after generation is born, lives, and dies; families are founded and again dissolved, while the clan persists unchanged.

The family is therefore distinguished from the family group and the clan as a group of kinsfolk established by contract, and only in a subsidiary sense by the tie of blood between parents and children; and yet it is precisely to this tie of blood that special weight is attached in the family. The family group has its origin in the family, starting from a married pair and their children. The part which contract plays in the organization of the family cannot be kept out of sight in considering the family group. This appears from the fact that such a group cannot in theory be restricted to its series of descendants. The blood of the family issues from two sources, both from the father and mother, and it would be absurd to look for only one source, one beginning of the family and the family group. There is, as we have already said, this distinction between the clan and the family group, that it is only the latter which considers the degree of kinship. Individuals are born into the family group on a definite condition which cannot be set aside; the homogeneous mass of the clan does not admit of any such definite distinction. While the family group extends in all directions and becomes connected with other groups, it is the tendency of the clan to shrink into its shell, and in proportion as it becomes allied with others, it is transformed into a family group. It is in this particular that the clan fundamentally differs from other communities allied by blood, and we shall attempt in the following pages to prove the extent of this difference.

The individual who is born a member of a clan, possesses given rights and duties. The clan consists of a group allied by blood, endowed with important juridical rights, and we find that when it is in its most flourishing state, the rights which are founded upon contract are extremely weak. The legal position of the family appears to be in proportion to the sacredness of the marriage tie, and when hereditary rights are mentioned in the regulation of the conflicting claims of parents and children, closer observation shows that a conception of the sacred claims of blood is less powerful than the consideration of the engagements which preceded the voluntary act of marriage. This contrast between the clan and the family seems to me to be of great importance. In the family the power of the ties of blood is of quite indefinite extent, and depends in each case on mutual sympathy; in the clan the rights are clearly defined, even though the tie of blood may eventually be regarded as doubtful.

For this reason we shall be justified in regarding with some scepticism the efforts which have been made to place the family on the same plane as the clan, as a community connected by ties of blood. I do not think it advisable, in the absence of irrefragable proof, to compare groups, in one of which the actual tie of blood is of comparatively slight legal importance, while in the other a tie of blood which is often imaginary has an important effect on the legal position. If the tie of blood were decisive, there would be an *à priori* reason for regarding the family as the foundation of the whole, and it is therefore remarkable that the importance of the family increases after it has ceased to insist on the tie of blood. The clan, however, loses its legal importance in the same proportion. The characteristic features which are here adduced will perhaps prove to be not unimportant. Enough has been said in this cursory estimate of our proposed inquiry into the way in which the clan became a group allied by blood, and the family became a privileged institution.

It has always been assumed as an undoubted fact that the tie of blood which keeps the clan together is founded on the same ideas as those which unite the family. The clan represents a group actually allied in blood, and it has been supposed to be a matter of indifference whether the common descent which is ascribed to the members of a clan is founded on reality or on fiction; it is enough that the life of the clan should be dominated by the idea of their common descent. Starting from this assumption, the attempt has been made to ascertain whether the family is a new formation in the clan, or if, on the contrary, the clan is an enlargement of the family. The rights of a clan and of a family must correspond, whether the clan be nominally or in reality a group allied by blood. In the former case, the fiction shows that it is only the tie of blood which supports the theory of rights, and thus enables the clan to act as a great family, and in the latter case the same remark holds good. In either case it would be possible to infer the organization of the clan from that which the family is, or was. Such an inference would be correct if the clan and the family were organizations of the same nature, but, as we have already said, we cannot begin by admitting this as an *à priori* assumption. We find groups of kinsfolk in the first beginnings of our communities, and this fact may be easily ascertained, but it is uncertain what is to be understood by the word "kinship." An inquiry into the original meaning and gradual development of the conception of kinship will constitute our first task, and only after this question has been decided can we apply ourselves to the special study of the family.

SECTION I.

THE DEFINITION OF KINSHIP.

One-sided definition of kinship—*À priori* and empirical
interpretation of the same.

IT has been already observed that, strictly speaking, a
family group can never be completely detached, since
the blood of the family flows from two sources. The
life of the child is given both by father and mother, and
if kinship is to be defined by descent, both parents must
be taken into account; the blood of both flows in the
child's veins. Yet it seems that this view, which appears to us to be in accordance both with nature and
with reason, is not accepted by many primitive peoples.
Wherever the clan is concerned, the child is either exclusively, or at any rate by preference assigned to one
or other of the parents. This fact has, especially of late,
been noticed by several learned men, who draw from
it conclusions with respect to the primitive form of the
family and of marriage. If the application is founded on
ideas of descent, it is easy to infer the nature of the
marriage bond from the general character of the mode
in which kinship is reckoned. If the child is referred
to both parents, or to the father alone, it has been assumed
that we may regard the connection between the sexes
as being so permanent that there can as a rule be no
doubt with respect to the fatherhood. On the other
hand, the fatherhood is not taken into account when the
sexual bond is a loose one, and under such circumstances
the descent can only be reckoned on the mother's side.

We find, indeed, a number of peoples in which this so-called female line prevails, and it has been inferred from this fact that the sexual relations of such races either still are, or were in not very remote times so unrestricted that there was no means of ascertaining the fatherhood; that is, that the primitive state was that of promiscuous intercourse.[1] This conclusion does not appear to me to be perfectly just. Although it must be admitted that a child whose father is unknown can only be assigned to the mother, as is still the case with illegitimate children, yet the converse does not necessarily hold good, namely, that the only reason for admitting female descent is that the father is unknown.

Agnation, or the reckoning of kinship through the father only, and not through the mother, is a fact parallel with that of female descent, yet no one has ever asserted that this is due to uncertainty with respect to the mother. The reckoning of kinship on one side only shows that, for some reason or other, no account is taken of one parent, but it in no way explains what that reason was. Here, if anywhere, an à priori interpretation is misleading, and no surmise is of any value except that which is supported by facts.

We meet with one obstacle in the investigation of questions with respect to the meaning of one-sided lines of descent. Many learned men are too much disposed to seek for the explanation of a given custom in conditions of former times which have now perhaps disappeared. It is certain that customs persist by the force of habit, even when the conditions which first gave birth to them have long ceased to exist; yet it is scarcely

---

[1] "It is inconceivable that anything but the want of certainty on that point (fatherhood) could have long prevented the acknowledgment of kinship through males" (McLennan, *Studies*, p. 129). Reference may also be made to other learned men—Spencer, Bachofen, some of Lubbock's writings, and, in a lower category, Engels, Lippert, Post, Wilken, Dargun, Giraud-Teulon, Kulischer, etc. Morgan takes up a position of his own.

necessary to remark that this appeal to early times can only be effective when it has been shown to be impossible to discover the cause of such customs in the conditions under which they still continue. If this main principle is not accepted, we shall be led astray by every idle delusion. If we are able to trace the cause of a custom in existing circumstances, we must abide by that cause, and nothing but a definite historical account of the prior existence of the custom can induce us to seek for another explanation. When we take the instance before us, we find that descent through the female line still occurs in cases in which the fatherhood may be ascertained, and if there are other circumstances which may explain the maintenance of the female line, we must for the present accept these as the cause. Definite historical accounts have in some instances pointed to promiscuous intercourse as the cause for tracing descent through the female line, yet this does not imply that it was the universal cause; for it is not an axiom, but an hypothesis which requires proof, that the primitive form of human communities was in all cases the same. Since the female line of descent has hitherto been explained by the *à priori* method, and this explanation has served as a basis for far-reaching theories, we must, in the first instance, carefully consider its historical forms. This study, however, requires such ample material, and it involves so many other questions that it may interfere with the proportions of this work. We propose to inquire what is implied by the female line of descent; what causes it involves; whether it is in every community the original line of kinship; and whether it does or does not essentially differ from agnation. As, however, we shall meet with many erroneous opinions, nothing but the most patient methods of induction can lead to certain conclusions. We must go step by step, from one land, from one race to another, and we must request our readers not to shrink from the trouble of following us.

CHAPTER I.

AUSTRALIA.

Hordes and clans—Isolated and mixed groups—Kobong group—Possession
and inheritance of land—The groups seek to effect local isolation—
Small groups more permanent than large ones—Australian prohibitions of marriage—One-sided definition of the clan, which is concerned with the latter, not with the family—The female line does not
imply promiscuous intercourse—The male line the more primitive—
Origin of female line.

It may appear to be arbitrary that I should choose to
begin with this quarter of the world, since we have no
accurate acquaintance with its primitive inhabitants. I
must admit that the choice is arbitrary, but this would
equally be the case with any other starting-point.

It is my object to inquire how far descent through
the female line prevails in Australia, and to which line
the child is assigned by its birth.

Many distinct tribes are scattered over the Australian
continent; each tribe inhabits a district of which the
limits are exactly defined, and no tribe ventures to exceed
those limits by violence, nor permits a stranger to invade
its own. They wander about within this territory, in
order to hunt game or collect roots, sometimes in detached
families, sometimes in large hordes. Such a horde is not,
however, a homogeneous mass, but consists of numerous
smaller divisions, the character of which is not fully
understood. The missionary Howitt states that the
Kurnai tribe in Gippsland [1] is divided into clans, each

[1] Fison and Howitt, p. 224. See Appendix I.

of which possesses its own portion of common land.
Howitt adds that the names of these clans express the
local position of each clan in the district. Thus one
clan is called *Brabrolung*, or "the men ;" another *Tatungo-
lung*, or "South men," and these inhabit the southern part
of the district; the third are men of the east; the fourth,
men of the west; the meaning of the fifth name, *Bratauo-
lung*, is not given. The inhabitants of each territory
believe in their descent from a common ancestor. Even
these groups are not homogeneous, but fall into minor
divisions, which are also called after the most important
localities in the district; only in one clan these subdivisions do not derive their names from the locality, but
from some man of note. It appears that a similar distribution occurs in other parts of the continent, but that
one of another kind, founded on quite different principles,
has interfered with it, so that it cannot now be clearly
traced.[1]

Nind states, speaking of the tribes in King George's
Sound, that they are divided into two classes, Erniung
and Tem, which do not, however, appear to be distinct
tribes. He mentions another distribution, into Moncalon and Torndirrup, and although one of these predominated in the east and the other in the west, yet it
could not be regarded as a tribal distribution. On the
other hand, the general mass seems to be divided into
tribes, one of which was in possession of a special name
and district, although such a tribe might include both
Torndirrups and Moncalons. These peculiar names seem
to be derived from the sterility or productiveness of the
soil.[2]

This last distribution, which has superseded the
former one, is apparently the same as the distribution

----

[1] *Monatsberichte der Gesellschaft für Erdkunde*, 11th series: Berlin,
1849, 1850. Ritter, *Brief*, p. 148. See Appendix II.
[2] *Journal Royal Geo. Soc.*, vol. i., 1832. Nind, *Description*, pp. 38, 42.
See Appendix III.

which was described by Grey, Eyre, and others, as derived from Kobong or Totem. The kobong of a man signifies the plant or animal from which he takes his name, and which he reverences in many ways as his protecting spirit. Both Nind and Grey state that the natives ascribe the origin of kobongs to the fact that individuals took the name of some plant or animal which was commonly found in the district.[1] These kobong groups constitute clans, since all those who have the same kobong are held to be in the same degree of kinship by blood. The character of the earlier groups does not come out so clearly, and very little can be ascertained of the relation which these two group-forms bear to each other.

We have only faint indications of the mode in which the kobong groups had their origin. Grey states that the people were afraid to kill an animal belonging to the species of their own kobong; but this was not the case with the tribes visited by Eyre, and he found that the kobong was not invariably inherited, although this was as a rule the case.[2] The kobong does not, in this instance, appear to cover the whole group of kinship. Waitz observes that individuals only appear to become connected with the kobong on attaining to the age of puberty.[3] Hence we may infer that the kobong group was established by sacred rights, not by heredity; and Spencer believes that the origin of the name must be traced to the custom which induced a mother to give the name of some animal to her child.[4] This does not, however, afford an explanation of the religious significance, and of the hereditary character of the kobong, for the names which the children receive at birth are not regarded with reverence, and are frequently changed.[5] Perhaps the meaning of the name as a tribal sign is not

[1] Grey, vol. ii. p. 228.   [2] Eyre, vol. ii. p. 328.
[3] Waitz, vol. vi. p. 788.   [4] Spencer, *Prin of Soc.*, p. 360.
[5] Eyre, vol. ii. p. 324.

unconnected with the relation of the individual to the district to which he belongs.

Each man possesses as his own a portion of the tribal land, and is able to define its limits with accuracy. The possessor has, indeed, only very moderate rights over this strip of land; in some cases he can sell it, and it is usually inherited, but this is because the father, in his lifetime, divides his portion among his sons.[1] Since the custom is widely diffused of naming the different districts after animals, etc., and the inherited land, at any rate in the south, generally has a peculiar name, which is also taken by its owner,[2] we are led to infer that the kobong name may be derived from this custom. If it could be ascertained that the tribal names of which Ritter speaks are in reality tribal names, and not those of families or clans, we might confidently assert that the nomenclature of distinct families followed the same principle as that of the whole tribe. The application of this principle to the larger circles gives us the tribes, and the subdivision of the tribe into smaller sections follows from its application to the smaller circles. This is, however, only a vague surmise; there are so many gaps in our knowledge that we do not even know whether each inherited portion has its special name, or if the father's portion retains its name, which thus serves as the tribal name of his children. We can only assert with confidence that there are subdivisions of two kinds, one of which takes its name from some characteristic of the land, and the other from its products. Our researches must be founded on these facts.

Among the Kurnai the clans are locally distinct; a clan is, as it were, a tribal division of the tribe. Nind, however, describes clans which are dispersed, and inhabit the territory of other tribes. On the other hand, it appears that the kobong groups show a tendency to local isolation, since its members belong to the same kobong.

[1] See Appendix V.   [2] Waitz, vol. vi p. 793.

Each horde has, as a rule, a predominating clan, and when the hordes break up, they fall into clans.[1] The kobong clan is, however, by no means bound to the tribe, as is the case with the Kurnai; one kobong may belong to individuals who live far apart. This, as we might have supposed, is only because the kobong names are to be found wherever the animals occur from whom the names are derived. Opossums, rats, lizards, eagles, snakes, etc., are everywhere common. The only fact which requires special explanation is that the lizard of the east appears to be confounded with the lizard of the west. This is to be explained by their having a common name; it is impossible for the primitive man to enter into detailed distinctions, and the force exerted on their imaginative faculty by the kobong name does not admit of any such distinction. It is, therefore, unnecessary to insist on the wide diffusion of the kobong names; the only important fact is the position of the kobong group within the tribe.

We find that the smaller groups are in all cases much more permanent than the large ones, since they have many more interests in common; among the Kurnai, the members of the smaller groups have stronger claims on each other than those of the large groups. The greater permanence of a kobong group, when tribes are brought into connection by the same kobong, must, however, impress on the tribe itself the character of its less important members, and in proportion to the attraction exerted on individuals by their common or allied kobongs, the bonds of the tribe are relaxed. These new groups show, as we have already said, a tendency to local isolation, and thus to form new tribes; and when no such isolation has occurred, it must have been thwarted by special circumstances, which we think it possible to ascertain.

The group to which a child is assigned by its birth is

[1] Grey, vol. ii. p. 239. McLennan, *Studies*, p. 89.

not the family, but the clan. We lay the greatest stress upon this circumstance, and it is only because this has not been done before that descent through the female line has been explained by ignorance of the paternity of the child. A clan is an exclusive group, and it is absolutely impossible for one person to belong to two distinct clans. In Australia, intermarriage between members of the same clan was never allowed, and hence it was necessary to define the clan to which the child belonged on one side only; either the father or the mother must be ignored. In Australia, it is usual to ignore the father, yet the male line is maintained by the Kurnai, Gournditch-Mara, Turra, Moncalon, and Torndirrup tribes, and by others visited by Eyre.[1] The line of descent has an important effect on the localization of the groups. If the child follows the parent on whom the family place of abode depends, the local isolation of the clan can be carried out; if otherwise, a fresh confusion of the clans will constantly occur. As a rule, the place of abode depends upon the will and humour of the husband, and the female line of descent, therefore, breaks down any fixed boundary between the territories of clans.

The female line of descent does not, however, affect the family. Among the Australians, indeed, the family has no fixed organization; the rape of married women, and divorces are of daily occurrence, and the bond which unites a father to his adult son is therefore unstable. Yet the tie of marriage cannot be regarded as so loose as to make it impossible for a father to feel any certainty with respect to the child, for all reports agree in declaring that the men are extremely jealous. Only the custom of hospitality, which leads a man to offer his wife to his friend or guest, can give rise to doubt; but the arrival of travellers is not of frequent occurrence. We shall presently consider the meaning of such customs, but we must pass over it now, as well as the strong affection which, accord-

[1] Fison and Howitt, pp. 276, 285. Nind, p. 44. Eyre, vol. ii. p. 328.

ing to all witnesses, Australians feel for their children,
since, as we shall presently see, such affection affords no
proof of the assurance of fatherhood. As an instance of the
sharp distinction between that which concerns the clan
and the family, we need only note that the obligations of
the blood-feud will sometimes place a father and son in hostile opposition to each other, since they belong to different
clans, and yet the father's land is divided among his sons.

Since, therefore, we find that the clan alone is affected
by the one-sided line of descent, the question arises
whether the circumstances of the Australians afford data
from which we can decide whether descent was originally
traced through the male or female line, and what were
the reasons for the transition from one to the other.
This may be premised: that either the reasons for adopt-
ing the female line were of universal application, or that
it may be adopted under all sorts of conditions; one or
other of these assumptions is warranted by its wide
diffusion. We find the male line in use among the Kurnai,
which are divided into clans in accordance with their
districts, not with their kobongs. The same line is in
use among the Moncalons and Torndirrups, who are no
longer quite distinct tribes, yet show traces of earlier
division. Their fusion seems to have been produced by
a subsequent kobong division. I have no idea how the
formation of groups dominated by the female line could
have arisen, since this line of descent interferes with the
permanence of the groups already formed. Hence I can
easily understand how groups which were formed and
maintained under the male line were confounded together
under the female line, without, however, altogether dis-
appearing. I am therefore inclined to regard the female
line as a later development; and this surmise seems
the more probable, since usually the female line only
appears in conjunction with the kobong groups. Among
the Kurnai, the only tribe which is without kobongs, the
female line is not observed.

If we venture to decide on the stage of civilization to which the Australian tribes have attained, we should assign those who maintain the male line of descent to the lowest place. The tribes visited by Eyre were on the whole more degraded than those visited by Grey; the former maintained the male, the latter the female line, and among the former, as we have already said, the kobong organization was only dawning. A single motive cannot be assigned for the adoption of the male line of descent by these tribes, and, indeed, we may infer the contrary, for the rights established by marriage appear to be less decided in the tribes observed by Eyre than in those described by Grey. Grey states that a widow becomes the property of her dead husband's brother, while Eyre reports that she returns to her own family after her husband's death.[1] Only among the Kurnai we find slight indications of her becoming the brother's property.[2] It is, on the other hand, possible to discover that the transition from the male to the female line was due to an urgent motive. As the family instinct became more developed, the importance of the distinction between brothers and sisters of full and half blood would become greater. When the husband was regarded as the only important person, it mattered little what became of the wife after the husband's death. Brothers and sisters born of one mother became an inconceivable idea. Yet polygamy led to the conception of such an idea. The daughters were subject to the father; on his death his brother took his place, and it was necessary to distinguish between the whole and the half brother, since the former must become the guardian. Among primitive men, as a rule, everything depends upon the first shock which their theories receive; the imagination is set to work in another direction, and cannot be restrained within due proportions and limits. In this way the

[1] Grey, vol. ii. p. 230. Eyre, vol. ii. p. 319. Waitz, vol. vi. p. 776.
[2] Fison and Howitt, p. 204.

unrestricted descent through the female line may have spontaneously arisen, although in the first instance it was only a feeling of convenience which induced the race to distinguish the children of polygamous families by their descent through their mothers.

We do not claim unconditional assent to these suggestions. We only assert that the conditions which exist among the Australians do not entitle us to regard the female line of descent as the primitive one, nor to explain it by the fact of promiscuous intercourse. Their circumstances do not afford proof of either opinion; they rather indicate that the female line was a later development, to which they were led for other reasons than those which referred to the question of paternity.

CHAPTER II.

AMERICA.

Exogenous totem-groups—General diffusion of female line—As to the primitive existence of the clan—The tamanuus of the peoples of Columbia—Tylor, Lubbock, and Spencer — Medicine and totem—System of names in clan—The Columbians the primitive tribes—Position of husband with respect to members of wife's family—Effect of this position on line of kinship—Influence of locality and household—Caribs—Non-existence of clans among them, and vague definition of kinship—Labour performed by son-in-law—Paternal authority and household among Brazilians—Tattooing a bond of union—Likewise a distinctive mark—Obligation of blood-feud—Slaves and freemen—Undeveloped clans—Forbidden marriages—Tribes of La Plata—No *patria potestas*—Hereditary dignity of chief—Araucanians—Coherence of the family—Female line not primitive—Origin of duties and privileges—Germ of development of groups—Nomenclature—Mexico—Paternal line and localized clans—The same in Peru—The couvade—Lubbock's hypothesis—Diffusion and meaning of the couvade.

WE find in North America very marked forms of clans which are distinguished by their totems or kobongs, and in that country as well as in Australia the clans are exogamous; that is, marriage between members of the L
same clan is not permitted. The formation of tribes is also more permanent than in Australia, when persons belonging to different tribes, but possessing the same totem, stand in close relations to each other; in America this is not the case. In some instances the clan organization is absent, and these exceptions will help us to understand its history—a history which reveals

the hidden causes of the lines of descent, and confirms the surmises suggested by our observation of the conditions which prevail in Australia. In both countries the social life of men is due to very simple causes, which are therefore universally applicable.

To the east of the mountain range, each of the tribes inhabits a territory of which the limits are strictly defined. The land may either be owned by the chief, or be the common property of the tribe. In the latter case, each tiller of a piece of ground has the use of it as long as he keeps it in cultivation, or else the tillage and harvest are undertaken in common; either the harvest and the animals killed in hunting are divided as they are required, or each man takes what he wants from the store in hand.[1] The tribal bond is a strong one; but, in spite of this, every tribe is divided into several clans, which, although not living apart, hold themselves to be separate corporations with the right of independent action. Wright tells us that in earlier times these clans showed a strong tendency to local exclusiveness.[2]

The female line of descent generally prevails in these tribes. The male line is, however, observed by the Punka, Omaha, Towa, Kaw, Winnebago, Ojibwa, Potawattamie, and Abenaki tribes, and by those of the Mississipi and the Rocky Mountains. Among these the Winnebagoes, Ojibwas, Potawattamies, and at least one of the Mississipi tribes, the Menominees, formerly followed the female line of descent, and the change has taken place under the influence of the missionaries. One of these tribes, the Choctas, is now in process of transition.[3] Morgan believes that in the other tribes also, the female line formerly prevailed, but he adduces no proof of this assertion. At the same time he states that the division into clans was a primitive one, and the fact that this division is not found among the tribes of Columbia does

---

[1] Waitz, vol. iii. p. 128.　　　[2] Morgan, *Anc. Soc.*, p. 83.
[3] Morgan, *Anc. Soc.*, pt. 2, ch. vi.

not disturb this belief; the tribes may have originally possessed the clan-organization and afterwards have lost it, since it is supposed that the American tribes migrated from the Columbian district.[1] I am more disposed to infer that the clan organization had its origin among the dispersed tribes at a later period, and I propose to try to decide the question by a different method.

Wilkes writes that the Columbians have a tamanuus, or medicine, which they reverence as their protecting spirit. Each man early in life chooses such a tamanuus, which is usually an animal.[2] I find in this custom the origin of totemism.

Tylor, in his work, "Primitive Culture," has spoken of totemism, which prevails throughout the world, in connection with the prevalence of animal worship.[3] He holds totemism to be that form of animal worship in which the animal is adored as the ancestor of the man himself, and he asks to what other cause we can ascribe the fancy that a man is descended from a wolf, a bear, or a tortoise. The hypothesis suggested by Lubbock and Spencer seems to him to be too rash. These learned men trace the cause of the so-called cultus to the prevailing custom of giving the name of an animal to an individual, and thence to a whole family. Such an individual at first regarded the animal with interest, then with reverence and superstition.[4] Tylor considers that this hypothesis may explain the obscure facts of totemism, but it is not warranted by experience, and its universal application may mislead us. We should do well not to rely too confidently on an hypothesis which accounts for solar and lunar nature myths by referring them to the heroic men and women who happened to be called after the sun and moon.[5] We shall revert to this point,

[1] Morgan, *Anc. Soc.*, pp. 109, 177. Appendix VI.
[2] Wilkes, *Narrative*, vol. v. p. 118. Appendix VII.
[3] Tylor, *Primitive Culture*, vol. i. p. 213
[4] Lubbock, *Orig. of Civ.*, p. 260. Spencer, *Prin. of Soc.*, ch. xxii.
[5] Tylor, *Primitive Culture*, vol. i. p. 215.

and are now only considering that part of Tylor's argument in which he lays stress on the distinction between totemism and the ordinary cultus of animals. He warns us against confounding the totem with the protecting animal which becomes the *medicine* of the individual.[1] I think that in this case he goes too far, for even if there is any real distinction between the totem and the medicine, the one might easily be evolved out of the other. We are in possession of facts which entitle us to infer that a totem was a medicine inherited from ancestors, to which a function somewhat different from that of ordinary medicine was ascribed.

It does not appear that the Columbian tribes are addicted to totemism, although it is found among the allied tribes on the Fraser River. Among the latter, the totem is carved on the beams of the house, and represented in all possible ways. Marriage is not permitted between persons who have the same totem.[2] I believe that the custom of carving the image of the owner's medicine on his house may have transformed its merely personal character into that of an hereditary totem.

Schoolcraft tells us that among the Sioux a clan consists of individuals who use the same roots for medicine, and that they are received into the clan by a great *medicine-dance*. He adds that it is the custom—and this is also the case with other tribes—to make a bag out of the skin of the medicine animal, which acts as a talisman, and is inherited by the son; it is only in this way that descent is reckoned through several generations.[3] This inheritance of the medicine may possibly explain the development of totemism, namely, by the reverence inspired by an inherited medicine. While Morgan is able to infer from a passage in Carver's "Travels" that in earlier times the Sioux were divided into distinct clans, I can only

[1] Tylor, *Primitive Culture*, p. 213.
[2] Mayne, *Four Years*, etc., p. 257. Appendix VIII.
[3] Schoolcraft, vol. ii. p. 171; vol. iii. p. 242. Appendix IX.

gather from Carver's narrative that their recollections of their ancestors were perhaps tolerably faithful.[1]

These clan-like corporations of the Sioux, consisting of persons who have the same medicine, may be placed in the same category as the kobong group which Eyre found in Australia. Descent is not so much the bond of union as the religious consecration by which a young man is admitted into the group. Such corporations were frequently formed in primitive communities, and the bond is one of great tenacity.[2] It seems probable that clans, together with their totem symbols, have in all cases been developed out of such corporations; were it otherwise, we should possess many facts with respect to the formation of clans which are now wanting. It is, however, certain that a development of groups occurs which is due to forces independent of the idea of common descent, and this development is found both in communities divided into clans, and in those which are without any clan organization. When the clan organization is fully developed, we always meet with usages which must be regarded as tokens of a period in which an individual was assigned to a clan for other reasons than that of his birth. Morgan states that it is no uncommon custom for a mother to enter her child into a clan which she selects at pleasure.[3] Each clan has peculiar names for its members, which no other clan is entitled to use; the possession of a given name therefore signifies that its owner is enrolled in a given clan. When a fixed rule has defined the limits of the clan, the right of name-giving loses its significance; on the other hand, it endows the name-giver, whether father, mother, or some other person, with great power, unless some definite law interferes with the arbitrary act. Morgan believes that in its time this right of name-giving favoured the

---

[1] Carver's *Travels*, p. 164. Morgan, *Anc. Soc.*, p. 154. Appendix X.
[2] Mayne, *Four Years*, pp. 260, 286, 289. Appendix XI.
[3] Morgan, *Anc. Soc.*, Shawnees and Delawares, p. 79; Sauks, Foxes, Miamis, p. 169; Delawares, p. 172.

5

introduction of the male line of descent, and he points to
the fact that it is now in use among the Delaware tribe.
Although the right in question may lead to the suppression of the female line of descent among the Delawares, other motives may also lead to its adoption.
Admitting this, we are led to the conclusion that the
right in question implies a comparatively loose connection between the clan and the line of descent.

From this point of view it is at any rate possible to
regard the condition of the Columbian tribes as the primitive one.　The observances of medicine prevail among
them, but there are no communities except those which are
defined by the locality and which keep together within
fixed limits.　Of late years these tribes have lived in peace
together, and have begun to intermarry.　In such cases
the husband goes to live with his wife's tribe, and the
wife takes an important position in the family.　She
acts as head of the household and takes charge of the
provisions.　When a man has several wives, or when
several families reside in the same lodge, each wife or
each family has a separate fire.[1]　Here we seem to find
the first beginnings of that state of things which is fully
developed in the eastern tribes.　Just as in this case the
tribe retains its women, and each wife of a polygamous
family is made locally independent by the possession of her
own hearth, so in the east the clan claims the right under
all circumstances of retaining and protecting its women.

Among the North American Indians, even after
marriage the man and wife usually belong to the huts
of their respective mothers.[2]　The man, however, appears
to be more dependent on his new family than on the
one to which he originally belonged.　He must share
the produce of his hunting with them, and his wife's
humour sometimes compels him to seek a new home for

[1] Wilkes, *Narrative*, vol. iv. pp. 447, 457.　Appendix XII.
[2] Bartrams, *Reisen*, p. 48.　Jones, *Antiquities*, p. 65.　Lafitau, *Mœurs*.
vol. i. p. 577.

himself. Even when he dominates over his wife, he continues to be a stranger in her family, at any rate until his children are born; his authority over these is not absolute, but he tries as far as possible to make them into active hunters and warriors.[1]

Among the Columbian tribes, the son remains with his father; both among them and the Sioux, when the son is left a minor, he is generally robbed of his inheritance, which his kinsfolk take for themselves.[2] In other such cases, where there are no clans, there can be no question of a distinct line of descent. We cannot agree with Morgan, who, as we have already said, seeks to explain the existence of the female line in so many of the other North American tribes from the fact that it prevailed at the time of their migration from Columbia. In the first place, there are no grounds for ascribing to the Columbians a primary and clearly defined line of descent, since they are, even in our day, still incapable of defining such a line. And, secondly, there are sufficient causes to account for the development and maintenance of the female line in the customs just described, by which the man inhabits his wife's home as a stranger, the children grow up in a house belonging to the members of the mother's clan, and the child is always, or at any rate generally, assigned to that clan when named. As the sense of clanship becomes ever more powerful, it would be difficult for the man under such circumstances to enrol his children in his own clan. We have every reason to think that this was not the position originally occupied by the husband, and hence we may affirm that the female line was adopted at a subsequent period. In this case polygamy may have had some influence, since it became more desirable to distinguish

---

[1] Lafitau, vol. i. pp. 475, 579. Carver, p. 314. Hunter, p. 251. Morgan, *Anc. Soc.*, pp. 72, 455. Giraud-Teulon, p. 192. Mackenzie, p. 96. Appendix XIII.
Wilkes, vol. iv. p. 448. Schoolcraft, vol. ii. p. 194.

between the children when the position taken by a husband in the family impressed upon marriage the character of a monogamy in which concubines were permitted. Yet, for reasons which I shall give presently, I think that the influence of polygamy was extremely slight.

In most cases the North American clan is strong enough to retain its members, and it becomes a political organization, with chiefs for peace (Sachems) and for war. Where the female line of descent is observed, the sons do not inherit dignity nor property; these always go to the son of the brother or sister. Here, again, we are presented with facts which cannot be explained by ideas about the tie of blood, but which arise from the usages of social life, formed under the influence which local circumstances exert upon the fancy. Morgan relates of the Iroquois that after a man's death, the brothers, sisters, and mother's brothers divide the property among themselves, but that a woman's property is inherited by the children and sisters, not by the brothers.[1] This custom may be formulated in general terms by saying that the inheritance falls to those who dwell together in one place. Owing to the faculty of memory, childhood and youth involve a young man in such a web of associations that he afterwards finds it hard to detach himself from them. The man who, when married, has lived as a stranger in the house of another, clings to the impressions of his former home, and his earlier household companions become his heirs. But the brother who has wandered elsewhere stands in a more remote relation to his sister than do the sisters and the children living with her in the parental home, and he is therefore excluded from the inheritance. It is evident that no ideas of kinship will explain why sisters should inherit from their brother, while brothers do not inherit from their sister. This order is due to the influence of

[1] Morgan, *Anc. Soc.*, p. 76. Bartrams, *Reisen*, p. 448.

locality, and the assertion must be wholly rejected that the relations of persons to each other are only decided by considerations of blood-kinship, and that consequently the female line of descent had its origin in a condition of promiscuous intercourse which has now disappeared. Even if the correctness of our hypothesis is still unproved, yet it is certain that all proofs of the other hypothesis are wanting. The female line of descent does not imply ignorance of the child's paternity, but only the invalidity of its legal rights; the female line does not sever the child from its father, but only from the father's clan.

Our assertion that the household is the source of legislative order, not from its character of blood-relationship, but from its local isolation, is confirmed by the circumstances of the South American Indians, where the causes at work are presented under somewhat different conditions.

Both among the Caribs, and in the southern tribes of Guiana and Brazil, we look in vain for any distinct clan organization, except in the case of the twenty-seven Arowak families, with which we are at present only imperfectly acquainted.[1] We find that clans are everywhere classified according to their villages, not by their families. The father or head of the household exerts unlimited authority over his wives and children, but this authority is not founded on legal rights, but upon his physical superiority.[2] Sons leave the parental roof when they grow up, but the daughters remain subject to their father until they marry. It is in agreement with these simple conditions that children are their fathers' heirs.[3]

In these countries the female line is only observed.

---

[1] Schomburgk, *Reisen*, vol. ii. p. 459. Brett, *Ind. Tribes*, p. 98. Traces exist among the Gês (Martius, vol. i. pp. 54, 283), the Guaycurus (Spix and Martius, vol. i. p. 268), and the Yameos (Martius, vol. i. p. 117). Yet the question is rather of communities than of race.

[2] Martius, vol. i. p. 122. Prinz Maximilian, vol. ii. p. 40.

[3] Martius, vol. i. p. 92. Waitz, vol. iii. p. 383.

by the Arowaks, Warraus, and Macusis.[1] Among the Arowaks, who are divided into clans, it is only the child's clan which is decided by the female line; the conditions in the other two tribes are somewhat obscure. Schomburgk states that tribal dependence is never derived from the father, but only from the mother, and that the offspring of an Arowak and of a Warrau woman would be reckoned in the Warrau tribe; he adds that the right of inheritance is in agreement with that of the tribal claims.[2] Nothing certain can be inferred from this fact; it is possible that the Warraus have followed the customs of the Arowaks, with whom they are closely connected. There is certainly no rupture of the relation between father and son, since the office of a wizard devolves upon his eldest son.[3]

The relations between father and son are so close among the Macusis that the simple assertion that among them, as well as among the other tribes of Guiana, the descent of the child is traced through its mother,[4] must be received with the greatest caution. The father fondly loves his child; it is completely in his power, and he can sell it, if so disposed, while the adult son is as a stranger to his mother.[5] Again, a strange light is thrown on the female line of descent by the prohibition to marry a brother's daughter, since this is regarded as the nearest degree of kinship among brothers and sisters. The father's brother is called papa as well as the father. On the other hand, it is permitted to all to marry a sister's daughter, a dead brother's wife, or a stepmother, after her husband's death.[6] The idea that the mother was more closely akin to the child than its father could not have resulted in such a state of things; on the other hand, it may be explained in accordance with our

---

[1] Schomburgk, *Reisen*, vol. i. 169; vol. ii. pp. 314, 459.
[2] *Ibid.*, vol. i. p. 169. [3] *Ibid.*, vol. i. p. 172.
[4] *Ibid.*, vol. ii. p. 314. [5] *Ibid.*, vol. ii. p. 315.
[6] *Ibid.*, vol. ii. p. 318.

principle, when we go on to consider the way in which the tribes in question lived.

The young husband usually lives for some time with his parents-in-law, and works for them.[1] The analogy between this custom and that which prevails in North America is apparent, but the distinction between them is not so plain. In the north, the custom was an expression of the clan sentiment, and this ideal character gave it greater weight. In the south it is reduced to a question of gain, and the son-in-law must serve for his bride as Jacob served for Rachel. The wooer may give other things for his bride besides his labour; when he has come to an understanding with the father, he gives a present and makes amends to him for the loss of his daughter by promising to give a sister in marriage to one of his sons, or, in default of this, he promises to give his own first-born daughter.[2] This mode of ransom is the true source of a custom in which, without further proof, the origin of a former observance of the female line has been sought. Waitz is surprised that among the Caribs the sons inherit from their fathers, " although they only appear to have regarded kinship in the female line as a true kinship." [3] This female line results from the claim made by men on the daughters of their father's sister,[4] and also from a similar claim made by the mother's brother. It is, however, easy to see that they merely follow from the ransom we have just mentioned; for if, when the first daughter is born, the mother's

---

[1] Schomburgk, *Reisen*, vol. i. p. 164; vol. ii. p. 318. Brett, p. 101. Martius, vol. i. p. 108. Gili, p. 344. Du Tertre, vol. iii. p. 378.

[2] Plogge, "*Reise in das Gebiet der Guajajara-Indianen*," quoted in Petermann's *Mittheilungen*, 1857, p. 206.

[3] Waitz, vol. iii. p. 383. Du Tertre, vol. ii. p. 400. Oviedo states that in Hayti the sons of the head wife are the first to inherit, next, the brothers, the sister's son, then the sons of the other wives (Sprengel, *Auswahl*, vol. i. p. 39). This does not imply a female line, but the dawn of a monogamous order of things, which regards the children of the inferior wives as illegitimate.

[4] Du Tertre, vol. ii. p. 377

brother maintains his right, and demands the child as his future wife, the father of the child is absolved from part of his duties towards his wife's parents, and the future husband must take them on himself.[1]

It would not be correct to say that the tribes just mentioned observe the male line; the child is bound by strong ties to both parents, but these do not distinctly involve ideas of common blood; all is still indefinite and fluctuating, since the groups of kinsfolk are still unformed. "The tribes of the Orinoco have no family names, by which one house is distinguished from another. They are so indifferent to their forefathers that they rarely know the names of their grandfathers."[2] Among these peoples the family is regarded only in its narrowest sense, and the power of the father is unlimited. Within this circle a desire is felt to distinguish the children by their mothers, and this is the more powerful since the polygamous family is no longer a homogeneous whole. It is only the first wife who is obtained by her husband's labour, and the rights of this head wife are predominant; her children sometimes enjoy special privileges.[3] Often each wife has her own hut, in which case the husband lives for a month with each of them.[4] The mother chooses her child's name, and is sometimes herself called after her child, and she exerts great influence over the choice of her son's wife.[5] If divorced, she seeks to retain the children, and if she is successful, she provides for their future.[6] The bond between the mother and child is esteemed to be so close that the children born of a connection between the men of the tribe and captive women are sometimes eaten.[7] Yet some authors assert that these children are placed on an equality with the

---

[1] Lafitau, vol. i. p. 557. Labat, vol. i. pt. ii. p. 5. See Spix and Martius, vol. iii. p. 133 (Mundrucus). Gili says that the word *avo* is used both for mother's brother and for father-in-law.

[2] Gili, p. 324. [3] Waitz, vol. iii. p. 383.
[4] Du Tertre, vol. ii. p. 387. [5] Gili, pp. 324, 342.
[6] Du Tertre, vol. ii. p. 376. [7] Waitz, vol. iii. p. 374.

others.[1] But however strong the tie between mother
and child may be, its force depends on their living
together in the same hut; the idea of this collocation
exerts a powerful influence on the fancy. There is
nothing to indicate that the idea prevails of a peculiarly
close tie of blood between mother and child.

Among the Brazilian tribes the claims of both parents
are considered, and in the more weighty questions the
father comes forward as the one in authority. It is
through him that the children are connected with the
tribe and its legal organization. The Brazilian household is more closely compacted than that of the Caribs,
and plays an important part as the fundamental element
of society. Only the fathers of families are admitted to
the general councils of the tribe.[2] The cohesive power
of the household is so strong that it is on the verge of
becoming a clan in the geographical sense, that is, with
local boundaries. Those tribes which are numerous are
subdivided into hordes and families, and there is a closer
union among the individual members of each section
than there is with the whole tribe.[3] Each of these subdivisions are groups of kinsfolk, while the others are
only groups by association; the former bear patronymic
names, while the latter derive their names from the
locality or from some special characteristic.[4] Among the
Gês such modifications are readily traced, but they seem
to disappear almost as quickly as they are formed.[5] The
cause of this swift disappearance lies in the difficulty
of maintaining tribal union between hordes which are
locally separated. A. von Humboldt observes " that
savage nations are divided into a great number of tribes,

[1] Du Tertre, vol. ii. p. 379. Rochefort, p. 327. Labat, vol. i. pt. ii.
p. 11.
[2] Martius, vol. i. pp. 64, 65.
[3] Martius, vol. i. p. 54. Spix and Martius, vol. ii. p. 821.
[4] Guaranis and Chireguanas (Azara, vol. ii. p. 54. Charlevoix, vol. i.
p. 294).
[5] Martius, vol. i. p. 283. Spix and Martius, vol. ii. p. 821.

between which there is a deadly enmity, and they never unite together, even when their language has a common origin, and their dwellings are only divided by a small stream or by a range of hills.   In proportion to the smallness of the tribe is the probability that the marriage between families, which has gone on for centuries, will produce a certain uniform modification, an organic type, which may be termed the national form." [1]   The scattered portions of the clan become distinct nations.

Only one bond is permanent enough to hold these portions together after their separation—the widely-diffused savage custom of tattooing, painting, and other personal adornments, by means of which the fancy maintains the local, graphic signs with which they cannot dispense, and to whose influence they involuntarily and absolutely surrender themselves.   The tattoo-marks make it possible to discover the remote connection between clans, and this token has such a powerful influence on the mind that there is no feud between tribes which are tattooed in the same way.   The type of the marks must be referred to the animal kingdom, yet we cannot discover any tradition or myth which relates to the custom. [2]   There is no reason for asserting that there is any connection between the tattoo-marks and totemism, although I am personally disposed to think that this is sometimes the case.   The tattooing, which usually consists in the imitation of some animal-forms, may lead to the worship of such animals as religious objects.   However this may be, tattooing is a plastic art which may be modified and altered, and if similar tattoo marks unite peoples together, any alteration of these marks may make the breach which has taken place between them irreparable.

Tattooing may also lead to the formation of a group within the tribe.   At all events, among the Uainumas the different families or hordes are distinguished by the

[1] A. von Humboldt and Bonpland, vol. ii. p. 192.
[2] Spix and Martius, vol. iii. p. 1279.

tattoo-marks of the face.[1] Among the Guaycurus a caste of nobles seems to have been formed in this way.[2] Yet the relations are so fluctuating that they lead to nothing certain, and do not give rise to a clan. The group may be associated in the cultivation of their fields, and live together in common in large dwellings,[3] yet the separate families are never lost in the group, but retain their independence. The household, not the group, constitutes the social element. There is only one circumstance which may point to an earlier or dawning kinship through the mother. The blood feud devolves on the son, brother, and sister's son ; the brother's son is not mentioned.[4] But we think that this order is due to the custom already mentioned, of retaining daughters in the parental home for some time after their marriage. In this way the daughter's children become attached to the household by closer ties than is the case with the son's children, born in another house. The origin of the subsequent observance of the female line may be sought in this custom, but it is in no sense the sign of one which has ceased to exist.

An instance of the wide influence of organizations which have gathered round the household like a somewhat indefinite crystallization may be found in the fact that the Guaycurus prohibit marriage between freemen and slaves.[5] Martius believes that this distinction of classes is an evident indication of hereditary rights, and he seems to found these hereditary rights upon descent from the ancestors they have in common. We do not accept this view, since it is easier to explain the prohibition from the custom of not tattooing slaves, that is, captives taken in war. It is natural that they should not have made use of the tattoo-marks of their own tribe,

---

Spix and Martius, vol. iii. p. 1208.
[2] *Ibid.*, vol. i. p. 268.   Martius, vol. i. p. 72.
[3] Martius, vol. i. p. 81.   [4] *Ibid.*, vol. i. p. 127.
[5] *Ibid.*, vol. i. p. 71.   Spix and Martius, vol. i. p. 268.

and also that they should not dare to. adopt those of their conquerors; and since the tattoo-marks are a sign of amity, they mark the limits within which marriage is possible, as well as those of the legal rights which they have in common. The child of a slave certainly inherits its father's lot, but it is because it belongs to its father, not because it was begotten by him.

It would be unreasonable to regard the organization we have just described of a tribe consisting of families and small family groups, as if it were derived from an organized clan of earlier date. The family shows no tendency to become more permanent, but is rather in constant danger of being lost in the family groups which finally constitute the clan. It may be inferred from the prohibition of certain marriages that the stream flows in the direction of the clan, and not against it. Throughout America the clan is exogamous; that is, marriage within the clan is forbidden. If in South America we had to do with the remnants of a clan-organization, we should expect to find a strictly prohibitive marriage law. And if we do not find such a law, or if it is only beginning to be formed within the family, we are entitled to regard the family as the first step to the clan. The Caribs see without a shudder the marriage of parents with their children.[1] " In Brazil it is generally held to be disgraceful to marry a sister or a brother's daughter. Morality with respect to such customs increases in proportion to the number of the tribe. It is very common for a brother to live with his sister in the small, isolated hordes and families. It may generally be said that incest is common among the numerous hordes and tribes of the Amazon and Negro rivers."[2] Among the Tupinambazes, the Puris, and the Coropos, the forbidden degrees appear to be those of mother, sister, and daughter. Among the Yameos, with whom, as we have already said, there are

---

[1] Du Tertre, vol. ii. p. 377. Labat, vol. ii. pt. ii. p. 5.
[2] Martius, vol. i. p. 116.

guilds which approximate to the clan, these guilds are exogamous.[1] Everywhere, however, marriage between members of different tribes is forbidden. The tattoo-marks define the limits of permitted marriages, and totemism defines those of prohibited marriages. Since we find that the North American tribes are just as averse from intermarriage with foreign tribes as those of the south, and the families in the south are as exogamous as the northern clans, we cannot avoid regarding the conditions of the South American Indians as the more primitive.

When we turn to the peoples south of Brazil, we observe the same social structure, characterized by some peculiarities which are very instructive, and which fully confirm our theory. The Brazilian family or household is subject to the authority of the father, and the woman, whether as mother, wife, or daughter, possesses neither rights nor property. The tendency to an exclusive line of descent only on the father's side, is in harmony with this order of things. As we go further south, we shall not find that the family has the same patriarchal character.

Each member of the family is independent. Marriages are dissolved arbitrarily and from caprice, and the children belong neither to father nor mother.[2] Among the Guanas the women make their stipulations before marriage—what they are to do in the household, whether the marriage is to be polygamous or polyandrous, and the like.[3] There is no social organization among the Morotocos; each family lives independently, and the women rule the house, but their authority does not extend beyond its threshold.[4] Among the Payaguas, when a divorce occurs, the children and the property belong to the

---

[1] Lery, p. 337. Spix and Martius, vol. i. p. 381.

[2] Charlevoix, vol. i. p. 312; vol. vi. p. 147. McCann, vol. i. 130. De la Cruz, p. 62. Smith, *The Araucanians*, p. 201. D'Orbigny, vol. iv. p. 92. Guinnard, p. 131. Dobrizhoffer, vol. ii. p. 268. Azara, vol. ii pp. 23, 44.

[3] Azara, vol. ii. p. 93.   Charlevoix, vol. iv. p. 283.

wives, and the husband only retains his weapons and his clothes; when the marriage is childless, each takes what is his or her own.[1] In all these tribes divorces only occur, however, when the marriage is childless.[2] Preference for the paternal line can only be traced in the hereditary dignity of the chief, which usually goes from father to son. The existence of hereditary chiefs is, however, no proof of the consolidated organization of the tribe, which always depends upon the functions of the chief, and in the cases in question these are insignificant. The formation of groups does not go beyond the combination of kinsfolk to maintain special rights.

The chief's dignity is hereditary among the Guaranis and some of the Carib tribes, but in other cases the strongest and bravest man becomes the chief. "It seems to me," Martius writes, "that the chief assumes the highest place among his companions, as much in virtue of his own personality as because he is called to it by the general voice of the tribe."[3] This remark, however, only applies to those tribes whose chiefs are hereditary, and even among them the dignity may devolve upon individuals distinguished for their valour or eloquence, or who are chosen by the still surviving chief.[4] Sometimes, indeed, it is open to women.[5] In times of peace the chiefs are for the most part only advisers and meditators, but during war they enforce a blind obedience.[6]

The Araucanians are in many respects more developed

---

[1] Azara, vol. ii. p. 132.

[2] Azara, vol. ii. p. 23. Dobrizhoffer, vol. ii. p. 259. Falkner, p. 157. Gili, p. 346.

[3] Martius, vol. i. p. 61. See Charruas, Tobas, Mbocobis, Patagonians, Fuegians (Azara, vol. ii. p. 15. D'Orbigny, vol. iv. p. 232. Wilkes, vol. i. p. 114. Parker Snow, vol. ii. p. 358).

[4] Guaycurus (Charlevoix, vol. i. p. 115), Abipones (Dobrizhoffer, vol. i. p. 130), Araucanians (Smith, p. 241). D'Orbigny, vol. iv. p. 183), Guanas (Azara, vol. ii. p. 95), Tehuelches, and Puelches (Falkner, p. 150. Smith, p. 196. Dobrizhoffer, vol. ii. p. 130. Azara, vol. ii. p. 96. Charlevoix, vol. i. p. 294).

[5] Smith, p. 242.

[6] Azara, vol. ii. p. 96. Dobrizhoffer, vol. ii. p. 136. Smith, p. 163.

than the other tribes, so that the description of their customs is of special value to us. The land is divided into four equal provinces, and these are again subdivided and, as Smith states, inhabited by clans ruled by hereditary chiefs ; these chiefs exert a patriarchal authority, and may be regarded as heads of families. They provide for the general good, enter into alliance with their neighbours, call the councils together, endeavour to arrange the disputes which arise from thefts, and decide on the purchase of tribal land.[1] We think that Smith is mistaken when he uses the expression " clan "; these groups are only local divisions of a tribe, still inspired by tribal sentiment, and the subdivisions are not groups of kinsfolk, but household groups which live together on ground which is locally isolated. Some of them are blood-relations, others not, and the fact of kinship is soon forgotten. The character of the hereditary chief's office by no means indicates that the group was originally a clan, or a family which was first ruled by the father, and afterwards by the eldest son. The limits of the family group are quite undefined, and are maintained, not so much by the recollections of their common descent as by the elementary conditions of their local distribution. The Araucanians inhabit large family dwellings, which is also often the case with other tribes, and as long as they all dwell together, there is great cohesive power in the family group; but as soon as the local bond is dissolved, the kinship is no longer recognized.[2] The hereditary dignity of the chief is merely the natural result of the fact that property is hereditary, and this again follows from living ✓ together in one place. Among the Araucanians, the word " ulman " or " guilman " signifies both a rich man and a chief, and when there is no heir, the new chief is chosen from among the rich.[3] We do not dispute the fact of hereditary rights ; it is enough to say that they afford no traces of an earlier clan-organization, and, still

[1] Smith, p. 240.   [2] Guinnard, p. 115.   [3] Smith, p. 242.

less, traces of an organization founded on the female line of descent.

An attempt is usually made to regard usages as the result of ideas of sacred rights and duties. This appears to me to be sometimes labour in vain, since it is much simpler to derive such ideas from the usages, and to trace the source of these to motives prompted by the claims of primitive life. When, for instance, Waitz writes that among the Peguenches all the kinsfolk must answer for a robber, too much stress is laid on the obligation; it is not the whole of the kinsfolk, but only those who are living in community with the robber, who are held to be responsible.[1] The injured person merely seeks to recover his property, and if the robber is unable to give him satisfaction, compensation must be made out of whatever is to be found in the house.[2] A common dwelling certainly produces a growing sense of having all things in common, and this is chiefly due to the fact that the mutual relations which subsist between neighbours are not so much with individuals as with the community of a given place.

Everything tends to show that the groups are in process of formation, and that they are not the survival of a more fixed order of things. We adduce a few examples, which we consider sufficient. The murder of a child by its father is, among the Peguenches, avenged by the mother's kinsfolk as any other murder would be,[3] and an adultress can only be safely killed by her husband after he has obtained her kinsfolk's consent.[4] This does not imply that kinship through the mother is particularly close, but merely that the groups, instead of being exclusive, overlap each other. Even after her marriage the wife is under the protection of her former companions, and her family extends the hand of friendship to her children. The father affords special protection to a

[1] Waitz, vol. iii. p. 517.　[2] De la Cruz, p. 38.　MacCann, vol. i. p. 127.
[3] Waitz, vol. iii. p. 517.　[4] De la Cruz, p. 38.

daughter because the price paid for a bride is a source of wealth,[1] and on this account he does not quite lose sight of her, even after her marriage.

The custom, which is in this case only beginning, of pointing out the child's family by its name shows that we have to do with the dawn, and not with the survival of usages which tend to the formation of a clan, and of the female line of descent, as it prevails in North America. Among the Araucanians, the last syllable of the father's name begins to be used as the family name.[2] Among the Tehuelches, hereditary names, with the exception of a few cases in which the Spanish custom is imitated, are altogether unknown.[3] Among the Peguenches, the child receives the name of his godfather in addition to that of his father, and there is a close connection between name-brothers, even when they have only part of the name in common.[4]

If we cast a hasty glance at the higher development of Mexico and Peru, we shall be confirmed in the belief that the social forms which we have just considered are antecedent to those of the clan, and that the clan organization naturally grows out of them ; and, again, that the clan which depends on the female line of descent cannot be explained from the facts of promiscuous intercourse.

According to the mythical account of the building of the city of Mexico, God ordered the priest to declare to the people that they should divide into four tribes which were to settle round the temple. Each of the four tribes was subdivided into smaller groups, each possessing its own district and god.[5] Morgan justly believes that this narrative points to a permanent division into clans.[6] We have many witnesses to the solidarity which exists

[1] De la Cruz., p. 59.   [2] Smith, p. 262.   Appendix XIV.
[3] Musters, p. 177.
[4] De la Cruz, p. 58.   See Spix and Martius, vol. iii. p. 1185
[5] Herrera, p. 156.   Appendix XV.
[6] Morgan, *Anc. Soc.*, p. 186, ch. vii.

between the different groups, both in their common responsibility for crimes, and in their maintenance of the rights of property.[1] But there is not a single witness which would entitle us to infer that there was originally a female line of descent. .The local isolation of the clans maintained by their distribution into districts is only possible where there is a male line; we have already shown that a confusion inevitably results from the female line. We are wholly ignorant how the clans arose; no conclusions can be drawn from the fact that the gods, or images of the dead, served as a centre for each clan, since it remains doubtful whether the severance into groups was due to their common worship of the same gods, or if men worshipped the same god because they were of the same blood.

Peru, before the Incas obtained possession of the country, was apparently inhabited by a number of peoples, whose organization resembled that found in Brazil and on the Pampas. Garcilasso's description of their rude state is perhaps overdrawn, yet this much I believe to be true. Each province and nation, and frequently each village, spoke a different dialect, which was unintelligible to their neighbours. Those who spoke a common language were in close connection with each other, while they lived at enmity and in perpetual warfare with those whom they did not understand.[2] This well-known classification into villages was maintained in a strongly-marked form under the Incas; no member of a given district or village could marry into another, and he was at the same time bound to the soil.[3] When we are confronted with these facts, it becomes impossible to find in the tribal forms of South America the survival of an earlier and diverse tribal organization.

[1] Herrera, vol. iii. pp. 321, 359, 370, 379. Waitz, vol. iv. pp. 76, 306.
[2] Garcilasso de la Vega, p. 31.   [3] *Ibid.*, p. 189.

THE COUVADE.

Before taking leave of America, we must consider some phenomena which are commonly supposed to be signs of the prior observance of the female line of descent; namely, the special customs which are included under the name of the couvade. This name is applied to the custom which obliges the father to occupy the lying-in bed instead of the mother. Lubbock attempts to explain this strange custom by saying that when the transition from the female to the male line of descent took place, the father assumed in all respects the position of the mother. Thus it was natural that he should refrain from everything which might hurt the child, both from certain acts and certain food. Lubbock ascribes the origin of the couvade to this abstinence, which the mother had really reason to observe, but in the father's case it was fictitious. The father was now, accordingly, regarded as the true progenitor, as the mother had formerly been so regarded.[1]

It is scarcely necessary to observe that the father would not submit to the couvade if he believed himself to be in no way connected with the child, and so far we agree with Lubbock. But the facts distinctly contradict his assumption that the couvade was due to the transition to the male line of descent, and a much simpler solution of the question is afforded by the later passages in the works quoted by him. Schomburgk states that the Arowaks agree with other tribes in the performance of these ceremonies of the lying-in bed by the husband together with the wife, and he says the same of the Macusis.[2] Yet we have seen above that these two tribes observe the female line of descent, and this fact makes Lubbock's explanation untenable.

[1] Lubbock, *Orig. of Civ.*, p. 154. Appendix XVI. See Tylor, *Early History*, p. 292. Bachofen, *Mutterrecht*, p. 419. Ploss, *Das Kind*, vol. i. p. 35, and ch. v.
[2] Schomburgk, vol. ii. pp. 314, 459. Brett, pp. 98, 101, states that the wife takes no part.

In order to find another explanation, an exact acquaintance with the phenomenon is necessary. I quote several accounts of this strange custom in the Appendix,[1] and they all show that the husband's lying-in bed is not regarded as a sick-bed, affording rest and strength after travail. The man fasts with extreme rigour, and abstains for a long while from certain meats which might injure the child; birds and fish would give it the stomach ache, turtle would cause it to be deaf, etc. As Tylor has already asserted, the couvade only expresses the belief in a secret mystical connection between the father and the child, a belief which does not go beyond what is known in other ways of the mode of thought in primitive man.[2] The belief that it is possible to inherit the courage of a dead man by eating his heart, or that a man may be bewitched by incantations over a lock of his hair, springs from ideas which will also include the couvade. "In order that the father's courage may devolve upon the child, the former subjects himself to the most painful ordeal on the birth of a son or daughter, and a young woman also submits to cruel rites on attaining maturity."[3] Among the Iroquois, a mother who shrieks during her labour is forbidden to bear other children, and some of the South American Indians killed the children of mothers who have shrieked, from the belief that they will grow up to be cowards.[4] The origin of the couvade cannot be traced to father or mother; the well-being of the child is its object; the father's powers of endurance are displayed on such occasions, and might thus be assured to the child, for no one who was deficient in courage and endurance would submit to this custom.

[1] Appendix XVII.
[2] Max Müller, strangely enough, traces the origin of the couvade to the derision of friends of both sexes (ch. ii. p. 278).
[3] Schomburgk, vol. ii. p. 431.   [4] Lafitau, vol. i. p 592.

CHAPTER III.

AFRICA.

The regulating forces universally simple—The female line a sign of the formation of more permanent groups—Scattered groups: slave-hunts —Conquest of Africa—Twofold line of descent—Bechuana clans— Patriarchal life—The kotla—Bantu and Negro villages—Their government—The village and the family—Women's prominent position—Bachofen and Giraud-Teulon—The wife and her family— Negroes—Female line—Description of West African community— Government of tribe and clan—Bechuanas the primitive type— Hottentots.

WE have endeavoured to show that the development of primitive social life lies between the Brazilian and North American forms. The social life of man begins with the partially agnatistic family, and the family group which is ruled by the father in virtue of his physical superiority; a strong man, or one who is pre-eminent in other ways, commands respect, and is obeyed by his associates, whether of the family or of the tribe. Clans are subsequently formed which, as their internal cohesion increases, gradually pass from the paternal to the maternal line of descent; the clan is then ruled by hereditary chiefs, and the family as a privileged group is lost. The organization of the community is not decided by considerations of descent, yet the same general causes also decide between the possible lines of descent. As in all cases which have to do with forces at work in wide circles, we find that here also the efficient causes are very simple and direct. It was the influence of locality which first assigned the child to its father, and afterwards, when the mother lived apart from the other wives, to its mother; this was still more the case when the woman's clan interposed between her and the husband who belonged to another clan.

When we take a general view of these facts, the preliminary condition of the successful establishment of the female line appears to consist in the distribution of the masses into several smaller societies. Our researches show that, in accordance with the principle of this distribution, all which is found in one locality belongs to the owner of that locality. Since their inclinations and passions are social, this law is adopted by men. Whoever is drawn to a locality owned by another forfeits his own independence, and we have already seen that the family served as the nucleus of this first crystallization. The man took his wife to his own abode, and ruled both her and her children. These first groups might either be dissolved, owing to continual disputes, and then always drift further apart, or they might live together in amity, until they were by degrees so closely united that they could not be severed without losing their existence. The vitality of the group was involved in maintaining the female line of descent, since it arose from its power of retaining and protecting its members, but it destroyed the natural basis of the family by its opposition to the will of the husband. Since the natural tendency to family life can never be wholly subdued, the clan which was organized in conformity with the female line had always to contend with an enemy at home; the local limits of the clan were confused by marriage, and this confusion undermined the dominion of the female line.

We do not deny that there may have been other starting-points for groups besides that of the family. Whatever produces community among individuals, whether they have in common their name, their tattoo-marks, or their *tamanuus*, may give the first impulse to the development of a still closer association. It is doubtful whether a different cause involves a different mode of life and different ideas, but this seems to us to be improbable.

We must now consider the Negro and Bantu peoples. Our knowledge of their ethnographical connection and historical development is scanty and uncertain; we know little beyond the fact of their mutual relations and nothing of their nature and extent. We must receive the reports of their communities with caution; since they are probably not in their primitive state, and since we are unable to ascertain what forces were at work in earlier times, it is impossible to draw any conclusion from that which has ceased to exist.

Since we are not able to revert to the primitive conditions, the hypothesis which has been hazarded with respect to the original character of the female line of descent is untenable, and even the internal probability of this or that hypothesis must remain an open question.

The Negroes inhabit the western parts of the Gulf of Guinea, and are surrounded by the Bantus on the east and south. The latter people seems to have made its way from the north into the territory held by the Negroes, of whom scattered remnants may still be found towards the north-east. All these tribes live by husbandry and the rearing of cattle, and trade is everywhere active. A special influence on these people must be ascribed to the slave-hunts, which cannot be left out of account in estimating the social conditions of Africa. This influence is particularly injurious in the east, because the Arabs who take up their abode on alien territory diffuse unbridled lawlessness in that district. The evil results of the slave-trade are not so apparent in the west, where it does not take the same form of devastating slave-hunts; the foreign slave-dealers remain upon the coast, and are not admitted into the interior.

The formation of groups has been particularly affected by this scourge, since every bond of tender feeling is ruptured by the love of gain, and we find accordingly that the groups are usually dispersed, or cohere very loosely together in the east. In the west they are much more compact and more sharply defined. While it is evident that we are presented in the east with the mutilated remains of groups, there is much to indicate that the formation of groups in the west is only arrested in one accidental particular. It must be our first object to obtain a clear idea of these groups.

The Negro communities and those of the Bantus are in most respects constructed alike. Taking the village as the starting-point, we find that it is usually governed by a chief and a council of elders, or of the heads of the most important groups of kinsfolk. Several such villages are again subject to a chief, whose authority varies according to circumstances. The original formation of the groups seems to have been by kinship, but this peaceful development has been interrupted by violence, and the very different forces of war and conquest have been brought to bear upon them. Swiftly arising, and as swiftly declining, the continuance of a kingdom depends upon the capacity of its ruler.[1] Fortunately, some communities are still in existence, of which the peaceful and natural development has not been materially disturbed, although the devastations of war have not been wholly absent. I am here speaking of the Bechuanas; the structure of their society, of which the lines are clear and simple, bears no trace of devastating forces.

It is probable that this people came from the north-east, and it now dwells on the borders of the Kalahari, and near the Hottentots. The chief source of Bechuana wealth consists in their great herds of cattle, and although they bestow a little culture on their barren soil, this labour is undertaken by the women. The people is to

---

[1] Livingstone, *Narrative*, p. 199. Appendix XVIII.

some extent a stranger in the land; it has authority over
several subject tribes, and is itself dispersed into sections
living apart, one or other of which suddenly overspreads
a new district, either for the sake of stealing cattle or in
search of a new dwelling-place.[1] The names of these
sections remind us of totemism, since they are called
after animals, such as the ape, alligator, or fish, and men
will neither kill nor eat the animal whose name they
bear. The word *bina* (to dance) is used to indicate their
dependence on a group; "What do you dance?" means,
"To what tribe do you belong?"[2] It seems probable that
these sections were originally clans, and I suspect that
they were torn asunder as the people advanced into the
country, and each conquered for itself its own strip of
territory. Let us now consider the organization of such
a clan-like section.

Each tribe has its own king, who inhabits the largest
village, and is reverenced in proportion to his hereditary
dignity. The tribe generally consists of several villages,
each with its chief, whom other lesser chiefs obey.[3] The
whole tribe may be regarded as a village, of which the
scattered villages constitute the different parts, although
the space which intervenes between them is sometimes
very wide. When the king has, with the consent of the
most important chiefs, selected a district, each chief, or
kosi (*i.e.* rich man) builds a house on his own portion, and
his kinsfolk, friends, and subjects build their houses round
it, sometimes so close together that it is hardly possible to
pass between the dwellings, but this is not the case as a
rule. In the same way the chiefs are sometimes separated
by wide tracts of open country, and sometimes not.[4]
Livingstone also tells us that they live in a patriarchal

[1] Livingstone, *Miss. Trav.*, p. 186. Burchell, vol. ii, pp. 348, 545.
[2] Livingstone, *Miss. Trav.*, p. 13. Appendix XIX. See the narrative of
the dancing Quimbandes by Serpa Pinto, vol. i. p. 231, Inaugural Dance
of the Sioux and Australians.
[3] Anderson, *Ngami*, p. 454.
[4] Burchell, vol. ii. pp. 513, 514.

7

way, and that each man is master of his children in virtue
of his fatherhood. The children build their houses round
that of their father, whose importance is increased by
their number, so that children are regarded as a blessing,
and are as a rule kindly treated. Near the centre of each
circle of houses there is a raised platform with a hearth-
place, called *kotla;* here they work, and eat, and talk over
the events of the day. The poor man builds his hut
close to the kotla of the rich, and is regarded as his child.
The under-chief has several such circles round his own,
and all these kotlas, with the king's large one in the
centre, form the village or tribe.   The circle of huts next
to the king's kotla consists of the huts of his wives and
kinsfolk.   We must add, in conclusion, that the king
endeavours to win over the subordinate chiefs, either by
taking their daughters to wife or by inducing his brothers
to do so.[1]

The kotla is the hearth-place of the Bechuanas, and,
more than this, it is a sacred spot, as the hearth was to
the Romans. It is the burial place of the chief, and
cattle are driven over the grave until the ground is
again level; the common man is, however, buried outside
the village, or the corpse is thrown upon the hill-side,
to be devoured by wild animals.   No one may enter
the kotla with his shoes on.[2] Some tribes, when they
migrate elsewhere, are said to erect a cairn of stones upon
the spot. It should also be observed that the bond which
unites the real and the adopted children of a patriarch
is not indissoluble, but rather displays tokens of its
voluntary character; families often forsake their own
chief and betake themselves to another village, and sometimes the whole village goes off in the night, leaving the
chief alone.[3]

[1] Livingstone, *Miss. Trav.*, p. 15.
[2] Burchell, vol. ii. p. 522.   Livingstone, *Miss. Trav.*, pp. 90, 314.   Le
Vaillant, *Voyage*, vol. ii. p. 216.
[3] Livingstone, *Narrative*, p. 292.

The partition of the tribe into patriarchal families is not restricted to certain given points, but extends through all parts of the tribe. The process of partition is carried on by an instructive combination of agnatistic and uterine kinship. A man has as a rule several wives, and no distinction can be observed among them, except that the first-comer, or the woman of highest rank, has the upper hand when they are unable to agree; a quarrelsome wife has a hut apart.[1] Nor is any distinction made between the children, except that the eldest son, or the eldest son of the woman of highest rank, inherits his father's position.[2] Even in the lifetime of a chief his subjects and herds of cattle are subdivided in proportion to the number of his wives, and each division of cattle has its distinguishing mark. After the father's death, the sons of a chief's wife inherit that portion of the subjects and cattle which was set apart in this way, and the mother takes an equal share.[3] These are probably the divisions of which Livingstone and Le Vaillant speak as the "Sun," the "Ruler," etc.[4]

The organization is as follows: the tribe is a system divided into greater and lesser circles, and each circle is defined by agnation, so far as it forms an independent whole; its position within the larger circle depends, how-

[1] Alberti, p. 107. Livingstone, *Miss. Trav.*, p. 185.
[2] Alberti, p. 131. Livingstone, *Miss. Trav.*, p. 185. Le Vaillant, *Voyage*, vol. ii. p. 215. Burchell, vol. ii. pp. 494, 553.
[3] Alberti, p. 138. Le Vaillant, vol. ii. p. 216.
[4] " Boguera is a civil rather than a religious rite. All the boys of an age between ten and fourteen or fifteen are selected to be the companions for life of one of the sons of the chief. . . . These bands or regiments (*mepato*) receive particular appellations; as the Matsatsi, the suns; the Mabusa, the rulers; equivalent to our Coldstreams or Enniskillens; and though living in different parts of the town, they turn out at the call, and act under the chief's son as their commander" (Livingstone, *Miss. Trav.*, p. 147). "Die Jünglinge, welche mit einem der Söhne eines Oberhauptes gleichzeitig beschnitten werden, gehören zu dessen künftiger Horde" (Alberti, p. 138). Anderson writes (*Ngami*, p. 446) "Children born of parents previously to their having been operated upon, cannot inherit regal power."

ever, on the female line of descent. We shall find that this type recurs in all the Negro and Bantu tribes, but often in such a mutilated form that it is difficult to identify it.

Among both peoples the village is the political unit. Each village is constructed on the same pattern. There is a large building for the council in the centre, called the palaver house, and an open square; as a rule, each family has as many huts, or as many sites for huts as the master of the household has wives; in many districts the family circle, as well as the whole village, is surrounded by a paling. Each village is subject to a chief who is more or less powerful, and who has obtained his office in many different ways.[1]

In some places the head of the village is appointed by the king, who generally chooses his brother, sister, or friend for such a post. After his death, disputes are apt to arise between his son and heir and these village headmen; the state falls into anarchy or is controlled by violence, and in the latter case the head-men give way in favour of the brothers and faithful friends of the new king. This state of things increases the authority of the king, and it shows that his will must prevail, although as a rule he maintains a good understanding with the village head-men. In the village itself the authority of the head-men is as absolute as that of the king in the tribe. But if in this way frequent internal disputes have given an air of conquering power to the kingship, yet the foundation of the kingly authority seems to rest on other ideas.

Magyar writes with reference to Kimbunda: "that the land is divided into several so-called soveta (circles), each ruled by a lesser chief, who is, however, in every

[1] Du Chaillu, *Journey*, pp. 254, 259; *Reise*, vol. i. p. 76. Cuhn, vol. i. p. 88. Palmer, p. 63. Degrandpré. vol. i. pp. 63, 102. Bastian, p. 72. Caillié, vol. i. pp. 36, 333, 439, 445. Bosman, p. 203. Barth, vol. iii. p 158. Cameron, vol. ii. p. 56. Vogel, Petermann's *Mittheilungen*, 1857, p. 138.

respect subordinate to the Soba, or prince. These vassal chiefs of the soveta are partly offshoots from the princely family, both of the male and female sex, partly elected by a majority of votes, over which, however, the influence of the prince is predominant. In the first case they bear the title of Sovan-erombe, and the dignity devolves upon their posterity; in the latter case they are called Erombe-an-Sekulu, and the dignity is elective. . . . The inhabitants of the circles in question are subject to the vassal chiefs. There is also a class called Muk-an-djamba (sons of the elephant), consisting of the prince's soldiers and servants, who are enrolled in five hundred libata and are about forty thousand in number; these are only subject to the prince." [1] It is easy to see that a military character is impressed upon the prince's rule by this horde of soldiers; yet this is not the basis of his power, but only a modification of it, as it appears from the general character of the community in other respects. From its highest to its lowest grades, the community is seen to consist of larger or smaller patriarchal family circles. Each is absolute master of his own household, and the internal affairs of the family are regulated by its head.[2] The dwelling-place of each chief is called *libata*, from the dwelling of the head of a family to the princely residence.[3] The Sova is, as among the Bechuanas, buried in the enclosed space round the huts, or in some cases on the highway.[4] The Sova appears to be the religious centre of his tribe; each family, and sometimes each person, has its peculiar and favourite fetish; the lion, panther, hyena, snake, and crocodile are also reverenced, reminding us again of the Bechuanas.[5] Yet the only real religion which they appear to possess consists in sacrifices to

[1] Magyar, p. 242. Serpa Pinto, vol. i. p. 167. The soldiers serve for booty (p. 279), with the king's sons for leaders (p. 316), and these plunder their subjects.
[2] Magyar, pp. 277, 281.   [3] *Ibid.*, p. 80. Appendix XIII.
[4] Serpa Pinto, vol. i. p. 170. Magyar, pp. 271, 337.
[5] Magyar, pp. 241, 335-337.

their departed forefathers, and the richest offerings are
made to the deceased Sova.[1] From this point of view it
is perhaps significant that some tribes, such as the Bihé,
take the name of a real or supposed ancestor.[2]

So far as our imperfect knowledge goes, we meet
with the same features everywhere.[3] In Njangwe, Rus-
suna's dwelling serves as the centre of the clan, and
almost forms a village in itself.[4] Each Warua village
has its peculiar fetish, but for the most part they reverence "Kungwe a Banza," an idol which ranks as the
ancestor of Kasongo's princely family.[5] In Kanjenje,
only the chief is buried, and all other corpses are
thrown into the bush.[6] The Shilluk invoke a hero as the
original leader and father of their tribe, and they believe
that the dead are invisibly present with the living.[7]
The Bongo and Bari carve small wooden images of the
dead.[8] Tattoo-marks serve to distinguish most of the
tribes and families.[9] We need only mention one other
feature, that there is the same change of lesser chiefs on
the Zambesi which has been described in the case of the
Bechuanas, and that we can trace a mixture of the male
and female lines of descent, since the Urungu bear their
mother's name, or assume that of their father after his
death.[10]

[1] Magyar, pp. 21, 271. Serpa Pinto, vol. i. pp. 168, 170.
[2] Magyar, p. 227. Appendix X.
[3] Schweinfurth, vol. i. pp. 94, 284, 484 ; vol. ii. p. 24. Cameron, vol. i.
p. 244; vol. ii. pp. 19, 68. Livingstone, *Narrative*, p. 108 ; *Miss. Trav.*,
p. 268. Bari, *Mittheilungen der k. Geographische Gesellschaft* (Wien,
1876), Neue Folge, vol. ix. p. 298.
[4] Cameron, vol. ii. p. 19.
[5] *Ibid.*, vol. ii. p. 71. "Banza" has the same meaning as "libata."
Degrandpré, vol. i. p. 67. Cuhn, vol. i. p. 37.
[6] Cameron, vol. ii. p. 71.
[7] *Ibid.*, vol. i. p. 120. Bari, Baker, vol. i. p. 89. *Mittheilungen der k.
Geographische Gesellschaft*, p. 296.
[8] Schweinfurth, vol. i. p. 98.
[9] *Ibid.*, vol. i. pp. 63, 326. Livingstone, *Last Journals*, vol. i. p 49;
Narrative, pp. 376, 524. Waitz, vol. ii. p. 25. Latham, vol. ii. p. 163.
[10] Livingstone, *Last Journals*, vol. i. p. 223.

The wife takes an important place among all the ✓ peoples of whom we have now spoken, but in some exceptional cases descent is reckoned on the father's side. The female line is observed among the Damaras or Herrero, neighbours to the Bechuanas. The tribe is divided into castes or *candas,* such as the Ovakueyuba (the people of the sun), Ovakuenombura (the people of the rain), etc., and each of them observes peculiar ceremonies and superstitions. These castes derive their descent through the mother, not through the father.[1] But the female line only applies to the castes, since we are told that the favourite wife takes precedence of the others, and that her son inherits the rank and property of his father.[2] The wives themselves fall to the man's brother, not to his sons.[3] We may add that in Bihé the king's sister's son appears to be his heir, which is also the case among the Banyai of the middle Zambesi.[4] With these exceptions, the child's position depends upon its father. But the female line is generally observed among the Negroes and the peoples of West Africa.

I suggest the following explanation of this fact. The Bechuana wives take, on the whole, an important position; the bond between parents and children is so strong that a man cannot marry without the consent of his parents, and even after he becomes a grandfather he can transact no business without their consent, at any rate without that of his father. The mother of the chief is present at councils, and he can hardly decide anything without her consent. A married man cannot dispose of

[1] Anderson, *Ngami,* p. 22.   [2] *Ibid.,* pp. 225, 228.   [3] *Ibid.,* p. 176.
[4] Magyar, p. 241. (At p. 284 the sons are said to be heirs, together with the female slave.) Serpa Pinto gives as heir the brother, and the eldest son of the eldest brother. (vol. i. p. 259. Livingstone, *Miss. Trav.,* p. 617). He says of the Balonda on the Upper Zambesi (p. 309), "All the Makalaka children cleave to the mother in cases of separation, or removal from one part of the country to another." Bachofen is not justified in the use he makes of this passage in *Mutterrecht,* p. 106. Among the Bangala on the Kongo, the uncle is bound to purchase his sister's son (*Miss. Trav.,* p. 434. Magyar, p. 284).

the property they hold in common unless his wife agrees to it, and on this point her husband often complies with her wishes. This remark applies to several of the Bantu peoples.[1] We are unable to draw from these facts such wide conclusions as those which Bachofen, followed by Giraud-Teulon, endeavours to draw from them, declaring that the important position occupied by women can only be explained by the female line of descent.[2] Such hypotheses are altogether groundless and visionary, and they are unworthy of the attention which has hitherto been given to them.

It is only possible to trace the half-mystical, half-real validity of the important position assigned to women, if we think it probable that they should exert a natural influence. We are not justified in assuming that the savage feels a contempt for woman in virtue of her sex; owing to her weakness, she has much to endure from the brutal passions of man, yet many ways of exerting influence are open to her. Owing to her lively fancy and more passionate feeling, it becomes her part to transmit to others the leading ideas of the primitive community; she begins by being what the bard afterwards became; she retains a faithful remembrance of traditions, and she stimulates the sluggish when they are slow to admit the claims of a bloody revenge. Hence women become the medium through which one clan asserts itself against another, and we have already observed many instances of the way in which unlimited power is placed in their hands. Besides, it is incumbent on Bachofen and Giraud-Teulon to show in what way the assertion that the wife enjoys greater privileges than the husband can be proved;

[1] Alberti, pp. 89, 92, 93. Livingstone, *Narrative*, p. 108; *Miss. Trav.*, p. 622. Schweinfurth, vol. ii. p. 96.

[2] Bachofen, *Mutterrecht, passim.* Giraud-Teulon, *Les Origines*, p. 215: "C'est à la constitution de la famille par les femmes qu'il convient sans doute d'assigner l'origine des prérogatives étranges et superstitieuses accordées a la femme dans le monde barbare, et en particulier à la sœur chez les Africains."

all that has been said only shows that women in some instances enjoy privileges which are always enjoyed by men. If a woman is found to be the head of a tribe,[1] these writers take it as a sign that a special sphere of ideas prevails, yet calmer consideration will show that it is merely an accidental and peculiar consequence of the usual conceptions. No community has been discovered in which women alone may bear rule. The female chief is either the sister or mother of the chief of the whole tribe, and exerts her authority in his name within a limited sphere; or she is the daughter and heiress of such a chief, who has left no sons. Wealth and uncommon intellectual power may also raise a woman to the dignity of a lesser chief.

Giraud-Teulon lays much stress on the sisters or aunts who enjoy the privilege of dethroning the king who is their brother or nephew, but his authorities for this statement are very weak. He tells us that a chief called Mazonda was dethroned by his sister Mata Yafa on account of his cruelty.[2] The story is taken from Cameron's book, which does not say that the sister was called Mata Yafa, but that this was "the title of the chief."[3] The narrative states that Mata Yafa had, by way of pastime, cut a pregnant woman to pieces; this enraged his sister, who was also his head wife, since she feared a like fate for herself. She won over a party to her side, and sought to surprise and kill the king. He, however, made his escape, and she then proclaimed another brother to be king.[4] No one who has not already made up his mind on the subject can see any proof of a sister's rule in this story. The references to the influence

---

[1] Schweinfurth, vol. i. pp. 140-143; vol. ii. p. 64. Livingstone, *Miss. Trav.*, pp. 179, 268, 273, 461, 502, 556; *Narrative*, pp. 108, 395; *Last Journals*, vol. i. pp. 32, 97. Cameron, vol. i. pp. 56, 178; vol. ii. pp. 56, 61. Magyar, pp. 242, 245. Andersson, p. 199. Bosman, p. 71.
[2] Giraud-Teulon, p. 218.   [3] Cameron, vol. ii. p. 58.
[4] *Ibid.*, vol. ii. p. 149. Appendix XX. I have no means of checking Giraud-Teulon's narrative of Mek-Nassr (*Les Origines*, p. 217).

exerted by the mother in councils are equally unsatisfactory. The Bechuana practice cited above shows us
that this may be due to the property which they hold in
common, and cannot, without special reasons, be referred
to mystical and religious ideas. The partition of property
which we have described enables the wife to be very
independent of her husband, and with regard to the
children she acts as the representative of their claims
upon their father. Similar conditions are found in
America, although we did not cite them.[1]

It is the woman's position with respect to property
which enables her to assert her equality with her husband, and which finally, among the Negroes and Bantus
in West Africa, makes the child's descent dependent on
its mother, thus establishing the predominance of the
female line. We have no reason to doubt that the conditions of the Damaras, with respect to the classes derived
from the female line, are similar to those of the Bechuanas. We have also sufficient evidence of the source of
the female line of descent in Bihé and among the Banyai.
A young man of the latter tribe must either buy his
wife or live with her in her home, and in the latter
case, if a divorce takes place, the children belong to their
mother's family. If the wife belongs to another village,
the husband nearly always goes thither, and is treated
by her family partly as a kinsman, partly as a servant.[2]
It is more easy to understand marriage into a strange
village, since we must remember that the Bechuana
village ranks as a family.

The significance of the way in which the wife's family
retains its hold upon her is most apparent in the case of
the Kimbundas. The Africans, in common with many

---

[1] We have already said that the children and property fall to the
Payaguan mother after a divorce. Among the Tehuelche, the father
points out which of his horses are to become the property of his new-born
son, nor can he afterwards dispose of them otherwise.

[2] Livingstone, *Miss. Trav.*, p. 622; *Narrative*, p. 285. Appendix XXI.
Comp. Ploss on the Marolong, *Das Weib*, p. 509.

other primitive peoples, believe that there is no such thing
as a natural death, but that it is caused by magic. It is
the most important office of the tribal magician to trace
out the criminal. On the death of a wife, her kinsfolk
endeavour to induce the magician to fasten the guilt on
her husband, since this will oblige him to pay to them
a large sum as damages.[1] The dread of such an event
induces him to treat his wife with a respect which is in
proportion to the power of her kinsfolk, and her insubor-
dination usually increases in the same degree.[2] Hence
it follows that the wife owns her own hut, her field, and
poultry, and that she is bound to provide for her husband's necessities; it is only the man's duty to give his
wife a new garment at every new moon.[3] Under such
circumstances the man is unable to rule his wife, and
submits to the domination of her whole family. It is
noteworthy that he has unlimited power over such of
his children as have a slave mother.[4] Notwithstanding
the wife's independence, the ground-idea is maintained
that she is the property of her husband, and this makes
her position so obscure and dubious that it is difficult
for her to rise from it.[5]

The conditions just described occur over a wide
range, and where they are most fully accepted, as with
the Negroes and the western Bantus, we find that the
female line of descent prevails. The wives are, indeed,
usually inherited, together with other property, but there
is no community of goods between them and the husband.
We are told that the Loango princesses seek to marry
rich men, whom they ruin as soon as possible and then
discard, and this is also said to have occurred in ancient
Egypt. In Egypt, as is now the case with the Beni-
Amer, daughters had to maintain their parents.[6] Du

[1] Magyar, p. 286.   [2] Ibid., p. 236.   [3] Ibid., p. 282. Bosman, p. 205.
[4] Magyar, p. 284.   [5] Ibid., p. 281.
[6] Klemm, Culturgeschichte, vol. iii. p. 282. Bosman, p. 363. Du Chaillu,
Journey, p. 427. Degrandpré, vol. i. p. 181.   Munzinger, p. 337. Giraud-
Teulon, p. 246.

Chaillu says much of the independence of the wives, and he asserts that when the father-in-law is dissatisfied with the husband, he often reclaims his daughter.[1] The influence of the family clearly appears in the rule that a man may buy his wives, but not those who are daughters of a prince, or even those of his own equals.[2] We find everywhere the fetish-worship which we have already described, but in connection with the tribe, not with the village; this change is the result of the transformed character of the village, which we shall presently consider more closely. In many villages the newly-born child is dedicated to a special fetish, a custom which gives a religious character to kinship, since we cannot doubt that it has to do with the worship of ancestors.[3] Du Chaillu states that the skulls of ancestors are preserved in a hut set apart for them, and that the dried powder of their brains, mixed with food, softens the heart of the eater.[4] The head of each tribe possesses an idol, which is worshipped by its members.[5] The nature of these tribes is somewhat obscure, and we shall presently give our opinion on the subject; the child belongs to them on one side only, and in this case the female line of descent generally predominates.[6]

Du Chaillu says that in Ashango, the brothers of the dead man successively inherit his property and rank. If no brother survives, the eldest son of the eldest sister is the heir. It is only in the Bakalai tribe that the son is his father's heir.[7] In Loango, and in many districts on the Congo, the same rule prevails.[8] According to Bosman, Accra is the only place on the coast of Guinea

[1] Du Chaillu, *Journey*, pp. 171, 197.
[2] Degrandpré, vol. i. pp. 101, 102.
[3] Bastian, p. 77. Bosman, p. 129.
[4] Du Chaillu, *Journey*, p. 199.　　[5] *Ibid.*, pp. 146, 362.
[6] With respect to families and family names, see Klemm, *Culturgeschichte*, vol. iii. pp. 288, 339. Isert, p. 180. Forbes, *Dahomey*, vol. ii. p. 73. Winterbottom, p. 170.
[7] Du Chaillu, *Journey*, p. 429.
[8] Degrandpré, vol. i. p. 109. Bastian, p. 71.

where children inherit their fathers' goods; yet even when the female line of descent is observed, the father's rank, shield, and sword devolve upon the eldest son.[1] Bosman's statements require, however, some explanation. He says, " The children of the brothers or sisters are the true heirs: the eldest boy of the family inherits from his mother's brother, or from his son (?), if he has one, and the eldest girl inherits from her mother's sister, or from her daughter, if she has one. No account is taken of kinsfolk on the father's side, whether father, brother, or sister, and nothing can be inherited from them." [2] Caillié states that in the tribes of Rio Núñez, the sister's son inherits the dignity of chief.[3]

Travellers usually trace the source of the female line of descent to the husband's want of confidence in his wife's chastity, but proofs of this assertion are wanting. The mode of inheritance described by Bosman certainly cannot be explained in this way, since dignity could not devolve upon the son if his exclusion from the property were justified by doubt as to his blood relationship. The simple explanation of the female line of descent is found in the Bechuana custom of distinguishing the different circles of the patriarchal families through the mothers,[4] and if we are able to show how the organization of district communities arose out of those of Bechuanaland, there can be no doubt that this opinion is just.

Du Chaillu gives the following detailed description of a West African community: "Tribes bearing different names considering themselves different nations, though speaking the same language. . . . These tribes were divided into a great number of clans, each clan indepen-

---

[1] Although in Accra property is inherited in the male line, the female line is recognized by giving the mother's name to the child.

[2] Bosman, p. 206.

[3] Caillié, vol. i. p. 127. See Waitz, vol. ii. pp. 123, 131. Klemm, *Culturgeschichte*, vol. iii. pp. 287, 288, 338.

[4] Winterbottom stands alone in his assertion that the female line is to be explained by polygamy.

8

dent of the others, and often at war with one or other of them. . . . The patriarchal form of government was the only one known; each village had its chief, and further in the interior the villages seemed to be governed by elders, each elder, with his people, having a separate portion of the village to themselves. There was in each clan the ifoumou, foumou, or acknowledged head of the clan (*ifoumou* meaning the 'source,' the 'father').

"I have never been able to obtain from the natives a knowledge concerning the splitting of their tribes into clans: they seemed not to know how it happened, but the formation of new clans does not take place now among them.

"Kings never obtain power over large tracts of country, as we see in Eastern Africa; the house of a chief or elder is not better than those of his neighbours.

"The despotic form of government is unknown; no one can be put to death at the will of the chief, and a council of elders is necessary before one is put to death. . . . Very few cases occur in which the father of the family is made to drink the *mboundou*, for he may compel any of his people to drink it. Every one is under the protection of some one. If, by death, a negro is suddenly left alone, he runs great risk of being sold into slavery. Pretexts for such a deed are not found wanting. Every one must have an elder to speak his palavers for him. . . . Any free man, by a singular custom, called *bola bonda*, which consists in placing the hands on the head of an elder, can place himself under the protection of the patriarch who is thus chosen, and henceforward becomes one of his people. Of course, the man under whose protection another places himself belongs to a different clan.

"Tribes and clans intermarry with each other, and this brings about a friendly feeling among the people. People of the same clan cannot marry with each other. The least consanguinity is considered an abomination.

... Slaves always belong to a different tribe from that of their. owner."[1]

It is plain that we here have to do with a mixed tribal and clan government, owing to the fact that each clan obeys its chief, and that one clan is constantly striving for the superiority over another.[2] On account of the frequent disputes, of the continual advance towards the coast, and of the diffusion of trade, it often happens that single clans separate from the rest, and also that one clan becomes dispersed into several villages, divided from each other by the villages of other clans. The connection between the fragments of the clan which is still maintained, shows that the separation is not of very ancient date.[3] We have reason to believe that the clans which obey a common chief were originally members of one large family group. Du Chaillu found that the heir changed his name on his accession to a higher dignity. Quengueza was king of Rembo, of the Commi tribe; he was subsequently called Oganda, after which no one dared to call him Quengueza. The head of the clan Aboga, in the Commi tribe, bears the name Oganda, the next brother that of Quengueza; the next is Kombe-Niavi, a name formerly given to the present Oganda.[4] This is apparently the same arrangement as that described by Bastian in Loango. The five princes who have a claim to the crown inhabit remote villages, and are not permitted to enter the capital. The first

---

[1] Du Chaillu, *Journey*, p. 424.

[2] Degrandpré (vol. i. pp 107, 189) gives the following instance of the power of the villages. Princes—that is, men whose mothers were of the blood royal—had the right of selling men at pleasure. But "Les droits des princes-nés cessent dans les limites de ces bourgades; ils ne peuvent les exercer sur leurs habitans, que dans la campagne où ils trouvent des prétextes pour les attirer lorsqu'ils veulent attenter à leur liberté; mais ils ne le peuvent dans le village même, où nul autre officier que le gouverneur n'a le droit de venir commander."

[3] Du Chaillu, *Journey*, pp. 16, 82, 233, 430.

[4] *Ibid.*, pp. 19, 429: "On my second journey, Obindji, the Bakalai chief, was called Ratenou, having taken the name of his father."

was called Mani-Kay, the second Mani-Bokke, the third Mani-Galloga, the fourth Mani-Kat, the fifth Mani-Ingarni. As soon as Mani-Kay succeeded the dead king, his name devolved on Mani-Bokke, and so on in succession down to Mani-Ingarni, for whom a new name was chosen.[1]

It is easy to show that the Bechuana community may under certain conditions be transformed into a community of the nature we have just described. Each of the Bechuana circles, both larger and smaller, is divided in accordance with the wives of the chief; the marks by which each division is distinguished have at first a natural tendency to change into clan-marks, and secondly, when no definite system of marks is in use, the mark already employed by the wife's family naturally presents itself as the sign of that portion which belongs to her. Supposing that two sisters are married into different families, their family circle falls into subdivisions, bearing the same name, and when, on the death of their husbands, the bond is broken which kept the circle together, those which bear the same name will have a tendency to reunite, so long as a nomadic mode of life keeps distinct social elements in motion.[2] As soon as this mobility diminishes, in consequence of the rising importance of agriculture and the consequent contraction of the territory necessary for the support of the tribe, each of the larger circles splits into a number of clans, which may be of the same race from circle to circle, and thus we have the villages described in West Africa.

It is a Bechuana custom for the king to try to unite the under-chiefs more closely to himself by intermarriage; either by marrying their daughters, or by giving his sisters or father's widows to them as wives. If the

---

[1] Bastian, p. 58.

[2] Livingstone, *Narrative*, p. 311: "In travelling, those belonging to one tribe (that is, clan) always keep by themselves, and help one another."

share of the king's property and dominion which each
son is to inherit comes to him through the mother, the
king's son inherits the fourth share of his mother's
brother; other shares may perhaps come to him, but this
is his in any case. The uncle may have sons of his own,
and may divide his property among them in the usual
way, but each son can only receive a part of his father's
territory, and the whole finally devolves upon the sister's
son. In this way he begins to appear as the true heir
in all circles below that of the king. The king's son
remains the heir, but he must be the eldest son of the
chief wife; and so much weight is given to the mother
by this qualification, that in the long-run the kingship
is also subject to the female line of descent. A woman
may obtain access to the highest command in more than
one way. It may either occur through the custom, so
widely diffused in Africa, of the king's marriage to his own
sister, or there may be some doubt about the hereditary
character of the kingly office, and this tends to put forward a family regarded as worthy to be elected; a custom
found among almost all the peoples we have mentioned.
Men who assert and exercise the right of abandoning
their chief and choosing another, are always on the
verge of an elective kingship. The promotion of the
sister's son to this dignity more usually occurs, however,
when the brother of a deceased king is able to set aside
his son. The brother is always able to urge the claims of
seniority, which constitutes an important advantage in
the eyes of primitive men. Among the Bechuanas,
when a king dies, each son receives that portion of goods
and subjects which had been assigned to his mother, but
the supreme command is given to the eldest son. During
the father's lifetime the sons bear the names of their
respective mothers, but after his death the eldest son
assumes his name. In this way the name and rank
disappear together, and it becomes easy for the eldest
of the surviving brothers to seize for himself the name

and rank of his lately deceased brother, or rather, of the father who died long before.[1]

In this way the singular mode of succession to names and dignities, which we described above, becomes intelligible to us. While the brother takes possession of the dead king's dwelling in the central square, the sons each inherit a portion of his wealth, and these portions are originally smaller than their uncle's kotla, and tend to grow less, since all the scattered elements of the community are attracted to the chief's kotla. In this way the sons of the deceased king become weaker under the uncle's rule, while, on the other hand, the sister's son is in the ascendant, since his mother's dignity makes him the most distinguished member of his father's circle. Even when the wealth of the king's sons equals that of the king's sister, yet after the death of all the father's brothers they are often set aside, and thus become sinking stars. Then the general tendency towards the female line of descent makes it easy for the sister's son to inherit the kingly power.

We have already said that in many instances the female line of descent is observed with respect to the inheritance of property without including the official dignity; the converse never occurs, except that the children of a slave mother occasionally inherit from their father. This is the necessary development from such a state of things as exists among the Bechuanas; first the property, afterwards official rank, devolve upon the female line. It is, on the other hand, impossible to trace the course of development if the female line is held to be the primitive line of descent in Africa.

When we attempt to classify the African peoples with respect to their civilization, we should place the Bushman and the Hottentot on the lowest plane, then

---

[1] Cameron, *Ugogo*, vol. i. p. 101 : "On the death of a chief, the son is supposed to look upon his father's eldest surviving brother as his new or adopted father."

the other Bantu peoples, and give the highest place to the Negroes. Such a classification compels us to seek for the primitive conditions among the Bechuanas, not among the Negroes. A hasty glance at the Bushmans and Hottentots teaches us that their social order is altogether primitive, since it is so extremely simple. The Bechuana communities can also be easily explained from the fact of their primitive condition. We see tribes or hordes gather round the most conspicuous person as their chief; and since this office depends upon personal advantages, it is not hereditary, although the son inherits his father's property.[1] The wife has a right to the property she has gained for herself, and in the event of a divorce, she retains the young children.[2] A girl who is marriageable, and not yet promised in marriage, cannot, among the Bushmans, be married without her own consent; but girls are, for the most part, promised to some member of the tribe from the time of their birth.[3] As soon as property increases in importance, and is less equally distributed, the question with respect to the sons' share in the inheritance leads to testamentary bequests, such as we noted among the Bechuanas, and the office of chief, which is combined with considerable wealth, becomes hereditary. The relatively high position of women may be assumed in this case.

A comparison between the primitive social life of African peoples, as it is found among the Hottentots, and that of the Brazilian tribes, shows that in both countries the single family, with the father as ruler, must be taken as the fundamental type of social development. Differences occur, however, in conformity with the differences which affect the natural conditions of life; some differences also appear during the process of development and

---

[1] Le Vaillant, *Voyage*, vol. ii. p. 72; *Sec. Voyage*, vol. iii. pp. 10, 11. Burchell, vol. i. p. 373.

[2] Burchell, vol. i. p. 373. Le Vaillant, *Voyage*, vol. ii. p. 43.

[3] Burchell, vol. ii. p. 50.

in the motive forces. The American Indian possesses nothing of value except his daughters, while in Africa the movable property of cattle plays an important part. In America, habit, the fear of their common enemy, the name, dwelling, and *tamanuus* which they have in common, create the first groups within the tribe; in Africa, men are associated together by their property. In both countries the formation of groups is due, not so much to ideas of descent as to their local boundaries; this principle begins by assigning to the mother a separate hut, placed within the father's kraal, and goes on to establish clans living in distinct quarters of the village. Our imaginative power is associated with objects of sense, and the thoughts of primitive men consist in imaginations; only those things are combined in thought which he has seen in local association, and at first that will appear to him to be hostile of which he fails to see the local connection.

CHAPTER IV.

ASIA.

Malayan Gezin—Semando and Djudur—Indian aborigines—Service and migration of bridegroom—Kasias—Process of development—Promiscuous intercourse of Nairs—Nair development—Limboos and Lepchas—Western Asia.

In China, and among the other Mongolian races, as well as among the Finns, we find clans, or, at least, clan-like groups of kinsfolk, who also possess the usual characteristic of exogamy. In all cases individuals are distributed into patriarchal families, and no direct traces of the female line of descent exist.

The primitive conditions are maintained in their greatest purity among the Malays of Sumatra, in the kingdom of Menangkabao. This people is divided into tribes (*Laras*) and subdivided into clans (*Sukus*). Each village has a chief for every sukus it contains. Each sukus is responsible for all the families of which it consists, and each family (*Gezin*) is responsible for the debts of its members, and the family holds and inherits property in common. Each individual belongs to his mother's gezin and sukus; even after his marriage, a man cannot form an independent gezin, but he, his brothers and sisters, still belong to that of their mother. He works for the gezin and is bound to provide for it; he is not bound in the same way to his wife, although he usually assists her as far as he is able to do so. These conditions now appear to be dying out; the male line of descent and individual property are fast spreading under European influence and that of Islam.[1]

The form of marriage which enjoins each man to remain in the house of his parents is only the extreme form of that which is in use in Sumatra under the name *Semando*. In such marriages the man and wife are on an equal footing, and their respective rights are protected by a contract between the relations of the two parties.[2] This form of marriage, however, is only common among the poor;[3] marriages are more commonly either *Djudur*—in which case a man buys his wife as his absolute property—or *Ambelanak*—in which the woman's family buys a husband for her, who is thereby completely detached from his own family; his new family becomes responsible for the debts he contracts after the wedding, and he lives with them as something between a son of the house and a slave.[4] Djudur involves the observance of the male, Ambelanak of the female line, and the question as to which was the original line of kinship among the Malays resolves itself into the question whether the man originally took his wife to his own home or established himself in her family.

It is certainly difficult to decide on the priority of this or that custom. In order to make our argument as conclusive as possible, we must also consider the primi-

---

[1] Bachofen, *Ant. Br.*, vol. i. p. 55. Waitz, vol. v. pp. 1, 141. Newbold, vol. ii. p. 220.

[2] *Ibid.*, p. 226.   [3] *Ibid.*, p. 300.

[4] Marsden, pp. 225-227, 236, 272. See Forbes, *Eleven Years in Ceylon*, vol. i. p. 333 : "In Cingalese marriages there is no community of property between the husband and wife; and the two forms, called Beena and Deega marriage, cause a great difference in the right of female inheritance. A woman married in Beena lives in the house, or in the immediate neighbourhood of her parents, so as to be able to cook for them, and render them assistance in times of sickness or in old age; if so married, she has a right of inheritance along with her brothers. If married in Deega, that is, to live in her husband's house and village, she loses her right of paternal inheritance, and acquires new rights from the patrimony of her husband." See also *Formosa*, Lambert, vol. i. p. 32.

tive peoples of India. In the case of these peoples, I
have only observed two instances of the man establishing
himself in the wife's dwelling; among the once-powerful
Koochs, and among the Kasias. We shall presently consider the Kasias more closely. We are told that a Kooch
woman owns the property, and it is inherited from mother
to daughter; the husband lives with his wife and her
mother, and is subject to both of them.[1] Although this
migration of the husband rarely takes place, yet it is very
common for the bridegroom to live for a while in his
bride's house;[2] and the reason for this custom is that,
as in America, the husband buys his bride by working
for her kinsfolk. Knox tells us that in Ceylon, where
the houses consist of only one room, the children, as they
grow up, are accustomed to pass the night in a neigh-
bour's house, which they prefer to their own home, and
where perhaps they find a bedfellow. These neighbours
are not displeased that young people in the same rank
of life should make acquaintance with their daughters
in this way, since they know that it will be the means
of inducing the young men to help them in their work,
and in other matters.[3] Among the Marianas, the wooer
who is unable to contribute to the support of his future
wife must become a servant to her family until he marries
her.[4]

We may be disposed to trace a connection between
customs which enjoin the bridegroom to earn his bride
by labour in her parents' house, and, again, to take up
his permanent abode with them. Yet it can be safely
asserted that no such connection exists, and that the
two customs spring from distinct ideas. Serving for
the bride is only a mode of purchasing a wife, while the

[1] *Journal of Asiat. Soc. of Bengal*, 1849, vol. xviii. p. 707; Hodgson.
See Appendix XXII.
[2] *E.g.* Kookies (*Butler's Travels*, p. 82. See *Journal of Asiat. Soc.
of Bengal*, 1855, vol. xxiv.; Stewart), Meckius (*Butler's Travels*, p. 138),
and Mishmees (Cooper, *Mish. Hills*, p. 236).
[3] Knox, p 192.   [4] Freycinet, vol. ii. pt. i. p. 386.

migration of the husband is due to the great cohesive
power of the several families, which causes them to
refuse to part with any of their members. Since men
are more independent, they are also less stationary; they
can no longer attract the women to themselves, and are
therefore attracted by them. It might be expected that
such a custom would gradually exert a destructive influence upon marriage whenever the husband gives up
the connection with his own family. We do not find
that in Sumatra the bond of marriage is easily broken
when the man remains in his mother's gezin, but the
tie appears to be a loose one among the Kasias whom we
have mentioned above.

The circumstances of this people have been altogether
misunderstood by Bachofen. He assumes that the bond
of marriage is so firm that the father's line of descent
must prevail amongst them, since the paternity is never
doubtful.[1] Bachofen bases his opinion upon two quite
unimportant treatises, of which the first contains nothing
about marriage, and the second gives an obscure and
doubtful report that marriages are contracted in a very
regular way, that conjugal infidelity rarely if ever
occurs, but that bigamy is practised.[2] Bachofen therefore concludes that they do not observe the female line
of descent, because no doubts are entertained with respect to the paternity.[3] We also believe that the female
line does not arise from doubt as to the paternity, but
we do not accept Bachofen's premisses, since competent
accounts by Yule and Fisher give a very different description of the Kasian marriages.

The licentious character of their marriages constitutes
the worst feature in the customs of this people; it can,
indeed, scarcely be termed a marriage, since the connec-

[1] Bachofen, *Ant. Br.*, vol. i. p. 213.
[2] *Asiat. Research*, 1832, vol. xvii. p. 501; Walters. *Journal of Roy. Geo. Soc.*, 1832, vol. ii. p. 94; Murphy.
[3] *Journal of Asiat. Soc. of Bengal*, 1840, vol. ix. p. 834.

tion is so frequently dissolved.   The man does not take
his wife home, but lives in her house, or pays her occasional visits; he appears to be only accepted in order to
add to the number of the wife's family.[1] The couples separate so often and so readily that it sometimes seems as if
the woman had two lovers at the same time, so that it has
been believed that polyandry is practised among them.[2]

Such a marriage resembles the pre-nuptial connections
described by Knox in Ceylon.   The assertion has often
been made that there was no marriage among primitive
men, who were contented with such a temporary connection, and the primitive character of the female line
of descent has been based upon this assertion.   The case
of the Kasias is, however, not conclusive, since neither
the primitive character of their female line nor the
primitive character of their free sexual relations are
established facts.   And we think it possible to show
that these customs, so far from being primitive were
introduced at a comparatively late period.

When it is asserted that a permanent tie of marriage
would be established with difficulty among primitive
men, it is in virtue of the maxim that social organizations
only become permanent and enduring after a lapse of
time.   In all places, however, in which man is found,
we find also that the family group, or clan, is highly
developed, and it seems to us that this organization
is much more cohesive than the individual family,
which is merely held together by the brute force of the
father.   We believe that the earliest development must
be traced to the father's claim to some equivalent for
the loss of his daughter; the next step in advance is the
attempt so secure for her a fair position with reference
to her husband, after the marriage has taken place;
and it is the father-in-law's intervention which finally

[1] *Journal of Asiat. Soc. of Bengal*, 1844, vol. xiii. p. 624; Yule. See
Appendix XXIII.
[2] *Ibid.*, 1840, vol. ix. p. 834; Fisher.
9

causes the woman to be the ruler of the household.[1]
Conditions such as those of the Koochs or those in
Menangkabao gradually arise, and these again yield to
those of the Kasias. It is only in this way that a
natural progress can be traced, and that this is really
the fact, and no idle fancy, appears from the further
development which is found among the Nairs on the
coast of Malabar. If we regard the social conditions of
this people as in the first stage of development, they are
as difficult to understand as they become intelligible
when we accept them as the latest phase of the development we have described.

[1] Freycinet writes as follows of the Marianas (vol. ii. pt. i. pp. 475,
477): "Une fille, en se mariant, n'apportoit jamais de dot à son mari:
c'était à lui ou à ses parens qu'il appartenait de pourvoir à toutes les
nécessités de l'entrée en ménage ; . . . à la mort du père, sa fortune et ses
enfans passaient entre les mains de la veuve; si, au contraire, c'était la
femme qui mourait d'abord, les parens de celle-ci s'emparaient non seulement des biens du mari, mais aussi des enfans qu'elle lui avait donnés. . . .
La veuve que son mari laissait sans enfans conservait non seulement
tous les biens de la communauté, mais avait droit en outre, à une espèce
de douaire, nommé fagahot (héritage) auquel toutes les parentes du défunt
étaient tenues de contribuer; en l'acceptant elle cessoit de demeurer
alliée à la famille où son mariage l'avait fait entrer, et lui devenait
entièrement étrangère." Laval gives a similar account of the Maldivians
(p. 113): "Les femmes n'ont rien en mariage et ne portent rien ; c'est
aux maris qui les prennent de les accommoder de tout ce qui leur est
nécessaire et de faire les frais des nopces, selon leur qualité. Aussi ils leur
constituent un douaire qu'ils appellent Raas, non pas selon les biens et la
qualité du mary, mais selon la qualité de la femme et selon que ses mères
et ayeulles en ont eu, car elle ne peut avoir moins. . . . La plus part des
femmes tiennent ce Raas, pour l'honneur et l'ancienneté de leur maison,
parce que la plus grande partie d'elles en quitte une partie ou le tout, si
bon leur semble, peu de jours après qu'ils sont mariez. Si le mary meurt,
il est permis à elle de prendre son douaire sur ses biens, mais les héritiers
composent avec elle, que si elle l'avoit quité durant la vie du défunt, elle
n'y pourroit plus rien demander." In both instances the child takes the
rank of its mother: "C'était ordinairement sur les femmes que s'établissait
l'échelle de la parenté mariannaise" (Freycinet, p. 372). "Les femmes
nobles, quoique mariées à des personnes de condition inférieure et non
nobles, ne perdent pas leur rang; mesmes les enfans qui en sont issus sont
nobles par le moyen de leur mère, bien que leur père fust de vile condition.
Aussi les femmes de basse qualité mariées à des nobles ne sont pas annoblies
par leurs maris, et elles retiennent leur premier rang, chacun demeure en
sa condition, et il n'y a point de confusion pour ce regard" (Laval, p. 151)

The Nairs constitute the ruling caste on the Malabar coast, and live as rajahs or warlike nobles. Like other Indian peoples, the Nairs jealously maintain their purity of caste, and their women are only allowed to marry men of their own or of a higher caste. Incest is abhorrent to them; all sexual relations are forbidden to members of the same household, which generally includes the whole family. But within these limits of the caste and the family the greatest liberty in sexual relations prevails. The family group—that is, the "joint family" which is so common throughout India—includes many allied families, which not only live together in large common houses, but also possess everything in common. There is a common tenure of land, over which the eldest male member of the community presides, while the mother, and after her death the elder sister, is in charge of the household. If a brother separates from the rest he is generally accompanied by his favourite sister, who takes charge of his house. The movable property which a man leaves behind him is divided among his sisters' children. The men do not marry, but may frequent other houses as suitors, without ceasing to live at home, and without being in any degree detached from the maternal family. As soon as a girl is marriageable, the mother invites her kinsfolk and friends, and presents herself with her daughter, arrayed in all her ornaments. She asks whether any one is willing to marry the girl, and if a suitor is found the wedding is solemnized with great splendour. The chief ceremony consists in winding a silken cord, to which a coin worth about two shillings is attached, round the necks of both, and the bridegroom then hangs the coin round the bride's throat. He is thus entitled, if so disposed, and if he is not too nearly related to the girl, to regard her as his wife for the space of one day; but thenceforward they see no more of each other than if no such union had taken place. He may have love passages in many houses: she chooses two, four, even as many as twelve husbands, on whom she bestows her favours, and receives in return small gifts for herself and her mother. Each lover remains at her command for twenty-four hours, and he must make himself useful to her during this period by fetching wood and the like, and he also enjoys the rights of a husband. Both parties are free to break off the connection without ceremony, and divorces are very frequent. The paternity of every Nair is unknown.[1]

McLennan believes that these conditions represent the first stage in the primitive life of man. We do not now undertake to examine this author's theory, but we are able to give our reasons for not regarding the Nair-type as primitive. This people is in no respect one of primitive culture, but has been developed in one direction by very varied external conditions. It is therefore probable that the singular customs we have described are final rather than primitive. Their promiscuous intercourse is not the primitive condition, maintained in some strange fashion, nor has it produced the female line of descent; this line is more probably due to the extreme concentration of the family group, and the fact that it had prevailed so long probably paved the way for promiscuous intercourse.

Our readers must have observed that the Nairs solemnize weddings, although they do not recognize the validity of marriage. It is impossible not to regard the ceremony by which a girl is dedicated to what is, according to our ideas, an unchaste life, as a wedding ceremony which has been degraded into a mere formality. The tying of the knot is found elsewhere as the symbol of the marriage union, and the coin is the symbol of the bridegroom's wedding gift. These symbols become quite unintelligible if the dedication ceremony is placed on the same plane as the festivities with which primitive men celebrate the advent of puberty. Even Bachofen

[1] Buchanan, vol. ii. p. 412. See Bachofen, *Ant. Br.*, vol. i. chs. xxviii-xxx.

recognizes a symbolical marriage in the ceremony we have described. We need not now consider the surprising assertion that the Nairs' marriage contract serves as the preliminary condition of his claim to sexual liberty; this follows from the mythological theory, which we shall discuss later on.

Among the northern Nairs, the women hold intercourse with the men as their lovers, and are very faithful to them, but they have nothing to do with the household management as long as the man's mother is alive. He may, if he chooses, send the woman away at any time, and on his death she goes back with her children to her brother, takes charge of his house, and her children become his heirs.[1] The same mode of life prevails among the Buntar, the highest class of the Sudras Tulavas; except that the eldest daughter of a Tulavan Rajah never marries, but takes now one, now another Brahman as her lover; her sons become Rajahs, and her eldest daughter carries on the family.[2] Similar conditions exist among the Mogayen (Tulavan fishermen) and the Biluares, who extract juice from palm-trees.[3] These are certainly transition forms, either of a waning or of a waxing Nair-type; and since it is difficult to obtain any certainty about them, they are of no use for our present purpose.

Lubbock's account of the Limboos will serve as an example of the inaccurate way in which these kinds of customs have sometimes been described. Limboo sons

---

[1] Buchanan, vol. ii. p. 513.   [2] Ibid., vol. iii. pp. 16–18.

[3] Ibid., vol. ii. p. 492; vol. iii. pp. 22, 53. "The wife works for her husband's master, who must maintain her and her children, until they are able to work; the eldest son then belongs to him, but all the other children belong to their mother's master, and return to the hut of her parents." The children of Catal or Curumbal slaves all belong to the mother's master (Ibid., vol. ii. p. 498). We are told of the Corar slaves to the Tulavas, who were formerly in possession of the country: "The master pays the expense of the marriage feast. When a man dies, his wives, with all their children, return to the huts of their respective mothers and brothers, and belong to their masters" (Ibid., vol. iii. p. 101).

belong to their fathers if a small sum of money has been paid to the mother; the child then receives a name and is admitted into his father's tribe, while the daughters abide with their mother.[1] In this custom Lubbock traces a survival of an extinct female line of descent. It is hardly necessary to say that we should rather trace in such a custom the dawning of a female line; but the custom itself has no existence. Campbell, to whom Lubbock refers,[2] only states that the Limboo bride is purchased, and, if such a stipulation has been previously made, is taken to her husband's home. Labour is often substituted for the purchase money. His account goes on to say that children born out of wedlock, and those born of a connection between Limboo men and Lepcha women, are called *Koosaba.* The father may obtain possession of the boys by purchase and by naming them, but the girls belong to the mother.[3] Here we are, in the first place, only concerned with children born out of wedlock, and, secondly, with the children of persons of distinct tribes, which are by the mode of naming them placed on a level with the illegitimate. It should be noted that the Limboos are strictly endogamous, the only exception being made in favour of the Lepchas.[4]

The existence of the female line among the peoples of Western Asia has been ascertained with respect to some ancient tribes; in other cases the inference of its existence is not wholly justified.[5] It does not now prevail in any part of that country. It would be lost labour

[1] Lubbock, *Origin of Civ.*, p. 149. Appendix XXIV.

[2] Lubbock quotes Campbell, *Trans. Ethno. Soc.*, New Series, vol. vii., which I have had no opportunity of consulting; but I think the same reference may be found in *Journal Asiat. Soc. of Bengal.*

[3] *Journal Asiat. Soc. of Bengal*, 1840, vol. ix. p. 603; Campbell. Appendix XXV.

[4] *Ibid.*, p. 596.

[5] Lycians (Herodotus, i. 173). In Northern Africa we may also cite the Ethiopians (Bachofen, *Mutterrecht*, p. 21), the Bega ancestors of the Bischari, and the Messophites (*Ibid.*, p. 108), Barea and Bazer (Munzinger. pp. 481, 484), Touaregs (Duveyrier, pp. 337-340).

to say more of these various accounts, since they afford
no material of any value in solving the question as to
the motives for preferring the one or the other line.
They are capable of being interpreted in whichever sense
has previously been adopted as the right one.[1]

[1] I may here direct attention to Wilken's attempt to trace the female
line among the Arabs. His conclusions are based upon the following
facts: 1. That polyandry and unchaste customs throw doubt upon the
paternity, so that it would be most natural to adopt the female line.
2. That the Arabs call the clan Batu, or belly, which points to the mother.
3. That some clans are called after the mother's tribe. 4. That the
character of the mother's brother is supposed to devolve upon the sister's
children. Wilken himself is of opinion that each fact, taken singly,
proves nothing, but that in the aggregate they are of weight. We shall
subsequently show that Wilken's opinions are untenable.

CHAPTER V.

POLYNESIA.

Polynesian classes—Marriage and class—Fijian Vasu.

THE Polynesian definition of kinship must be added to the conditions we have described in the last chapter. The dividing line which is usually drawn between the Polynesian and Melanesian is in this case without significance.

In Polynesia, the distinct classes constitute a similar state of things to the family group in the peoples we have just considered, since they form an exclusive organization, holding property in common. It is not very clear how these classes arose, but we may assume that they are connected with an earlier distribution into clans, so that the chief represents the eldest line of the posterity of their common ancestor. In some cases this ancestor is supposed to be of Divine origin ; but we lay no stress on such a supposition, since it probably arose after the chief's position was established. The people are usually in possession of small plots of ground, either as comparatively independent proprietors, or as serfs ; the nobles are owners or rulers of small districts, and the king is ruler of the whole. The conditions are in many respects confused and indefinite, yet the type is undoubtedly that of the joint family, or village community.

The classes differ from clans in a natural way. The

nobles of different clans belong to one class, and while the clan is usually exogamous, the class always tends to become endogamous. In Polynesia, the definition of the class depends upon the line of kinship, and the classes are not isolated with the exclusiveness of castes in India : marriages between the different classes are not absolutely forbidden.

The position of a child born from a marriage between persons of unequal rank may be decided in several ways. The child may either be always assigned to the superior or inferior class, or always either to the father or mother. Polynesia offers us examples of all kinds.

If the father or mother alone belongs to the ruling class, the child is, in the Caroline Isles, assigned to that class.[1] In the Tonga Isles, the highest class—the Egi, or nobles—inherits rank and property through the mother ; the children of the common people (Mataboulas and Tuas) inherit from the father, but belong to the mother's class.[2] In Otaheite, the children of a marriage between a noble (Hui-Arii) and a woman of a lower class are set aside, unless numerous ceremonies are performed in the temple at the time of the wedding, so as to raise the rank of the inferior person.[3] Both among the nobles and in the intermediate class of landowners the father abdicates in favour of his new-born son, because the son has an additional ancestor, and is therefore of higher rank than his father.[4]

Marriages are dissolved in the Sandwich Isles at the wish of either party ; only in the case of the chiefs there is no divorce, but they form a connection with other women, and their wives take other lovers. These are usually of inferior rank, and the children begotten of

---

[1] Chamisso, vol. ii. p. 241.
[2] Martin, vol. ii. p. 101. Rienzi, vol. iii. p. 45. Morgan, *Systems*, p. 559.
[3] Ellis, vol. iii. p. 98.
[4] *Ibid.*, vol. iii. p. 100. Cook, vol. i. Hawkesworth, vol. ii. p. 243.

such marriages are almost always put to death, probably by the kinsfolk of the higher class, in order that their own importance may not suffer from intermixture with an inferior rank.[1] When we are told that in Hawaii the dignity of chief is inherited through the mother, it must be understood that preference is given to those of the chief's children whose mother is of the highest rank.[2] " The wife does not share her husband's rank. The rank of the child is decided by certain definite laws, generally by that of its mother, but also in some cases by that of the father. A woman of noble family who marries one of the common people loses her rank in the event of bearing children to him, in which case she and her children are degraded to her husband's class. The right of inheritance is not decided by priority of birth, but by the fact that the mother is of higher rank than the other wives."[3]

This is also the case at King's Mill and in New Zealand.[4] In the latter country, the man who marries into another tribe or clan takes up his abode in it, and is thenceforward reckoned with his wife's family. It is also usual for the wife to raise her husband to her own rank, while this is not done by the husband.[5] This fact has been regarded as a survival of a clearly established female line, and a sign of the earlier pre-eminence of the wife ; but it seems to me to imply precisely the opposite. Only the prevalent custom of ascribing the child to its father would induce the kinsfolk of a woman of high rank to adopt her husband, in order not to lose their hold upon the children. If the female line were about to disappear, the growing claims of the husband would lead to the adoption of his wife by his own family.

It has been supposed that the strongest proof of the

---

[1] Ellis, vol. i. p. 256; vol. iv. p. 411.   [2] Varigny, p. 14.
[3] Chamisso, vol. ii. p. 275.
[4] Wilkes, vol. v. p. 85.   Rienzi, vol. iii. p. 142.
[5] Thompson, vol. i. p. 176.   Brown, p. 34.

female line is to be found among the Fiji Islanders, but here also the spirit of mature criticism is wanting. We are told that the king is succeeded by his brother, and by his eldest son only in the event of his leaving no surviving brother. The mother's rank and some other circumstances may, however, cause this rule to be violated, so that the younger is preferred to the elder brother.[1] The chief's practice of extensive polygamy makes it desirable to establish the child's rank by a reference to its mother.[2] The female line cannot be deduced from these customs, but a stronger proof is afforded by the institution of the Vasu, which is described as follows :—" Most prominent among the public notorieties of Fiji is the *Vasu*. The word means a nephew or niece, but becomes a title of office in the case of the male, who, in some localities, has the extraordinary privilege of appropriating whatever he chooses belonging to his uncle, or those under his uncle's power. Vasus are of three kinds : the *Vasu taukei*, the *Vasu levu*, and the *Vasu ;* the last is a common name, belonging to any nephew whatever. *Vasu taukei* is a term applied to any Vasu whose mother is a lady of the land in which he is born. The fact of Mbau being at the head of Fijian rank gives the Queen of Mbau a pre-eminence over all Fijian ladies, and her son a place nominally above all Vasus. No material difference exists between the power of a *Vasu taukei* and that of a *Vasu levu*, which latter title is given to every Vasu born of a woman of rank, and having a first-class chief for his father. *Vasu taukei* can claim anything belonging to a native of his mother's land, excepting the wives, home, and land of a chief. . . . However high a chief may rank, however powerful a king may be, if he has a nephew he has a master, one who will not be content with the name, but who will exercise

---

[1] Williams and Calvert, p. 18. Appendix XXVI. Rienzi, vol. iii. p. 286. Morgan, *Systems*, p. 582; *Anc. Soc.*, p. 375.
[2] Williams and Calvert, p. 26. Appendix XXVII.

his prerogative to the full, seizing whatever may take his fancy, regardless of its value or the owner's inconvenience in its loss. Resistance is not thought of, and objection only offered in extreme cases. Thokonauto, a Rewa chief, during a quarrel with an uncle, used the right of Vasu, and actually supplied himself with ammunition from his enemy's stores." [1]

It cannot be denied that this great power of the sister's son is very remarkable, and at the first glance it seems only possible to explain it by assuming that there was a peculiar sanctity in the tie of kinship between the man and his sister's son. The extent of the claim is astonishing—a claim which no son would venture to put forward; and this is the more remarkable since the sister's son is not the uncle's heir. In all other cases in which the female line divides father and son, in order to tighten the bond between the mother's brother and sister's son, the analogy with the male line is maintained; that is, the uncle exerts his authority over the sister's son, whereas in this instance their positions are reversed. This arouses a suspicion that ideas unconnected with the female line may have produced the Vasu rights.

On examining more closely the whole institution of the Vasu, we are first struck by the fact that no legitimate rights belong to the common Vasu. These claims can only be made by the Vasu whose mother's brother possesses people and land. It may be assumed that the power of the Vasu in its extreme development was first directed against the mother's brother after it had become an integral part of the political machinery of Fiji, since we are told that the Vasu-right becomes an instrument in the king's hand for ruthlessly plundering the land. The king makes use of the Vasu, and shares the plunder with him. [2] There can be no doubt that the institution of Vasu arose out of the natural reverence with which the subjects regarded the king's sister's son when he

[1] Williams and Calvert, p. 27.   [2] *Ibid.*, p. 27. Appendix XXVIII.

visited his uncle. They honoured the king through his kinsfolk. The king and his sons ruled after no gentle fashion, and the ruler was entitled to commit all sorts of acts of violence. In this way the honour paid to the king's sister's son enabled him to rob the people freely. The Vasu-right was gradually transformed into a fundamental institution, and that which was at first serviceable to the king was now turned against him. It certainly affords no indications of a mystical and religious belief in any special sacred bond between the mother's brother and sister's son.

10

CHAPTER VI.

ARYAN PEOPLES.

Maine and McLennan—Patriarchal family group—Joint family group—
Economic interests—Property in land and cattle—Comparison between Hindus and Bechuanas—Primitive character of agnation—
Hindu female line—Sapinda and Samanodoka—Agnates and cognates
—Germanic female line—Marriage and guardianship—Physical relation between mother and child—Class inheritance—Inheritance of
property—Arms and accoutrements—Precedence taken by female
heirs—Rejpus—Woman hands down family tradition—Orestes.

THE endeavour to grasp the meaning of the line of
descent is in no case more important than in that of the
Aryan peoples, for since we ourselves are Aryans, these
peoples possess a special interest for us. The primitive
records are also more abundant, consisting of very ancient
laws committed to writing, and not merely of everyday
customs and usages. But the very abundance of the
material increases the difficulty of dealing with it. And
the special question with which we are now concerned,
whether the Aryan community was originally agnatistic
or not, has been treated in an unsatisfactory manner,
owing to the imperfect and obscure mode in which it
has been stated.

Two theories, completely opposed to each other, have
been presented to us. Philologists generally hold that
the primitive character of Aryan communities was exclusively agnatistic, and this theory has been supported
by Sir Henry Maine in a manner which entitles us to

regard him as the representative of the patriarchal theory. This theory asserts that the child was originally ascribed to the father only, and kinship through the mother was not counted at all. On the other hand, learned men like McLennan, Bachofen, etc., hold it to be an undoubted fact that the Aryan tribes originally lived in promiscuous intercourse, and only counted kinship through the mother.

This apparently irreconcilable contradiction must not, however, be estimated too highly, since the word "originally" is used in a different sense by the two parties. Sir Henry Maine understands by the primitive Aryan community only the one of which the type is found in the earliest collections of laws; while McLennan undertakes to describe the primitive community in its literal sense. It was McLennan's object to examine the salient features of the patriarchal state which may be deduced from the most ancient laws, in order to ascertain how far they have arisen from an altogether different social condition. Maine sets aside such inquiries as wholly irrelevant, and, whatever results they may afford, he holds his own theory to be firmly established.[1] On this point we do not agree with Maine, for if it can be shown that a community in which there was promiscuous intercourse and a female line of descent preceded the agnatistic community, it would undoubtedly be a much more arduous undertaking to trace the causes which effected such a transformation. The strife between the two theories which still subsists must be referred to an imperfect estimate of the mode in which kinship should be reckoned.

The family group, or joint undivided family, constitutes the typical feature of the Aryan community; that is, an association of persons who dwell under the same roof, who own their property in common, and who offer a common sacrifice to the same ancestor. Such

[1] Maine, *Early Law*, ch. vii. p. 192. See Hearn, p. 153.

kinsfolk are termed Sapindas, or persons joined together
by the cake of sacrifice. These family groups are further
distributed into clans (Gotra), and members of the same
Gotra are called Samanodocas, or persons joined together
by the same libation of water. The Sapinda kinship
ceases with the seventh person, that is, with the sixth
degree of kinship; the Samanodoca connection only
ceases when the birth and family name are no longer
known.[1]   As long as the family group holds together,
it is under the guidance of the eldest male of the eldest
line, and the amount of power possessed by this patriarch
is shown to us in the case of the Roman heads of families.
This patriarchal community, a reduced form of the
modern family in one respect, and its enlargement in
another, is considered by Maine to be the first step
in primitive jurisprudence.[2]   The patriarchal power
extends over the life and liberty of the members of the
family.   The wife and children are absolutely in the
power of the head of the family, and he has not to give
account to any one for his actions. We saw that the
Brazilian community was constructed on these lines,
which afford the typical form of brute force. The Aryan
groups only differ from those of Brazil in their greater
permanence; they are not, like the latter, dissolved when
the son grows to manhood.   In this more permanent
structure a force silently arose which prescribed limits
to the arbitrary power of the patriarch.   Habit and
custom gradually constrained him to act under a deep
sense of responsibility to the presiding spirit of the family.[3]
The women, in particular, as the most defenceless, were
placed under the protection of this spirit, and the head
of the family no longer dared to kill his wife before he
had proclaimed her guilt to the domestic tribunal.   The
patriarch always tended to become merely a judge who
decided causes in accordance with custom and usage; he

[1] Hearn, p. 168.   [2] Maine, *Ancient Law*, pp. 133, 138.
[3] Hearn, p. 97.   See Grimm, p. 450.

ceased to be the master whose arbitrary will was law. So likewise his position as ruler of the family property was changed. As the family grew into an undivided family group, he was no longer regarded as the owner, but only as the steward of the property. As it has been truly said, he no longer inherited a property, but an office.[1]

The joint family group appears as soon as the children of the same father continue to live together after his death. The brothers and sisters then possess in common what had previously belonged to the father alone, and under these circumstances the patriarchal power was necessarily modified. We have seen that the Brazilians took the first step towards the joint family group, but in their case the organization had no stability, since it lacked the power which is maintained by the interests which members of the same family have in common. Property and religion riveted the connection among the Aryans, but both were wanting to the Brazilians, or only existed in their faint beginnings. We are told, for example, that "the Macuanis used to bury the corpses of their young children in their huts, and those of adults at a distance from the village. On the graves of the latter, which were surrounded by a ditch, they placed flesh and fruits, and lighted a fire, in order that all the needs of the departed might be satisfied. They subsequently struck a lance into the grave, or built a hut upon it."[2]

The worship of ancestors, which we here find in the germ, became of such importance among the Aryans that it may be termed the bond of union among the groups; its force was owing to the fact that it was able to work under material conditions which had, at any rate in part, produced the formation of the joint family groups. Economical interests first led to the formation of such

[1] J. D. Mayne, pp. 198-200. Hearn, p. 82.
[2] Spix and Martius, vol. ii. p. 492.

groups. We can readily understand that many different circumstances had their effect on this development; it would be unwise to ascribe to one or other of them, taken singly, the power of producing such a compact organization. It was an organization of which the stability depended upon the manifold ways in which its members were useful to each other: their common share in matters pertaining to attack and defence, the impressions to which they were subject during their common growth, that thorough community of spirit which arises from living together in one place,—all these things had their influence on the formative process, and, as I have repeatedly said, local union is the chief condition under which primitive consciousness is able to maintain the idea of the interdependence of individuals. The circumstances we have enumerated are found in every form of social development, but this special form, the joint family group, is only produced by special economic interests.

J. D. Mayne asserts that it is only the great ease with which a family can obtain as much wealth as it desires which hinders the simple patriarchal family from becoming a joint family group.[1] But he lays too much stress on land as the only form of wealth. For although the scarcity of land may, in a growing population, often have promoted the development of the joint family group, as well as of the village communities, Sir Henry Maine justly urges that in primitive communities the possession of the soil is not the main point; it is not the soil, but the means of turning it to account which are valuable.[2] Land may be abundant in cases in which a lack of the means of cultivating it makes it desirable that it should be held in common. J. D. Mayne has himself cited the Kandhs as an instance of such a state of things. We have seen that among the Bechu-

---

[1] J. D. Mayne, p. 198. Appendix XXIX.
[2] Maine, *Early History of Institutions, passim.*

anas the large herds of cattle pass from mothers to children; each of these groups already forms something like a family group, and whenever monogamy smooths the way for it, as it does in the Aryan race, similar conditions of family communism necessarily arise. The owner of a large herd commands respect; the social position of the individual does not make it desirable to divide this herd among many heirs, partly because the sole possessor of a small herd is less powerful than the joint possessors of a large herd, and still more because the profitable use of the soil becomes more difficult through such a partition.

In Maine's excellent work on the "Early History of Institutions," he dwells upon the importance of the custom of giving and receiving stock; the great proprietor lends his cattle to the poor, who thereby become his dependents. As we have said, this custom is not unknown to the Bechuanas.[1] Cattle are not everywhere essential for the profitable use of the soil; simple individual labour becomes a means of wealth, and thus defines the limit of the property which each individual can hold. The culture of the soil is, among most primitive peoples, carried on in common, and among many of them the value of this common labour leads to the development of a community of property. We must therefore choose between two possibilities. The Aryan joint family group was either developed from the Bechuana form, according to which cattle constitute the essential wealth, or from the form in which wealth consisted in the possession of the soil.

The distinction between the family groups which owe their existence to one or other of these conditions is not unimportant. An agricultural community lays much more claim to the capacity of each individual for labour than is the case with a community which is

---

[1] Burchell, vol. ii. pp. 348, 515.

wholly or chiefly occupied with the rearing of cattle. In the former case a diminution in the number of a household is a loss which it is difficult to supply, and they are chiefly concerned in keeping up their numbers, that is, in retaining their hold on the individual. But in a cattle-breeding community men make it their first object to increase the number of stock. In the former community the head of the family opposes the departure of his daughter, and seeks to induce her wooer to become one of the household; but in the latter he will sell her as early, and for as high a price as possible. The agricultural community will therefore display a natural tendency to the female line of descent, which we accordingly find in America; the rearing of cattle is favourable to the male line, as in the case of the Bechuanas, where this tendency offers a strong resistance to all those tendencies which endeavour to introduce the female line into the polygamous family.

The Hindu communities are almost exclusively agricultural; but this was not the case with our Aryan forefathers, who were wholly occupied with the rearing of cattle. Starting from the assumption that the Hindu clans were developed from families and family groups, an organization into clans which Lyall describes as still existing in Rajputana,[1] the word used for a clan reminds us of conditions analogous to those of Bechuanaland. Gotra (a clan), as well as the Bechuana kotla, signifies a cow-place; and the part which it plays in Bechuanaland probably affords a true picture of the part it played in the times of our remote ancestors. Squatters establish themselves round the huts of the large proprietor, and although not entitled to inherit with those who are really his children, they are all called his children. They hold together for the sake of protection, and the sons

---

[1] Lyall, *Asiat. Stud.*, p. 152. The process described by Lyall is so far unsatisfactory that he speaks throughout of the institution of the clan as already existing, and says nothing of its origin.

remain with their father, in the hope of becoming his heirs. It was a custom of comparatively late date that sons who withdrew from their father's authority should not inherit from him, just as a Bechuana is disinherited who migrates to another kotla.

The religious character of these cow-places, as centres for the mystical ideas of each separate circle, and their use as a burial-place for the dead patriarch, to the exclusion of all others, present facts from which it is not difficult to explain the Aryan worship of ancestors, the worship of the hearth, the Lares and Penates. The further development of ancestor-worship leads also to the further development of groups in an agnatistic direction, and the right of inheritance becomes inseparable from the duty of offering sacrifices to the dead. We wholly accept McLennan's view, which is vehemently opposed by Maine, that the marriage of the father and mother is not the basis of agnation, but that this is due to. the father's patriarchal power.[1] Since the Aryan clans are exogamous, like nearly all other clans, the child's assignment to the clan must have been on one side only, either agnatistic or uterine, and we find nothing to indicate that a female line of descent had given place to the agnation now found in Aryan races. Every attempt to point out a primitive female line is based upon the erroneous belief that through agnation the child was severed from all relations to the mother and her family. It is, however, evident that agnation only excludes the child from its mother's clan and from the concerns of that clan.

McLennan bases the opinion that the Hindus at one time observed the female line of descent on the marriage prohibitions which existed among them. According to Manu, a Hindu might not marry within his father's clan, and the subsequent edicts of Kulluka extended this prohibition to the mother's clan.[2] As this

[1] Maine, Anc. Law, p. 149.   [2] McLennan, Pat. Theor., p. 219.

latter edict was issued by the later authority, it seems impossible to deduce from it the prior existence of maternal kinship, yet this is what McLennan ventures to do. He is of opinion that the bond which held together the individual members of the same gotra became weak as soon as the gotra included large and scattered groups only sharing the same family name. Hence he thinks it probable that the prohibition dated from a remote period, when the gotra constituted a small and closely united community. It could not have been invented by Kulluka, but it was merely more strictly defined, after having been in general use. McLennan naturally brings forward all the signs of the great importance ascribed by Manu to the mother as confirmations of his opinion; for instance, that when Manu speaks of both parents, he always puts the mother first. It is, however, difficult to ascertain the antiquity of this prohibition of marriage into the maternal clan.[1] I am myself disposed to think that it was of early date, without, however, attaching much importance to the matter. There is nothing surprising in such a prohibition; the facts of religion and kinship are at first identical, but as they gradually become more distinct, a medley of ideas arise, in which this prohibition necessarily has its origin.

We mentioned above the Sapinda and Samanodoka degrees of kinship, and must now consider them somewhat more closely. Persons who are associated in the chief sacrifice to the dead are Sapinda, so that their relations are always mutual. The man who offers sacrifice is Sapinda to the dead man to whom it is offered, and the converse is also the fact. Each man serves as the centre of seven persons, of whom he is the first, and the other six are his Sapinda. But these six are not all Sapinda to each other, for the Sapinda of each consist in three superior and three inferior members. We must also observe that the dead Hindu not only profits

[1] Schrader, p. 385.

from the sacrifices offered to himself, but from those which were not offered to him, but to persons to whom he himself had been bound to sacrifice during his lifetime.[1] Since such sacrifices were offered to the mother's father, etc., those who do not stand in agnatistic relations to each other may mutually become Sapinda, and these cognates are termed *Bandhus*. The maternal ancestors of the agnate may, however, be either the paternal or maternal forefathers of the Bandhu, and the agnate thus becomes the Bandhu or Bhinna-gotra (member of another clan) Sapinda to the Bandhu, since both sacrifice to the same person.[2] This, however, is a later consequence of the religious development of the Hindu community. As a rule, and in primitive times, all agnatistic Sapindas and Samanodokas started from very closely cognate Sapindas (Bhinna-gotra).[3] A Bandhu never takes precedence of an agnate of the same degree. If, as J. D. Mayne observes, the Sapinda did not originally imply that persons were associated by sacrificing to the dead, but by being parts of the same body, we shall easily understand that man and wife become Sapinda because their union has produced one body;[4] and from this beginning the other conditions of maternal kinship can be explained without difficulty. It is therefore not necessary, although always possible, that Kulluka's prohibition against intermarriage with the maternal clan was based upon a prevalent custom; he may only have deduced the consequence of such an act from the ideas which were entertained by his contemporaries.

Dargun, another writer on this subject, has much stronger reasons for showing that the female line was formerly observed by the Germans. He undertakes to establish the thesis, "that the ancient Aryans at the time of their dispersion regarded kinship through the mother as the sole or chief basis of blood-kinship, and

---

[1] J. D. Mayne, p. 477.   [2] *Ibid.*, p. 478. Appendix XXX.
[3] *Ibid.*, p. 489.   [4] *Ibid.*, p. 487.

all their family rights were governed by this principle."[1]
This thesis is, indeed, not quite adequately supported by
the facts which he adduces, but it seems to him warranted
by the fact that the peoples among whom he traces the
existence of the female line must otherwise have adopted
it instead of agnatism after the dispersion, and he asserts
that throughout the world there is not a single instance
of such a transition, while there are, on the other hand,
numerous examples of the converse transition from the
mother's to the father's line. Dargun, as usual, regards
the doubtful paternity of primitive times as the original
cause of the female line,[2] and he lays special stress on
the fact that the relationship between mother and child
appears to consist only in the tie of blood, while, on the
other hand, a juridical character, derived from the conditions of holding property, forged the link between
father and child, and only gave place to a deeper feeling
as time went on. "In the same proportion as the
popular conscience began to recognize the tie through
the father as equal to the tie of blood through the mother,
men began also to use the names, hitherto only applied to the maternal kinsfolk, for the paternal kinsfolk
in the same degree."[3]

Our foregoing investigation contradicts these reflections in every respect. We have endeavoured to show
that the female line was, as a rule, a transition form, and
it is a familiar thought that the definition of kinship was
an essentially juridical act, produced by the exclusive
and exogamous character of the clan. It is a question
which we must leave unsolved for the present, whether
the primitive consciousness of peoples enabled them to
see any distinction between the tie of blood and the
legal tie; it is a question which would throw no light
on Dargun's views, since his argument only regards the
tie of blood as a tie of the heart, of sentiment, and mutual
sympathy. Dargun states that the Germans always

[1] Dargun, p. 13.   [2] *Ibid.*, p. 76.   [3] *Ibid.*, p 75

acted on the principle that the child must share its mother's lot, for the child always followed the person to whom the mother belongs.[1] The German was obliged to buy his wife. A marriage did not, however, become invalid if the purchase-money was not paid, and the wife in such case still owed obedience to her husband, and must accompany him to his home.[2] Such a marriage only differed from the marriage which was wholly founded upon purchase, in the fact that the wife was not absolved from her old legal conditions ; both she and her children remained under the guardianship, *patria potestas*, of her father ; the children did not inherit from the father, but from the mother's family, and if wife or children died under the husband's roof, he had to pay damages.[3] The purchase-money served as payment for the *mundium*, by which the man obtained juridical rights over wife and children. It is in harmony with this train of thought that illegitimate children belonged to the mother, since the father had no claim upon the woman ; and it was due to the same fundamental ideas that the Romans only obtained authority over wife and children when all the marriage rites were fulfilled (*confarreatio* and *coemptio*).

It seems to me that it would be rash to deduce a female line of descent from these conditions.[4] Dargun states that the child followed the mother, and that who-ever had authority over her also had authority over the child ; that is, the fact that it was the offspring of the father invested the latter with no legal obligations, while, on the other hand, the mother's claims were founded on the circumstance of her having given birth to the child. But this does not imply a female line, still less does it give a more sacred character to the maternal

---

[1] Grimm, p. 420.
[2] Dargun, p. 27. Laband, *Zeitschrift für Völkerpsychologie*, 1865, vol. iii. p. 174.
[3] Grimm, p. 449. Laband, p. 174.   [4] Schrader, p. 389.

11

than to the paternal kinship. The child came into the world and into the enjoyment of its earthly privileges through the mother, and this fact will always serve as the starting-point for every possible definition of kinship. The mother who brought forth the child was in possession of it before its birth, so that her master is also master of the child. As the Hindu says, "Whoever owns a field, owns also all that grows thereon: the seeds brought thither by the wind, the water, or in any other way, do not belong to the sower."[1] The idea of begetting plays in this case a minor part. The saying we have quoted is not founded upon the idea that the child's body is a part of its parents, but upon its local conditions; the offspring lay hid in its mother's womb, and whoever owned the woman owned also that which was contained in her.

Whenever the fact of begetting is the central thought, the merely juridical relations become of less importance. Both among the Germans and the Aryans we note the struggle between the husband and the father, between the present and the former owner of the woman, for the possession of the child; it is not the maternal relations, the mother's brother, or the uterine brothers, who contend with the husband, but the woman's father, and this fact suffices to set aside all question of a female line. The father's claim on his daughter and her children may, as we have repeatedly said, have been the germ of a dawning female line, but it cannot be regarded as the survival of such a line, since its predominance inevitably weakens the paternal rights.

Dargun finds in the fact that the child inherits its mother's rank a further confirmation of the theory that the mother's relationship to her child is a blood relationship, of more primitive origin than that to its father.[2] The child of a free father and of a slave mother becomes a slave. In earlier times marriage between a free woman and a slave was not sanctioned, and the slave

<hr>

[1] Bachofen, *Mutterrecht*, p. 200.   [2] Dargun, p. 32.

was put to death if he took the free woman by force.
Dargun adds that it was subsequently ordained by the
law of Zealand that the child of a slave father and of
a free mother should itself be free. Dargun does not
fully understand these facts. It seems to have been the
original principle that the child should be a slave, because
whoever, whether man or woman, married a slave,
thereby forfeited his or her freedom.[1] This principle
is only an expression of class feeling, and has nothing
to do with considerations as to whether the child's blood
was derived from the father or the mother. When more
humane views prevailed, or when a rapid increase of
the family seemed desirable, these definitions lost their
sharpness, and were subject to modification in many
ways. When the Zealand code (111, 112), declared
the child of a free woman to be free, this milder edict
may have been borrowed from the Roman law. In
Sweden the child was free, if either parent was free. In
Denmark, even up to quite recent times, the marriage of
a woman of noble birth with one of the burgher class
was regarded with displeasure, since the estate of a noble
was thus transferred to burgher hands, and the woman
was generally obliged to sell her property. A woman of
the burgher class who married a noble was also compelled to do the like, and yet her children were not
allowed to inherit their father's rank and estate.[2] In
Champagne, on the other hand, as late as the sixteenth
century, the mother's noble rank was, under certain
circumstances, inherited by the child.[3] No special preference for the mother's blood is apparent in the definition of the child's position ; the definition is generally
in agreement with the special arrangement which the
class interests of the time in question have established
as the most suitable for mixed marriages.

The preference of uterine to agnatistic kinsfolk,

[1] Grimm, pp. 324, 326. Stemann, p. 278.
[2] Stemann, p. 318. [3] Chiruël, p. 861.

which Dargun believes that he can trace in some instances in the order in which property is inherited, is of greater importance.   But before we turn to his account, we must describe the usual mode of inheritance.   The soil, the common property of the joint family group, as well as of the village, was originally only inherited in the agnatistic line ; and if that line became extinct, as far as the family was concerned, it lapsed to the larger circle.[1]   The intrusion of aliens was opposed, and it was therefore decreed that the descendants of women who had married into alien families should not inherit the land of their maternal kinsfolk.   Wherever the *sippe*, or joint family, was dissolved, these considerations lost their force, and the land was in this case inherited by women.

The woman established her claim on movable property at a much earlier period.   Such property soon came to be regarded as the property of the individual, and was subject to the natural law of inheritance.   Among the Hindus, movable property was in primitive times held in common ; but subsequently, as family communism became less strongly marked, it was inherited by those to whom it had been left by its original owner.[2]   We believe that the same principle was maintained by the Germans, and was only not thoroughly carried out because the family communism of the nearest kinsfolk was observed up to a late period, so that the inheritance was rarely in accordance with the *stirpes*.   The order of succession was : son, daughter, father, mother, brother, and sister.

As soon as the wife became capable of holding pro-

---

[1] Grimm, p. 467.   Among the Germans the clan (gotra) soon disappeared.   *Sippe* is the joint family group of seven generations.

[2] J. D. Mayne (p. 238) gives a detailed account of these conditions. Among the Germans also there was a current classification of ancestral or unobstructed property, in opposition to obstructed property.   See Roepell on the Poles, vol. i. p. 601.   Marsden (pp. 230, 244) states that in Rejang the brothers of the deceased share with their nephew the inheritance which had been their father's property.

perty, her legal position with reference to it and to her husband had to be defined. There was usually a community of goods in marriage, or the woman owned as private property her *dos* or *mundium*, the gift made by the bridegroom, and probably the household furniture ; the husband could enjoy the use of her goods, but they were not reckoned as part of his own property.[1]

A special share of the property was assigned to the wife in Saxony and Westphalia, and could only be inherited by women ; this share was termed *Gerade*.[2] The word was originally applied to the wife's ornaments, that is, to things which were by their nature only adapted for women. In contrast to these, all which was used by the man only—weapons, and all kinds of armour—were termed *Heergewäte*. The Gerade was only inherited by women, and the Heergewäte by men, as we should infer from the nature of things. But these conceptions were subsequently enlarged, and all which bore a special reference to man or woman was assigned to the categories in question. The sheep which were shorn by the wife, the poultry which was fed by her, were included in the Gerade ; the horses on which the man rode, and other like things, were Heergewäte. If there were no male or female heirs, both the Gerade and Heergewäte fell to the Sippe or joint family, " in order to increase the common good, in accordance with the ancient law of succession."[3] The usual partition of the property into male and female was sometimes carried out so logically that male animals counted as Heergewäte and female as Gerade. Heergewäte and Gerade were separated from the rest of the property before it was divided among the heirs.

After these explanations, which we do not give in

[1] Grimm, p. 449. Maciejowski, vol. i. p. 216 ; vol. iv. p. 13. Stemann, p. 328.

[2] Grimm, p. 568-599. Froste-Things Lov., vol. ii. ch. ix. Paus, vol. ii. p. 123.

[3] Grimm, p. 485.

any detail, we return to Dargun. The general character of the order of succession we have described testifies to the gradual elevation of the wife into a person capable of inheriting property, so as to become placed almost on a level with the male heir. When the Salic law names the mother as the nearest heir to a childless man, we are disposed to think that the father is understood to be included with her.[1] This may also be the case when the law puts the mother's sister, but not the mother's brother, after the brothers and sisters ; but this does not seem to me to be quite so clear. Dargun, as well as Waitz, wishes to take the law literally, so that the succession of heirs to a childless man would be in this order : mother, brothers and sisters, mother's sister, father's sister. We will not go into the question how far his opinion is justified, but will only inquire whether this order of succession entitles Dargun to infer that it indicates an earlier observance of the female line.[2]

The fact that the parents inherit to the exclusion of the brothers and sisters, introduces us to the patriarchal family. The paternal patriarch is, indeed, the ruler and sole possessor of property, and the son is only withdrawn from his authority by emancipation, which entitles him to become the independent possessor of property. Whatever the son possesses within the family, he possesses only at his father's pleasure ; and if in later times this rule became less arbitrary, yet the brothers and sisters could always be excluded from the inheritance.[3] We think that the state of things in a Bechuana camp may explain the preference given to the mother. The portion which a man would inherit from his father is, among that people, included in that of his mother. As long as the son inhabits his father's kotla, he possesses nothing of his own ; he buys nothing

---

[1] von Amira, p. 5.   [2] Dargun, p. 61.
[3] According to the laws of the Werinian Angles, the brothers and sisters inherited before the parents.

without his father's consent, and he only enjoys the use of certain things. In the event of his dying childless before his father, these things again become the father's property, but they are assigned to the mother's portion. This might easily lead to the special mention of the mother in the text of the law. We think that this would be more particularly the case in a polygamous family, and it is generally admitted that polygamy was practised by the Franks as well as by other Germans.

Our explanation may serve to reconcile the two opposite views. The father is, as master of the family, the sole heir, but the mother decides on the ultimate fate of the property inherited from the child. Amira forgets that the law of inheritance must have been modified when polygamy disappeared, but Dargun is altogether mistaken in declaring a female line of descent to be the only possible explanation of the special mention of the mother. The whole character of the child's position in the family is in agreement with our interpretation. Thus, in Denmark, children shared the common property of their parents, but the fact that they did so only became apparent when the inheritance was divided. That which devolved upon the child was not regarded as an inheritance, but as something which already belonged to the child, and that portion only was considered to be inherited which had been the private property of the parents. Grandchildren, whose father was already dead, were often disinherited by their uncles, that is, they inherited nothing from their grandfather.[1] Maciejowski writes that "among the Slav peoples the community of goods which subsisted between father and son had no legal consequences during the father's lifetime, for the son possessed nothing of his own as long as the father lived. Elsewhere, as in Poland, Bohemia, and Hungary, so long as no injury was inflicted on the paternal property, the son might with-

[1] Stemann, pp. 3C0, 411. Amira, p. 5.

draw his private property from the rest, and especially those goods which he inherited from his mother." [1]

Tacitus gives the brother and the father's and mother's brother as the next heirs of a childless man. [2] The uncles are not named by the Salic law, but the mother's sister and then the father's sister follow the brothers and sisters. Dargun takes this as an indication of a primitive female line, in which we do not agree with him. Another explanation may afford the desired solution, and the female line will not explain the exclusion of the mother's brothers in favour of the mother's sister. When a man dies without leaving children, parents, or brothers and sisters, only remote kinsfolk remain, and his relations to these may be influenced by all sorts of ideas. The paternal and maternal kinsfolk usually enjoy equal rights, in accordance with their degree of blood relationship to the heir. But it may happen that the heritage may be regarded on the one side as the property of the dead man's mother, and on the other as Gerade. The relations between the Bechuana mother and child, which we adduced by way of analogy, suggest such a conception. The Franks had not, indeed, the precise definition of the Gerade, yet Amira writes, "The traces of a Franco-Salic Gerade cannot be ignored. This was the widow's property, and after her death it devolved upon her children, or, if there were no children, on some member of the family to which she belonged." [3]

Taking as our starting-point the legal relation with respect to property which existed between mother and child in a polygamous, patriarchal family, the complete dissolution of the family which would result from the death of a man who had neither children, parents, brothers, nor sisters, would bring forward the mother's side before the father's side, the aunt and female cousin before the uncles. It is evident that this regard for

---

[1] Maciejowski, vol. i. pp. 227, 228.
[2] Tacitus, *Germany and its Tribes*, p. 15.   [3] Amira, p. 35.

women, as well as this different mode of inheritance, must be regarded as an innovation, and Dargun argues in a circle when he infers from the rules in question that there was a female line of descent. We know nothing of the date of these rules; Dargun takes them to be ancient survivals, because he holds them to be survivals of the female line; and, again, the existence of the female line is held to follow from the great antiquity of these rules.

Dargun has also made use of the rejpus to support his theory. The rejpus is the fine which was paid by a bridegroom on his marriage with a widow. The persons to whom this fine was to be paid seem to have been strangely selected, and the reasons for such selection have never been satisfactorily explained. Neither do we venture to explain them, and we only give our reasons for rejecting the explanation suggested by Dargun. Rejpus was paid (1) to the son of the widow's daughter, (2) to her sister's son, (3) to the daughter's son of her mother's sister, (4) to her mother's brother, (5) to the deceased husband's brother, (6) to his nearest kinsfolk, as far as the sixth degree, if the person in question was not his heir.[1] Dargun regards the rejpus as a fine which was imposed at a time when the marriage of widows was still illegal, and he can only explain the fact that it was not paid to the husband's kinsfolk, except in default of uterine kinsfolk, because the latter were held to be the only true kinsfolk.[2] The assumption of an earlier observance of the female line will not explain the two most striking peculiarities of this sequence, namely, that the mother's brother comes after the cousin's son, and that only those of the husband's kinsfolk had a claim who were not his heirs.

Amira has justly estimated these facts, which he

---

[1] Grimm (p. 425) gives the son and brother's son as the first recipients of the rejpus.

[2] Dargun, pp. 71, 141. Giraud-Teulon, p. 336.

explains by regarding the rejpus as a recompense paid
to the widow's kinsfolk, on account of the injury inflicted
by this second marriage on the expectations they entertained of sharing the widow's property. *Lectus stratus,
lectavia condigna, scamnum coopertum, cathedrae* were
furniture belonging to the wife, and by the rules of the
Gerade they would fall to precisely those kinsfolk who
could claim the rejpus. The widow was, however, upon
her second marriage, bound to leave these objects in the
house of her former husband. It must be assumed that
some indemnification was required by the female kinsfolk for this loss, as well as for the disturbance of the
expectations arising from the *dos,* and the rejpus may
have served for such indemnification.[1] We believe that
the meaning of this singular arrangement is truly given
in this suggestion, and it is confirmed by the limitation
of the payment of rejpus to such of the husband's kinsfolk as were not his heirs, which thus becomes intelligible. For the husband's heirs were fully indemnified
by the *achasius* which was paid to them out of the
mundium, when they gave up the widow.

The wife was not quite cut off from her family by
marriage; several ties between her and her former family
still subsisted, and only those which were legal were
dissolved. She had grown up under the influence of her
own people, and could not withdraw from it without
difficulty. The greater the power of traditions, and of
the way in which the popular fancy was busied in the
creation of myths, legends, and poems, the more unreasonable would it be to suppose that marriage put an end
to all the feelings which had previously been so active.
A married woman retained a faithful recollection of her
own people, and she would hush her child to sleep with
the songs of her former home, until it was inspired with
the same loves and hatred. The final reasons with which
Dargun seeks to support his assumption of a primitive

---

[1] Amira, pp. 30-36.

female line ignore the force of this passion and sentiment, and in this he shares Bachofen's point of view.[1] In the old legends it was not legal but spiritual bonds which constituted the relation between mother and child ; it is the patriarchal family which is actuated by passion and sentiment. The child may be more dependent on the mother than on the father, and the wife may be more dependent on the brothers and sisters than on her husband; yet, however deeply rooted the sentiment which attracts the child to its mother's family, it is still the family of the mother's *father*. It is easy to understand Tacitus's narrative : " Sister's sons are held in as much esteem by their uncles as by their fathers ; indeed, some regard the relation as even more sacred and binding, and prefer it in receiving hostages, thinking thus to secure a stronger hold on the affections and a wider bond for the family." [2]

Before bringing these researches to an end, we must mention the Orestes myth, to which some writers have ascribed great importance, as a proof of a primitive female line.[3] The well-known mythical story is as

[1] Dargun, p. 50. Bachofen, *Mutterrecht; Antiq.*, vol. i. The bond between brothers and sisters is adduced as being especially noteworthy and primitive. For the brother's sake the sister sacrifices not only the husband, but the children which belong to her husband. This, again, cannot be explained by the female line. Gudrun slays her husband Atli because he had slain her brother. Signy helps her brother Sigmund to avenge himself on her husband Siggeir, who had slain her father and her other brothers ; but when the vengeance was accomplished she ascends the funeral pile as a faithful wife, and is burnt with her husband. Kriemhild, after long conflict, sacrifices her brother in order to avenge her husband Seigfried. In this Bachofen traces the growing development of marriage, which was primitively of no account. We, however, see nothing in it but tales of the various and conflicting passions of the human heart, and their different issue in different characters. The more the mother is affected by the passions she had cherished in her patriarchal home, the less we should feel disposed to connect this fact with decadent customs. It is rather the growing life of a community which is always becoming more firmly organized, and which bursts the bonds formerly imposed upon the heart by the conditions of patriarchal life.

[2] Tacitus, *Germany and its Tribes*, p. 15. See Schrader, p. 389.

[3] Bachofen, *Mutterrecht*, p. 45. McLennan, *Studies ; Kinship in Ancient Greece*. Fison and Howitt, p. 122.

follows : Clytemnestra slew her husband Agamemnon ; Orestes avenged his father by putting his mother to death. The furies, on whom it was incumbent to avenge blood-guiltiness, appear to have ignored Clytemnestra's act, but wish to wreak vengeance on Orestes for his mother's murder. Orestes spurns them from him, and the complaint is brought before a tribunal, over which Pallas Athene presides. Orestes affirms that there is no tie of blood between him and his mother, but only with his father, and that he ought not, therefore, to be punished for the murder of Clytemnestra. Apollo defends him, and Athene gives her sentence in favour of Orestes, adducing her own birth without the aid of a mother. Here, undoubtedly, Æschylus treats of the same problem as that put forward by Plato, in accordance with which the mother contributes nothing to the child's being. The mother is to the child what the soil is to the plant ; it owes its nourishment to her, but the essence and structure of its nature are derived from the father. We do not, however, believe that this justifies the assertion that a growing agnatism was thus prevailing over the waning female line. We have already repeatedly opposed the idea that it is the power of begetting which defines the ties of kinship ; we trace a different world of thoughts and conceptions in the poet's description. In the Homeric community, woman played a more active part than was accorded to her in that of the later Greeks. The Orestes myth shows that she was so little esteemed as to be degraded into the mere nourisher of the child. But there is a difference which must not be overlooked between a respect for woman and the observance of the female line of descent.

It is hardly worth while to consider the other proofs which have been adduced of a female line. Polybius states that among the western Locri all the fame and glory of descent were derived from the women, not from the men. Bachofen confidently interprets this statement as a proof that the Locri observed the female line.[1] But if we look more closely into the matter, we find much reason to question this assumption. In their native country there were a hundred families of distinction among the Locri, from among whom the maidens desired for sacrifice at Ilium were selected. Some of these women accompanied the colony in its migration westward, and their posterity were held to be of noble descent up to a late period. This statement does not, therefore, afford any proof of a female line of descent; that is, we cannot infer from it that descent was at any time usually made to depend upon the mother. These women were the most distinguished among the colonists; and we have already seen that when the parents were of unequal birth, the child's descent was usually reckoned from the nobler of the two.

In order to appease the wrath of Poseidon, it was decided at Athens, under Kekrop's rule, that women should no longer have the right of voting in the assembly, that children should no longer bear their mothers' names, and that the women themselves should cease to be called Athenians. Bachofen infers from this a prior existence of the female line.[2] We are only concerned with the second decree, that children should no longer bear their mothers' names. But this decree does not imply that children had up to that time been called after their mothers only; it only justifies us in inferring that they might also bear their mothers' names. The existence of the female line of descent would only be manifested by this decree if the mother's name had been used exclusively.[3]

[1] Bachofen, *Mutterrecht*, pp. vi., 309.   [2] *Ibid.*, p. 41.

[3] It has even been attempted to make use of the contrast between patricians and plebeians. " The patricians, some say, were so called because they were the fathers of lawful children; others, because they could give a good account who their own fathers were, which not every one of the rabble that poured into the city at first could do" (Plutarch's *Lives*, Romulus, p. 53). The traces of a female line have also been discovered in the fact that at the plebeian feast of Ceres neither the father nor the son might be named.

12

We shall presently consider many questions which affect the problem of the line of descent, but they extend far beyond our present limits, and we cannot treat of them yet. The great simplicity with which our explanation of the definition of kinship may be applied to all races throughout the world, and the uniformity with which, as we have seen, the same forces exert the same influence, are a pledge, at any rate for the moment, of the justice of our conception. The definition of kinship results from the conflict between clans, and teaches us nothing further with respect to the child's relation to its parents. The choice between the two possible lines is decided by the economic organization of the community and by the local grouping of individuals; but there is not the slightest trace of the fact that considerations with respect to the sexual relations had any influence in the matter.

SECTION II.

THE PRIMITIVE FAMILY.

THE conclusions to which we have come in the foregoing section are so completely opposed to those which have generally been accepted as correct, that we are bound to take the utmost care in establishing our premisses. The insignificant part assigned to ideas of blood-kinship and of the conditions of propagation appears, indeed, to contradict all previous theories. It has been supposed that the tie of blood, still so powerful in modern society, and a common descent, must have had an irresistible force in primitive times; and that these alone would have been sufficiently powerful to control the conflicting elements, and to effect a social development. It has been assumed that the blood-feud, the tenacious cohesion of the family group, the sacrifice to the dead, the inheritance of the property of parents by their children, are simple facts which teach us that the tie of blood served as the central point for the ideas of primitive consciousness. Round this fixed point all the other ideas which bind one man to another gradually clustered, and taught him to adapt his own desires to those of others. It cannot, however, be overlooked that in some cases the relations of fathers to their children were rather of a legal character than such as are due to the tie of blood. This has been taken as a proof that the sense of fatherhood was of later development, and that in primitive times the child was held to be allied by blood with the mother, and not with the father. We have, however, seen that the definition of kinship is nothing but a definition of the clan, which is necessarily one-sided, since the clan forms an exclusive group; it has nothing to do with the primitive organization of the family. Yet the forces which dominate the clan-life of men will also influence family life, and the organization of the primitive family displays many peculiarities which can only be explained in this way.

CHAPTER I.

FATHER AND CHILD.

Different position of father and mother—Fatherhood and procreation—
Licentious customs—*Jus primae noctis*—Juridical children.

THE relation to the child is by no means the same in the
case of each parent, so that in communities constituted
on the uterine principle, the mother takes somewhat the
same position as the father does in those which are agnatistic. The mother's position is, with all its significance,
nearly always one of retirement, and the main interest
gathers round the father and his child.

Mackenzie tells us that among the Knisteneaux, fathers
are very indulgent to their children. Although the
father never comes forward as a dictator, yet he always
endeavours to train his sons to be efficient warriors and
hunters; at the same time the mother seeks to teach her
daughters all which it is necessary that they should know.
It does not appear that the husband makes any distinction between his wife's children, even if they were begotten by other men. Those children only are held to
be illegitimate whose mother has not yet lived with a
man as her husband. Chastity is, to all appearance, not
regarded as a virtue, nor is conjugal fidelity a condition
of domestic happiness. When unfaithfulness is punished
by cutting off the hair, by biting off the nose, or by

death, this is always because the woman has acted without her husband's permission, for a temporary interchange of wives is not uncommon, and it is one of the duties of hospitality to offer the wife to a stranger guest.[1] The Knisteneaux is therefore not influenced by considerations of paternity in his relations to his children. The female line of descent is undoubtedly accepted by this tribe, and this fact has been referred to their lascivious customs. Such a theory is, however, indefensible, since the customs in question are widely diffused and prevail indifferently among uterine and agnatistic peoples. They were found in Australia among the tribes visited by Eyre;[2] among the Dieri and Wa-Imbio;[3] among the

[1] Mackenzie, p. xcvi.

[2] " Foeminae sese per totam pene vitam prostituunt. Apud plurimas tribus juventutem utriusque sexus sine discrimine concumbere in usus est. Si juvenis forte indigenorum coetum quendam in castris manentem adveniat ubi quaevis sit puella innupta, mos est; nocte veniente et cubantibus omnibus, illam ex loco exsurgere et juvenem accedentem cum illo per noctem manere unde in sedem propriam ante diem redit. Cui foemina sit, eam amicis parte libenter praebet; si in itinere sit, uxore in castris manenti aliquis ejus supplet ille vires. Advenis ex longinquo accedentibus foeminas ad tempus dare hospitis esse boni judicatur. Viduis et foeminis jam senescentibus saepe in id traditis, quandoque etiam invitis et insciis cognatis, adolescentes utuntur. Puellae tenerae a decimo primum anno, et pueri a decimo tertio vel quarto, inter se miscentur. Senioribus mos est si forte gentium plurium castra appropinquant, viros noctu huic inde transeuntes, uxoribus alienis uti et in sua castra ex utraque parte mane redire. Temporis quinetiam certis, machina quaedam ex ligno ad formam ovi facta, sacra et mystica quam foeminas aspicere haud licitam, decem plus minus uncias longa et circa quatuor lata insculpta ac figuris diversis ornata, et ultimam perforata partem ad longam (plerumque e crinibus humanis textam) inscrendam chordam cui nomen *Mooyumkarr*, extra castra in gyrum versata, stridore magno e percusso aere facto, libertatem coeundi juventuti esse tum concessam omnibus indicat. Parentes saepe infantum, viri uxorum quaestum corporum faciunt. In urbe Adelaide panis praemio parvi aut paucorum denariorum meretrices fieri eas libenter cogunt. Facile potest intelligi, amorem inter nuptos vix posse esse grandem, quum omnia quae ad foeminas attinent, hominum arbitrio ordinentur, et tanta sexuum societati laxitas, et adolescentes quibus ita multae ardoris explendi dantur occasiones, haud magnopere uxores, nisi ut servas desideraturos" (Eyre, vol. ii. p. 320. See Fison and Howitt, p. 202).

[3] Fison and Howitt, pp. 205, 290.

Polynesians,[1] the Fijians,[2] and the Mikronesians;[3] among
the Eskimos, the Kamskatchans, the Ischuktese, the
Mongols, and the Tartars;[4] in Ceylon,[5] in Africa,[6] and
in North and South America.[7]

It is inevitable that wherever such customs prevail,
it must be difficult, if not altogether impossible, to point
out the actual father of the child. Yet nothing can be
confidently inferred with respect to the relations between
the father and son from these customs alone. The savage's outlook is very limited, and ideas which appear to
us to be in close connection may in this case remain
detached from each other in his consciousness. When
he makes over his wife to his friend or guest, he does
not necessarily think of the consequences which may
result from this act; the idea of a possible child does
not enter his head at the time, and possibly not at a
later period. On the other hand, the idea of procreation
is quite apparent in other customs.

We are told that the Eskimos are very willing that
the Angekoks should have intercourse with their wives,
since in this way they believe that they shall obtain sons
who will excel all others.[8] The same thing is said of
the Keiaz of Paropamissus.[9] And of the Arabs we are
told "there is one form of marriage according to which

[1] Waitz, vol. vi. p. 130. Meinicke, vol. ii. p. 305. Varigny, p. 14.
Freycinet, vol. ii. pp. 587, 599.

[2] Williams, p. 147.

[3] Waitz, vol. v. pp. 106, 130. Chamisso, vol. ii. pp. 209, 243.

[4] Ross, p. 517. Klemm, *Die Frauen*, vol. i. p. 52. Lesseps, Forster,
vol. iv. p. 214. Wood, p. 201. Lubbock, *Orig. of Civil.*, p. 122.

[5] Knox, p. 194. Percival, p. 122.

[6] Magyar, p. 282. Serpa Pinto, vol. i. p. 62. Isert, p. 222. Munzinger,
p. 525.

[7] Von Martius, p. 121. Spix and Martius, vol. ii. pp. 492, 825. Waitz,
vol. iii. pp. 111, 314, 388, 422. Gili, p. 293. Lubbock, p. 122. Herrera,
p. 336. Falkner, p. 157. See also, with respect to the excesses which
accompany festive gatherings—Eskimos, Bastholm, vol. i. p. 162; Abyssinians, Bruce, vol. iii. p. 303; Californians, Venegas, p. 80. Also the Massagetes, Strabo, book xi. p. 912; Troglodytes, Strabo, book xvi. p. 1404.
See also Plutarch's comparison of Lycurgus with Numa.

[8] Bastholm, vol. i. p. 162.   [9] Latham, vol. ii. p. 246.

a man says to his wife, when menstruation is over, 'Send a message to such an one, and beg him to have intercourse with you.' And he himself refrains from intercourse with her until it is manifest that she is with child by the man in question. The husband acts in this way in order that his offspring may be noble."[1]   The consideration of these facts makes it impossible to insist on the question of blood-relationship.   On the one side stands the father who begets the child, and transmits his qualities to it; on the other, the simple fact of procreation involves no rights, and a man does not hesitate to call himself the father of a child whom he knows with absolute assurance to have been begotten by another.

We must here mention the well-known custom, *jus primae noctis,* as a characteristic example of this twofold view of fatherhood.   This term is usually applied to the right of the feudal lord to sleep on the first night with his vassal's bride; but in its wider sense the term includes all the customs which permit one or more persons to pass the first night with the bride.   Karl Schmidt, in his work entitled "Jus Primae Noctis," has made a thorough and intelligent study of the subject, and he has come to the conclusion that it is not proved that such a right, namely, a legitimate claim to the first night, existed either in Europe or elsewhere, at any time or in any place.   The custom prevailed, sometimes as an abuse of power, sometimes for other and better reasons, but never as a right which might eventually be confirmed by law; and it is not creditable to Giraud-Teulon that he asserts it to be useless to look in Schmidt's book for the reasons of his scepticism, or for any explanation of the current tradition with respect to the so-called right.[2]

Schmidt does not attempt to deny the fact, but he wishes to define the clear distinction between right and might, which has not hitherto been taken into account. In words inaccurately quoted by Giraud-Teulon, he directs

---

[1] Wilken, p. 26.   [2] Schmidt, p. 41.

attention to the fact that the connection between the
jus primae noctis and the hypothesis of a primitive state
of promiscuous intercourse is by no means certain. This
hypothesis is so visionary and uncertain that it demands
much further proof before it can be taken as the basis
of wider deductions. The *jus primae noctis* must be
shown to have had an historical existence, and cannot be
inferred from the assumption of a primitive state of promiscuous intercourse. It is unintelligible that a people
which lived in sexual communism should exchange such
a practice for their lord's sole claim to all women, or that
the lord should restrict his previously unlimited rights
to the evening of the wedding. As far as we are able
to follow the process of thought of primitive men, we
must assume, either that savages were so uncivilized as
to surrender their wives to the chief's pleasure at all
times, or that they were sufficiently civilized to protect
themselves against any invasion of marital rights, and
especially on the wedding night.[1] In other matters we
find that usages tend to become extinct as soon as they
are limited to special occasions. Even if we set aside
Schmidt's evidence on this subject as insufficient, his
main argument is only the more firmly established: the
jus primae noctis must be historically proved before
we can give credit to it.

It is not difficult for our modern consciousness to
understand that in the Middle Ages the feudal lord might
put in his claim to the wedding night, but it is too
readily forgotten that this kind of brutal jest would be
unintelligible among savages. Such an immoral custom
implies no slight advance in civilization, since its origin
would be inexplicable in the case of a people whose
unmarried girls were passed from hand to hand. If the
jus primae noctis is found among uncivilized peoples,
the chief is certainly not exercising a right, but rather
doing a service to the bridegroom by sleeping with his

[1] Schmidt, p. 41.

bride.[1] By this act of the chief, or of the priest, the marriage at once received a special consecration, and a numerous and distinguished family was promised to the married pair. On the Malabar coast, for instance, the bridegroom pays for such an act of coition.[2] The custom is founded on the same ideas which induce the Eskimos to surrender their wives to the Angekok, and, in connection with ideas of the value of friendship, it is easy to explain the custom by which the bridegroom surrendered his bride to the wedding guests before he himself had intercourse with her.[3]

These facts throw a strong light upon the bond between the father and child, and we must go back a long way in order to understand this bond. Father and child are united together by certain privileges, and the latter is usually, but not necessarily, begotten by the former. In addition to this legal relation and to the stream of ideas deduced from it, there was a sense of the influence of the actual father on the child's character, and as time went on these two groups of ideas, which were originally quite distinct, necessarily became intermingled. We can adduce some curious particulars on this subject.

The Liburni had their wives in common, and the children were all brought up together until they were five years old. They were then collected and examined in order to trace their likeness to the men, and they were assigned to their fathers accordingly. Whoever received a boy from his mother in this way, regarded him as his son.[4] It was customary among the Arabs for several men, sometimes as many as ten, to own one

---

[1] Azara, vol. ii. p. 141. Spix and Martius, vol. ii. p. 574 ; vol. iii. pp. 1189, 1211. Herrera, p. 336. Garcilasso, p. 31. Waitz, vol. v. p. 111. Schmidt, pp. 216, 309, 366.

[2] *Ibid.*, pp. 313, 358.

[3] Baleares, Bachofen, *Mutterrecht*, p. 12. Nasamones, Herodotus, book iv. chap. 172. Schmidt, p. 38.

[4] Bachofen, *Mutterrecht*, p. 20.

wife; she afterwards decided to which of them the
child should belong, or else the woman was constrained
to pitch her tent by the road side, where every one,
except the men in question, might have access to her.
The child was then assigned by an expert to one of the
joint husbands, to be regarded as his own, which, in fact,
it was not.[1] When a Hindu marries, all the children
previously born from his wife become his own; and in
Pakpatan, even when a woman has forsaken her husband
for ten years, the children which she brings forth are
divided between him and her lover.[2] Among the Marianas, when a divorced wife or an unmarried woman
with children marries, the husband is regarded as their
true father.[3]

It is not due to promiscuous intercourse and the
female line that blood-relationship is not the ground
for the legal connection between father and son. If the
female line—that is, a legal connection dependent on
the mother—had at any time its origin in the exclusive
recognition of the maternal tie of blood, this would
involve the thesis that the juridical relation was in
accordance with the facts of procreation. But in that
case the growing power of fatherhood would have displayed the same tendency, and would not have obtained
the superiority merely as a juridical order of things,
quite independent of considerations of blood.

[1] Wilken, p. 26.
[2] Wade, *Journal of Asiat. Soc. of Bengal,* vol. vi., 1837, p. 196.
[3] Freycinet, vol. ii. p. i. pt. 476.

CHAPTER II.

POLYANDRY.

McLennan's theory—Child murder and polyandry—Scarcity of women and polyandry—Stages of polyandry—Transition to male line—Child murder without significance—Promiscuous intercourse and polyandry —Polyandry of Nairs—Polyandry of Thibetans—Eldest brother— Limitations of marriage—Causes of polyandry—Forms of polyandry —Family communism.

EXACTLY the same features are presented to us by the external form of marriage; and the inquiries which we are about to make will complete the materials furnished in the former chapter, and will carry us a good step further.

McLennan believes that nothing has had so much influence on the development of the family as polyandry, which he holds to have been the first stage of progress, and necessary as a transition from promiscuous intercourse to monogamous marriage. Polyandry alone made such progress possible, and can itself become intelligible merely when we regard it as a stage of transition. McLennan's researches and theory have been received with a consideration which is in many respects well deserved, for although his estimate of polyandry has not been altogether accepted, and is scarcely entitled to be so accepted, since the theory is too loosely constructed, yet all that he has adduced displays such sound judgment and perspicacity that hardly any other writer

on the subject is equally instructive. Even if the conclusive value of his suggestions is negative, a careful and
critical examination of them will repay us.

McLennan affirms that men originally lived in hordes,
in which there was much internal strife, in consequence
of which they were broken up into smaller hordes. It
is certain that these conflicts usually occurred about
women, and probably between groups of the horde, and
not between individuals; the individual was compelled
to practise promiscuous intercourse, since he was unable
to take a wife for himself alone, to isolate himself,
and to found a family.[1]

McLennan goes on to say that child-murder was
extensively practised by the hordes, the female infants
being usually put to death, since women were held
to be a source of weakness to the clan. This custom
made women scarce, and led both to polyandry and to
the introduction of alien women within the clan.[2] The
later custom led to exogamy and to the symbol of rape
which is part of the wedding ceremonies of many peoples,
and polyandry subsisted independently as the germ of
the regular marriage forms of later times. It was the
first faint limitation of promiscuous intercourse, and was
called into being as soon as a scarcity of women made it
necessary to group the sexes. The first mode of grouping is found by McLennan among the Nairs, as it has
been described above; one woman lived with several
men, strangers to each other, and these had access to
more than one woman.[3] McLennan adds that it was a
step in advance when the woman, while still living
among her own people, no longer dwelt under her
mother's roof, but had a hut of her own, in which she
received her lovers.[4] The woman's migration to her
husband's house followed, that is, she was taken away
from her mother's dwelling in order to become a wife

[1] McLennan. *Studies*, pp. 131, 134.   Appendix XXXI.
[2] *Ibid.*, p. 111.   [3] *Ibid.*, p. 142.   [4] *Ibid.*, p. 152.

13

common to a circle of brothers. In the two earlier stages, the female line of descent is necessary, since the father cannot be ascertained; but in the latter stage, the paternal line may begin to appear, since in this case the husbands are brothers, so that the paternal blood, although not yet the individual father, may be ascertained.

McLennan, however, only regards considerations of paternity as a secondary cause; he holds it to be a much more important fact that now that the woman inhabits another house the course of succession in the female line which has hitherto been followed will no longer keep the property in the family, but must lead to a general dispersion of the family possessions.[1] Even in the earlier stages it was possible for the man who had special reasons for regarding himself as the father of a given child to assign the inheritance to his son, to the exclusion of the sister's son, since he was at liberty to give as much as he pleased to the son before his death. If such an attempt had played any important part in history, we must admit that the question of the paternity would be decisive, and considerations as to the property would only be the consequence, not the cause.

In his latest treatise, McLennan holds that in addition to considerations as to the property, the consecration of the dead was also a means of introducing the paternal line of descent, so soon as there was a physical certainty of fatherhood. By this consecration the child, or the mother and her child together, were admitted into the father's clan.[2] It appears that, while McLennan holds that the final impulse towards the introduction of the paternal line was given by pecuniary interests, the wish for such legal order was prompted by ideas of paternity. He believes that men had originally no idea of kinship,

---

[1] McLennan, p. 154. As we have already said, such conditions are still to be found. Buchanan, vol. ii. p. 513; vol. iii. p. 16.
[2] McLennan, *Patr. Th.*, ch. xiii.

although they may always have been attracted to each other by sympathetic feeling. Individuals were at first assigned to a group, and not to another individual, and the first idea of kinship did not regard men as belonging to distinct families, but as brethren. The tie of blood which is first apparent—that between the mother and child—made the children of the same mother kinsfolk by blood ; and as soon as fatherhood began to be as certain as motherhood, it might be expected to obtain recognition also.[1] The force of this idea of kinship by blood was so great that it overcame the tribal feeling. The tribe could only retain its firm consistency as long as the children to which alien and captive women gave birth were assigned to the tribe and not to the mother.[2] We shall consider in succession all the points included in this theory ; for the present we must content ourselves with discussing the point which refers to polyandry.

It is not proved that the tribes which practise child-murder put to death the female infants by preference. Lubbock and Darwin regard this as an open question,[3] while Giraud-Teulon says with decision that there was no motive for killing the girls rather than the boys; the women kept house for the tribe, and were of great use.[4] He adds, in agreement with Spencer, that poly-andry was not the necessary consequence of the prevailing custom of putting female infants to death, since in primitive communities many men died by violence, and in this way the respective balance of the sexes was automatically adjusted.[5] Spencer justly remarks that if female infants were put to death in all the tribes, the scarcity of women could not be supplied by capture from without.[6] In addition to these remarks, it must be stated that it is an untenable assumption that female

[1] McLennan, *Studies*, pp. 121, 122. Appendix XXXII.
[2] *Ibid.*, p. 184. Appendix XXXIII.
[3] Lubbock, *Origin*, etc., p. 129. Darwin, *Descent of Man*, vol. ii. p. 364.
[4] Giraud-Teulon, p. 115.   [5] Spencer, *Principles of Soc.*, p. 646.
[6] *Ibid.*, p. 648. Giraud-Teulon, p. 113.

infants are put to death in some tribes and not in others, and that the former obtain women by capture from the latter. It has been suggested that the motive for the murder of female infants is the fear of becoming the object of the predatory instincts of other tribes; whence we must conclude that the tribe which keeps its women alive is tolerably strong; those tribes which lack women cannot, therefore, obtain them by violence to any great extent. It also seems to be a strange thing to kill the female infants from a dread of being exposed to attack, and at the same time to seek to increase the number of women by carrying them off by violence from other tribes.

This does not, however, affect the main point of McLennan's theory, which is as follows:—There is nothing in a scarcity of women which could lead a community accustomed to promiscuous intercourse to adopt polyandry; on the contrary, such a scarcity would make it more difficult to set limits to promiscuous intercourse. The latter is indeed polyandry, inasmuch as the woman has more than one lover, and this characteristic would be encouraged rather than checked by any scarcity of women. Marriage, or the exclusive possession of one woman by one or more men, would become more easy in proportion to the increase in the number of women, since the conflict between the lusts of the men would necessarily become less intense. It therefore becomes necessary to trace the transition from promiscuous intercourse to polyandry to other sources than the scarcity of women.

The promiscuous intercourse of the primitive community is the fundamental assumption of McLennan's theory; and to this assumption another is added—that there is a blood-tie between the child and its mother, while uncertainty with respect to the father does not admit of any tie of fatherhood. McLennan considers that these assumptions may be taken for granted, so that he does not trouble himself about proofs. We have shown that such an assumption is erroneous, and we think it open to question whether polyandry affords the proofs of promiscuous intercourse, and whether polyandry was generally practised and developed through the stages given by McLennan. The Levirate, the Niyoga, and the inheritance by brothers, are regarded by McLennan as proofs of polyandry; he holds that whenever these are found, polyandry must at some time or other have been practised. McLennan has dwelt so exclusively on this point that he has almost lost sight of the previous condition of promiscuous intercourse. And thus it appears that the assumption of promiscuous intercourse only forms an essential part of McLennan's theory as the basis of polyandry; and this makes it more necessary to discover whether polyandry affords any clear indications of promiscuous intercourse.

We have shown above that this is not the case with the Nair-type. This type is, indeed, that of men living in promiscuous intercourse, but it is certainly not to be regarded as a primitive, but rather as an ultimate type. If we have to distinguish between the two forms, the distinction is merely quantitative, since the Nair woman only holds intercourse with from ten to twelve at a time; the limit set to the freedom of sexual intercourse is, however, not so much legal, as one which arises from the transitory nature of things. If we could agree with McLennan in regarding the Nair practice as the primitive and very slight limitation set to absolutely promiscuous intercourse, we should be compelled to admit that his theory was a plausible and successful *à priori* construction. Nothing would be more natural than the conversion of this quantitative limit into one of quality, such as we find in the polyandry practised in Thibet, where the woman is not restricted to a definite number, but to a definite group, that is, to several brothers. But everything depends on the question whether experience justifies the *à priori* inference that there are indications in the polyandry of Thibet which show that promiscuous intercourse and the polyandry of the Nairs are its regular and necessary preliminary stages.

The polyandry of Thibet is described as follows:— "When an eldest son marries, the property of his father descends to him, and he is charged with the maintenance of his parents. They may continue to live with him if he and his wife please; if not, he provides them with a separate dwelling. A younger son is usually made a Lama. Should there be more brothers, and they agree to the arrangement, the juniors become inferior husbands to the wife of the elder; all the children, however, are considered as belonging to the head of the family. The younger brothers have no authority, they wait upon the elder as his servants, and can be turned out of doors at his pleasure, without its being incumbent upon him to provide for them. On the death of the eldest brother his property, authority, and widow, devolve upon his next brother."[1] "Nor is this sort of league [living together] confined to the lower ranks of people alone; it is found also frequently in the most opulent families."[2] "The Kunawarees are all polyandrists, *i.e.* one house or family has usually but one wife only, and she is considered as more particularly the wife of the eldest brother."[3] Cunningham describes the arrangement somewhat differently from Moorcroft; he says that the father does not give way to the son on his marriage, and that the younger brothers have the right of demanding their share of the inheritance, if they wish to build houses for themselves;[4] but the latter arrangement is, as we observed in our remarks on India, merely to be regarded as a variation in the way in which the property of the joint family group is ordered.

[1] Moorcroft, vol. i. p. 321.   [2] Turner, p. 349.
[3] Cunningham, *Journal of Asiat. Soc. of Bengal*, 1844, vol. xiii. pt. i. p. 178.   [4] *Ibid.*, p. 203.

The character of polyandry is adapted in every respect to this organization of the joint family group. The eldest brother is in all things the representative of the family, and McLennan admits that this position of authority is the reason for assigning the children to him by preference. I do not see, however, why this position of authority may not also have affected the mutual relations of the brothers in their quality of husbands. The accounts that we have quoted show that, strictly speaking, it is only the eldest brother who is married, and that the younger ones are not husbands, but merely specially authorized lovers. There is nothing to indicate that the band of brothers, as such, take a wife in common; that is, that the marriage is the act of the whole community. Whoever maintains the primitive character of promiscuous intercourse, must be able to explain how a woman's right to bestow her favours on any man whatever gave place to the obligation of contenting herself with the brothers of the family group. Such a problem is not presented by the facts, but one which is altogether different, namely, how the woman's right to hold intercourse with one husband, which was involved in the marriage tie, could have been extended to a right to hold intercourse with several. The causes are the more easy to find, since we already know that the surrender of a man's own wife was a natural expression of friendly feeling among primitive peoples; and hence we understand that if a joint family group wished for any reason to have only one woman in the family, they had no choice but this—either one of the male members of the family could marry, while the others either remained celibate, or contracted illegitimate connections in alien families; or else the household wife became common to all the brothers.

In some districts the eldest brother's privileges with respect to marriage are very remarkable. Butler states that in Assam the younger brother may not marry before the elder, unless the latter has given his permission in writing ; after which the elder brother is himself forbidden to marry, since he has thereby forfeited the right to form any such connection. If he should, notwithstanding, subsequently marry, he is usually shunned as an outlaw.[1] The Brahmans on the Malabar coast are afraid of injuring their position by too numerous marriages, and for this reason the younger brothers rarely marry, but live with the Nair women as their favoured lovers.[2] In Thibet there are valid reasons which make it desirable to restrict the number of marriages. The unfruitful soil inspires a dread of any rapid increase of the population ; during the man's absence, the wife enjoys greater protection if she has more than one husband, and when she is shared by several persons the children also are better cared for.[3] The younger brother cannot, like the Malabar Brahman, seek to solace himself outside his family, since he must in that case maintain his wife and child, or pay a fine to his family.[4] Polyandry thus becomes the necessary consequence of restrictions on the liberty of marriage.

Spencer does not regard these facts as reasons which will account for the origin of polyandry, but only for its persistent continuance ; he thinks that its origin is due to the growing tendency to restrict promiscuous intercourse.[5] Spencer cannot agree with those who regard poverty as the efficient cause, since we find that in Ceylon polyandry is practised by the nobles, not by the common people.[6] I do not see, however, why we should assign precisely the same reasons in all cases. The polyandry of brothers arose in a joint family group, under the pressure of varying circumstances, and it cannot be

---

[1] Butler, p. 227. Spix and Martius, vol. iii. p. 1185.
[2] Buchanan, vol. ii. p. 425. Duncan, *Asiat. Res.*, 1798, vol. v. p. 13.
[3] Spencer, *Prin. of Soc.*, p. 677.
[4] Cunningham, *Journal of Asiat. Soc. of Bengal*, 1844, vol. xiii. pp. 1, 204.
[5] Spencer, *Prin. of Soc.*, p. 665.   [6] Knox, p. 197.

doubted that among these pecuniary interests played an important part. We are told that among the Shinar, those who are wealthy have each their own wife, but that the poor content themselves with a wife for each circle of brothers.[1] It was also the case in Sparta that brothers whose wealth just sufficed to provide for their common meals were content with a joint wife.[2] In that country it was likewise thought seemly for a husband to choose a brave and distinguished friend to sleep with his wife.[3]

Among the Kolosch people, the man kept a substitute, whose duty it was to protect his wife and dwelling during his absence, and this was also the case with the Aleuts.[4] Ross states that when the Eskimos have no children, the husband has the right of taking another wife, and the wife another husband.[5] We cannot doubt by what motive they were actuated in these cases.

In Nukuhiva, one of the Marquesas Isles, where there is a great deficiency of women, the women, and specially those of higher rank, live in polyandry; yet the first man with whom they live is regarded as the husband, the others are only lovers.[6]

We learn from Strabo that the Arab conditions resembled those in Thibet. "A man's brothers are held in more respect than his children. The descendants of the royal family succeed as kings, and are invested with other governments, according to primogeniture. Property is common among all the relations. The eldest is the chief. There is one wife among them all. He who enters the house before any of the rest has intercourse with

---

[1] Buchanan, vol. ii. p. 416.
[2] Schömann, p. 140. Bachofen, p. 198.
[3] Grote, vol. i. p. 609. Plutarch, comparison between Lycurgus and Numa.
[4] Waitz, vol. iii. p. 328. *Ibid.*, p. 308.
[5] Ross, *Voyage of Discovery*, p. 72. The Avanos and Maypures (Humboldt and Bonpland, vol. iv. p. 477).
[6] Waitz, vol. vi. p. 128.

her, having placed his staff at the door ; for it is a necessary custom to carry a staff. The woman, however, passes
the night with the eldest.   Hence the male children are
all brothers.   They have sexual intercourse also with
their mothers.   Adultery is punished with death, but an
adulterer must belong to another family."[1] The fact that
the wife passed the night with the eldest clearly shows
that he was held to be the actual husband.   Even at the
present day the Arab women are very unchaste after
marriage, while they are perfectly chaste when still
unmarried.[2]

There is another form of polyandry, according to
which several brothers have intercourse in common with
several sisters. Cæsar[3] states that he found this to be
the custom among the Britons.   Dargun acutely remarks
that since philology shows that the Aryan race lived in
monogamous union before their dispersion, this polyandry of the Britons must have been of subsequent
origin, and as this conclusion seems to him to be absurd,
he rejects the monogamous marriage of Aryans.[4]   In this,
as in other cases, we do not agree with him.   On the
contrary, Cæsar's report confirms our belief that fraternal
polyandry in the joint family group was not due to a
licentious view of the marriage tie, but it was an expression of the communism which is characteristic of this
organization ; different reasons lead at different times to
this interpretation of marriage.   Indifference with respect to the actual progenitor makes polyandry possible,
without destroying the relation between father and child.
I find no grounds for the doubts which Hearn throws on
the truth of Cæsar's account.[5]

---

[1] Strabo, book xvi. p. 213.   [2] Burkhardt, p. 110.   Munzinger, p. 226.
[3] " Uxores habent deni duodenique inter se communes, et maxime fratres
cum fratribus, parentesque cum liberis : sed, si qui sunt ex his nati, eorum
habentur liberi, a quibus primum virgines quaeque deductae sunt " (Cæs.,
De Bell. Gall., Lib. v. xiv.). See Dio. on the Picts, "Caledonians and
Meates."
[4] Dargun, p. 130.   [5] Hearn, p. 150.

We can to this day observe this form of polyandry flourishing among the Todas, together with the recognition of juridical fatherhood.[1] The usual communism of the village and family with respect to property is practised by this people in its most essential features. The brothers generally live together, and the eldest of them has the right to select a wife as soon as he comes to man's estate. The other brothers, however, take part in the wedding ceremonies, and as they grow up, they are received by her as her husbands. If the wife has sisters, these become, as soon as they are marriageable, the brothers' wives, without any further ceremonies. In this we simply see the connection of one household with another. The children are so distributed among the brothers that the eldest brother takes the eldest child, and so on in succession. If a man has no children, he is derided and despised, and he is therefore willing that his wife should try to supply the want by means of other men. The Todas are undoubtedly altogether indifferent as to the actual paternity. Polyandry has become a necessity, because they usually put the female infants to death, and women are scarce; but it may be doubted whether polyandry was induced by this deficiency, or whether polyandry, which made many women unnecessary, did not rather lead to the extensive practice of child-murder.

We think that we have now shown that polyandry belongs to the category of facts which have to do with the ordinary family communism, and especially with the joint family group. The date of its origin cannot therefore be earlier than that of the aforesaid communism, and polyandry does not forfeit its character of a marriage in which there are authorized lovers, while the individual never quite loses his personality in that of the family. There is no warrant for the attempt to regard polyandry

[1] As described by Spencer. See also Wilkes, vol. i. p. 54. With these the Agathyrsis may perhaps be classed (Herodotus iv. chap. 104).

as a survival of promiscuous intercourse. Neither of these conditions is implied by the general indifference with respect to fatherhood; it is, on the contrary, the indifference which already existed which made it so easy for polyandry to arise in every circle of which the members lived in a joint household. But the readiness with which it was adopted does not entitle us to declare that polyandry was at any time the universal form of marriage. McLennan, who believes in such universality, deduces other facts from it; as we have already said, he traces a connection between polyandry and the Levirate and Niyoga, so that where these occur, polyandry must formerly have prevailed. We must now consider these two phenomena.

CHAPTER III.

THE LEVIRATE AND NIYOGA.

The Levirate—Jews and Hindus—Maine's theory—Mayne's theory—Son of appointed daughter—Juridical character of fatherhood—Niyoga—Marriage and *patria potestas*—The Levirate and Polyandry—Spencer's theory—Iranian Levirate and Niyoga—Ossetian Levirate—Juridical motherhood.

The term Levirate is given to the strange custom which enjoins a man to marry the widow of his brother, if he die childless, in order to raise up children to the dead man, to whom the children produced by such a marriage were supposed to belong. This obligation only existed if the man was altogether childless, for if he left a daughter the matter took another turn, and the daughter's son took a son's place.

There is no good reason against the opinion that the constraining duty of raising up seed to the deceased brother was prompted by the eager desire to have a son who might offer the needful sacrifices to the dead man. But why such a wish should impose this duty of the Levirate on the brother is altogether unintelligible if we forget the juridical character of fatherhood among primitive men.

The phenomenon is best known among the Jews and the Hindus, and is given in the following words :—

"If brethren dwell together, and one of them die, and have no child, the wife of the dead shall not marry
14

without unto a stranger: her husband's brother shall go in unto her, and take her to him to wife, and perform the duty of an husband's brother unto her. And it shall be, that the firstborn which she beareth shall succeed in the name of his brother which is dead, that his name be not put out of Israel. And if the man like not to take his brother's wife, then let his brother's wife go up to the gate unto the elders, and say, My husband's brother refuseth to raise up unto his brother a name in Israel, he will not perform the duty of my husband's brother. Then the elders of his city shall call him, and speak unto him: and if he stand to it, and say, I like not to take her; then shall his brother's wife come unto him in the presence of the elders, and loose his shoe from off his foot, and spit in his face, and shall answer and say, So shall it be done unto that man that will not build up his brother's house. And his name shall be called in Israel, The house of him that hath his shoe loosed."[1]

It is also written in the Manu, that "On failure of issue by the husband, if he be of the servile class, the desired offspring may be procreated, either by his brother or some other *sapinda*, on the wife, who has been duly authorized: Sprinkled with clarified butter, silent, in the night, let the kinsman thus appointed beget one son, but a second by no means, on the widow *or childless wife:* By men of twice-born classes no widow, *or childless wife*, must be authorized to conceive by any other man than her lord."[2]

We may here note that the Hindus combine the Levirate with the Niyoga, according to which the childless wife might be espoused in her husband's lifetime. This practice was unknown to the Jews; by the Jewish law the Levir was actually married to the widow, but this was not the case with the Hindus. It has been asserted that among the Jews the Levir obligation was only incumbent

---

[1] Deut. xxv. 5-10. See also Judah and Tamar (Gen. xxxviii.).
[2] Manu, chap. ix. 59-64.

on the brother who had lived in the same city or district with the dead man, by which, perhaps, the joint family group is meant; or, again, that it was only in force when the surviving brother was unmarried.[1] We shall presently be able to estimate the force of this distinction.

Sir Henry Maine, in his work on "Early Law and Custom," has attempted to explain the Hindu Levirate by their desire for offspring, and he connects it with other customs which are still in force, and which enable the soulless man to obtain sons without having begotten them. He mentions as the most important of these customs, adoption and the consecration of daughters, that is, constituting the daughter's firstborn son the son and heir. He regards these two usages as the most primitive, and he believes that the Levirate, and subsequently the Niyoga, were only degenerate forms, arising from misuse of the legal fictions which are customary in primitive communities. The conflict between belief and actual facts is really amazing, but it proves to us what power is exerted by legal ideas in primitive communities. And to none of these is a man more indebted than to those which established an artificial production of kinsfolk.[2] We shall see presently that our view of its connection with these ideas differs from that expressed by Maine; but for the present we lay no special stress upon this fact, since the thing itself, adoption, etc., actually occurs, and the child thereby becomes responsible to the new father, as if he were really its progenitor. It may, however, be questioned whether a blood-tie was supposed to be created by this expedient, and not rather a merely legal connection, which would be of equal strength and validity, whether it took place at the child's birth or at some later period.

J. D. Mayne has put forward a theory with reference to the character of the paternal relation which is in agreement with the point of view advocated by us.

[1] Michaelis, vol. ii. p. 207.　　[2] Maine, *Ancient Law*, p. 130.

According to law, the man to whom the mother belonged counted the son to be his own. And the son's owner could give him up to be the son of another man, just as an emancipated son might give himself up to any one he pleased to be his father.[1]   Starting from this juridical point of view, the Levirate and the Niyoga present no special difficulty. Sir Henry Maine thinks that the Niyoga is of later date than the Levirate, but J. D. Mayne is, I believe, justified in regarding the Levirate as merely an, enlarged form of the Niyoga, which came into effect after a man's death.   The indissoluble character of marriage would explain why the Levir child was ascribed to the dead husband, just as the Niyoga child was ascribed to him when he was still alive.   Sir Henry Maine's process of thought on this point does not seem to be quite clear ; we cannot fail to remark a certain vagueness in his conception of the part played by the tie of blood.   Maine himself considers that kinship was, speaking generally, based upon authority ; and yet he seeks to connect the Levirate and Niyoga with an imaginary tie of blood between father and son.   In order to do this, he selects as his starting-point the father's right of appointing the firstborn son of his daughter, that is, the dedication of the daughter. (See Table, next page.)

J. D. Mayne explains this classification of sons by the supposition that it was in accordance with the old order that a girl without brothers should return to the men of her own family and be to them as a son.   In this way the father continued to be the guardian of his married daughter, and might take her son, if he so pleased.   This only took place when the contract of marriage included an express reservation of the right of guardianship.[2]   McLennan expresses a similar opinion, and he is directly opposed to Maine's attempt to prove that by a fictitious arrangement the mother's father was able to regard his daughter's son as the fitting represen-

---

[1] J. D. Mayne, p. 59.   [2] *Ibid.*, p. 68.

TABLE OF THE DIFFERENT MODES OF PROCURING SONS, AND THEIR SUCCESSIVE ORDER, AS GIVEN BY DIFFERENT AUTHORITIES (J. D. MAYNE, p. 60).

	Aurasa. Legitimate son.	Kshetraja. Son begotten on wife.	Putrika putra. Son of app. daughter.	Kanina. Damsel's son.	Gudhaja. Secretly born.	Paunarbhava. Son of twice married woman.	Sahodha. Son of pregnant bride.	Nishada. Son of Sudra woman.	Dattaka. Adopted son.	Kritrima. Son made.	Kritaka. Son bought.	Apaviddha. Son cast off.	Svayamdattaka. Self-given son.
Baudhayana, ii. 22, §§ 10-23	1	3	2	8	6	11	9	13	4	5	10	7	12
Gautama, xxviii. §§ 32, 33	1	2	10(ᵛ)	7	5	9	8	—	3	4	12	6	11
Vasishta, xvii. §§ 9-21 / Vishnu, xv. §§ 1-27	1	2	3	5	6	4	7	12	8	—	9	11	10
Manu, ix. §§ 158-160 / Kalika Purana, 3 Dig. 155	1	2	(ɩ)	7	5	10	8	12	3	4	9	6	11
Yajnavalkya, ii. §§ 128-132	1	3	2	5	4	6	11	—	7	9	8	12	10
Narada, xiii. §§ 45, 46	1	2	3	4	6	7	5	—	9	11	10	8	12
Sancha and Lichita, 3 Dig. 151	1	2	3	5	6	4	8	11	9	—	10	7	12
Harita, 3 Dig. 152	1	2	5	4	6	3	10	—	7	12	8	9	11
Devala, 3 Dig. 153	1	3	2	4	5	8	7	—	9	11	12	6	10
Yama, 3 Dig. 154	1	2	3	5	6	4	8	—	9	10	11	7	12
Vrihaspati, 3 Dig. 162, 171	1	8	2	10	12	9	11	7	3	6	5	4	—
Brahma Purana, 3 Dig. 174	1	2	3	7	5	10	8	12	4	—	9	6	11

(ᵛ) Mitakshara (i. 11, § 35) explains the low position assigned by Gautama to the son of an appointed daughter as being relative to one differing in tribe. (ɩ) The son of an appointed daughter is not specified in Manu's list of twelve sons. He had been already described, and stated to be equal to an actual son (Manu, ix. §§ 134-136).

tative of an actual son.[1] Sir Henry Maine writes that the daughter served as the channel through which her

[1] McLennan, *Patr. Theor.*, p. 288. On p. 269 he finds fault with J. D. Mayne for admitting that it is less easy to explain this class of sons than the others. We do not think that this blame is deserved. Mayne must, indeed, first explain how the father was able to retain the guardianship of his married daughter. It cannot, however, be denied that this last work of McLennan's is characterized throughout by an embittered tone, and a petty and contradictory spirit which makes a painful impression on the reader.

father's blood flowed into her son, and that this was originally, as he supposes, accompanied by an express declaration of the father's will, together with some religious ceremonies. This was the case in Athens, where a son derived from such a marriage appears to have been received into his mother's family with the customary forms of adoption; he received the family name together with the rights of guardianship over his mother.[1] The daughter's son thereby became an adopted son, and when Maine thus strongly insists on the fact that the mother was the channel through which the father's blood was transmitted to the son, I think that he does so in order to explain why the men of early times displayed a special preference for the adoption of the daughter's son. This power of adoption is connected with the clan, with the Sapindas and Samanodocas, and the position of the sister's son would therefore indicate a recognition of cognate kinsfolk, like that already described as Bandhus or Bhinnagotra.[2] McLennan has paid little attention to this fact, but has simply rejected the whole theory, because it does not agree with the fact that there was a total dissolution of any connection between uterine kinsfolk in the agnatistic community.[3] We have already pointed out that this last assertion is altogether erroneous. At the same time Maine is mistaken in basing the adoption of the daughter's son on considerations of the ties of blood, instead of simply connecting them with the custom which prevails among so many peoples, in virtue of which the firstborn child was surrendered to the father-in-law as purchase money for the wife.

The same remarks apply to Maine's views with respect to the Niyoga-son. He writes that when a man dies without children, neither the adoption nor the dedication

[1] Maine, *Early Law*, p. 92.
[2] McLennan, *Patr. Theor.*, p. 275.
[3] Maine, *Early Law*, p. 107. See Appendix XXXIV.

of the daughter can take place, and another method of preserving the dead man's name is adopted. The force of analogy will represent the Niyoga-son (in this case equivalent to the Levir-son) as strongly resembling the actual son. Both are born from the wife or widow, and although her husband's blood may not flow in the veins of the Niyoga-son, yet it is at any rate that of his race.[1] To this we add that the law demanded that the Niyoga should be a Sapinda or Sagotra of the deceased man; if otherwise, the child belonged to the former, and not to his dead brother.[2]

McLennan makes the following objections to this opinion: (1) that the Niyoga or Levir-son could not, in the case of a people which set a special value on fatherhood, be held to be the same as an actual son, and (2) that it is incumbent on Sir Henry Maine to show how the blood of the individual could be preserved by Niyoga; the preservation of the family was not the question, since there was no danger of its extinction. He infers that Sir Henry Maine has missed the true bearings of the question.

These objections are not valid, since Maine only proposes to explain how it was possible to feign the validity of the Niyoga sonship. Such a fiction became possible (1) because the Niyoga-son, born from the dead man's wife, is Sapinda to him, and (2) because his blood is in reality that of the family McLennan's criticism would only be well founded if Maine had undertaken to explain the reason of the Hindu belief that the Niyoga or Levir-son was actually begotten by his fictitious father; he is, however, not concerned with the unreasonableness of the idea.

There can be no doubt that the considerations suggested by Sir Henry Maine influenced in many respects the growing development of Hindu family life; the idea of blood-kinship did not, however, produce, but rather

---

[1] Maine, *Early Law*, p. 102.   [2] McLennan, *Patr. Theor.*, pp. 277, 279.

limited the Niyoga, inasmuch as it reserved for the kinsfolk that which was previously open to every one, and gave a definite purpose to the intercourse with the wife, which had before been altogether purposeless.[1] As we have already observed, to regard fatherhood as belonging to an altogether juridical category is most in harmony with the patriarchal theory advocated by Sir Henry Maine, who himself seeks to explain the position of illegitimate children from this point of view. They were all born of women who were within the household sphere, or who then entered into it, and the legal position of these children was therefore decided by the well-known rule which applied to Roman slaves. There is no distinction between the power of a father and of a protector.[2]

McLennan undertakes to oppose this view also. He says that the father's authority over the mother is the basis of his authority over the child, and that this authority was the foundation, but not the consequence, of the protection afforded by the father to the children of the unmarried daughter. And when the illegitimate children were transferred to the husband of their mother, her marriage was certainly the bond which united stepfather and children, whence his protection followed.[3] In this case McLennan has been unable to distinguish between the protection and the authority of the protector; his remarks only apply to the former, while Sir Henry Maine is speaking only of the latter. When Maine, as we have already seen, considers that agnation is not based upon marriage, but on the paternal authority, McLennan, who so zealously advocates the primitive female line, will not refuse his assent; for he is of opinion that the female line was suppressed by the ever

---

[1] See Grimm, p. 433, and Weinhold, p. 308 with respect to Niyoga among the Germans. See J. D. Mayne, p. 58, for the fact that in earlier times the custom of permitting strangers to have access to their wives was widely diffused among the Hindus. At p. 63, he shows that at a later date this privilege was restricted to the Gentiles.

[2] Maine, *Early Law*, p. 98.   [3] McLennan, *Patr. Theor.* p. 281.

increasing predominance of the husband. We do not, indeed, find the existence of paternal authority when the father and son belong to different clans. We agree with McLennan that mere protection is insufficient to incorporate any one into a clan to which he does not belong;[1] but we believe that a mere marriage between the mother and a man who was not the child's father was equally insufficient to effect such incorporation.

The main point at issue between Sir Henry Maine and McLennan is whether the Levirate and Niyoga are of comparatively late origin, or if they date from a primitive state of things, so that they are now only maintained by force of custom, after development has produced a civilization which is hostile to them, and by which they must ultimately be suppressed. We believe that the truth lies between these two theories. Everything tends to show that the Levirate and Niyoga belong to the customs and ideas which prevail in primitive communities. But there is no reason to suppose that the Hindu communities which afford the earliest accounts of these customs entertained ideas which were opposed to them. The earliest Hindu community is, however, patriarchal. The Levirate and Niyoga do not spring from any less binding form of marriage; they find a fitting soil wherever fatherhood is of a predominantly legal character, as it continues to be in comparatively modern times. The weakness of McLennan's standpoint consists in the altogether unproved assertion that monandry necessarily involved that special interest for fatherhood, with which such customs as the Levirate and Niyoga are incompatible. This is a very common opinion, and if it were correct, McLennan would be justified in his assertion that the reason of both customs is to be found in whatever form of marriage prevailed before monandry was universally accepted.[2] We readily admit that it is most

[1] McLennan, *Patr. Theor.*, p. 282.
[2] *Ibid.*, p. 158. See *Fortnightly Rev.*, 1877: " The Levirate and Polyandry," and *Studies*, p. 160.

natural to regard polyandry as this primitive form of marriage, and McLennan's explanation resembles that already given by Michaelis and Bachofen.[1]   But if the fundamental theory, which declares that monandry is incompatible with these customs, is erroneous, the whole explanation which relies upon it must also be set aside.

We agree with McLennan that the Levirate and Niyoga present many points of contact with polyandry.[2] The Levir-child was ascribed to the dead man in virtue of the same ideas according to which, in Thibet, the eldest brother and ruler of the house was held to be the father of all the children of the household.   In the Thibetan family we find the same feature which distinguishes the Jewish Levirate from that of the Hindus, namely, that the Levir married the widow, instead of merely holding intercourse with her; for in Thibet the brother of the dead man inherits his property, his authority, and his widow.   This agrees with Mielziner's assertion that the Jewish Levirate was connected with the old agrarian law of Israel, which aimed at retaining the undivided property in the tribe and family.   The brother-in-law took with the widow and sister-in-law his brother's whole property, which must otherwise have been divided among all the brothers.[3] The story of Judah's son Onan shows, however, that the Levir obligation was not always willingly fulfilled, and that the thought that the child which was begotten must bear the name of another man was distasteful.[4]

But the most important point of contact between the Levirate and polyandry, together with the strongest motive for assigning to them a common origin, consists in the setting aside of the direct fatherhood which is common to both of them.   The causes for such an act

[1] Michaelis, vol. ii. p. 198.   Bachofen, *Mutterrecht*, p. 200.

[2] McLennan, *Patr. Theor.*, pp. 159, 267.

[3] Mielziner, p. 55.   The Levir-brother did not precisely inherit the dead man's property, but he managed it as guardian of the unborn child.

[4] Gen. xxxviii. 8-10.

must, however, be determined by other facts. We flatter ourselves that we have shown that no special explanation of this setting aside is required, but that it is the natural practice of primitive men, and that the causes both of the Levirate and polyandry are to be traced to the authority of the husband, which is the legal foundation of marriage. McLennan finds fault with J. D. Mayne for regarding the Niyoga as the primitive form, and the Levirate as its derivative; the Levirate implied the fiction that the child was begotten by the dead man, and this was wholly different from the Niyoga, which implied the man's rights of property with respect to his wife and child.[1] McLennan misunderstands Mayne in this matter; he does not, as McLennan supposes, assert that the notion of material fatherhood, valueless for the Niyoga, was all-important for the Levirate; but he chiefly insists on the fact that the husband's ownership did not cease on his death.[2] It does not appear how McLennan explains the transition from the begetting of children in common by polyandrous brothers, children which belonged to the eldest brother, together with everything else in the house, to the begetting of children by the surviving brother which should be accounted as those of the brother who was dead. In whatever way this fact is wrested, it only becomes intelligible from the legal point of view, and no consideration of the actual fact of begetting nor any classification of the relative circumstances can avail to explain the fiction which represented the dead man to be the begetter of children.

Spencer has attempted to explain the Levirate from the prevailing custom that the brother should inherit his

---

[1] McLennan, *Patr. Theor.*, p. 270.

[2] J. D. Mayne: "After his death the ownership had ceased, unless, indeed, by another fiction he was considered as still surviving in her. Therefore, unless the husband had given express directions during his lifetime, the process to be adopted was to be as like as possible to an actual begetting by him, or was to be such a substituted begetting as he would probably have sanctione l."

dead brother's widow. We shall explain presently the main facts of fraternal inheritance, and will now only consider whether it has anything in common with the Levirate. After referring to McLennan's theory, Spencer briefly observes that it would be more to the purpose to seek for the explanation of the Levirate in the fact that the wives formed part of the inheritance, since they were in primitive communities regarded merely as property. He does not, therefore, consider that the custom of marrying the brother's widow bore any reference to polyandry.[1] McLennan justly replies that the Levirate wholly differed from the inheriting of the widow by her brother-in-law, since the Levir was thus excluded from the inheritance of the dead man, inasmuch as he had to raise up heirs to him.[2] His further remark, that Spencer's explanation does not destroy the relation between the Levirate and polyandry, is more doubtful; he says that inheritance from a brother follows from polyandry, since all the rules of the mode of inheritance are based on marriage laws and the modifications of the family. Spencer, on the other hand, is of opinion that inheritance by the brother was produced by one of the conditions of the female line of descent.[3]

Spencer disputes McLennan's criticism in a singular manner. He contradicts it by a statement which is inserted in the "Principles" amid quite other matter, and he holds that no one can fail to see that this constitutes the essential point of the explanation he has undertaken to give. This statement is to the effect that the Hebrew injunction to raise up seed to the dead brother may possibly be explained by the prior obligation of providing for the children which the brother leaves behind him.[4] This suggestion, which finds no place in the ten pages

---

[1] Spencer, *Princ. of Soc.*, pp. 679-681.
[2] McLennan, *Fortnightly Rev.*, 1877, p. 701.
[3] Spencer, "A Short Rejoinder," *Fortnightly Rev.*, 1877, p. 897.
[4] Spencer, *Princ of Soc.*, p. 692.

which contain the aforesaid explanation of the Levirate, is now constituted its essential point. Under the influence of the paternal line and filial inheritance, which were beginning to prevail against the female line and fraternal inheritance, the old obligation of maintaining the children which the brother had begotten in his lifetime was transformed into the obligation of providing the brother with posterity, and this obligation was expressed by the Levirate. He thinks this explanation more satisfactory than that of McLennan, which fails in the point adduced by McLennan himself, since it does not appear how the organization of a polyandrous family, in virtue of which the next brother inherited the deceased's property, authority, and widow, could lead to the institution which ordained that the next brother in a polygamous or monogamous family should renounce the inheritance and raise up the heir which was lacking to the dead man.[1] Spencer has, however, still to explain the most obscure point in the Levirate—how it was possible to raise up posterity to the dead. He has contributed something towards the explanation of this duty, but he does not go beyond the general statement that it was always the brother's duty to contribute to his elder's well-being. This is, however, a subordinate point with respect to the question how far it was possible to carry out the Levirate.

I must here adduce some of the characteristics of the Levirate, as they are found among the Jews and Hindus, since they present features which have nothing to do with the conditions of polyandry, and which cannot be explained by them. Other facts might perhaps be adduced, but these decisively confirm the theory I have advocated, namely, that the Levirate and polyandry may both be explained by the juridical character of fatherhood, but that they are not necessarily related to each other.

There were five distinct forms of marriage in ancient Iran. The second was termed Yogan-zan, in which the

[1] Spencer, *Fortnightly Rev.*, p. 896.

15

wife stipulated that her firstborn son should not be regarded as the son of her husband, but that the inheritance of her father or brother who has died without male heirs should devolve upon him. In such a case the woman obtained a son's share of her father's property, and she was remarried to her husband when her firstborn son was fifteen years old. Satar-zan, the third form of marriage, resembled the former, except that the stipulation was not made in favour of one of the kinsfolk, but of some other person, in return for a certain sum of money.[1] In this case, as in the Levirate, we find that children were ascribed to the dead, and it is evident that the conditions were made effective by means which were wholly juridical.

McLennan asserts that the Levirate occurs among the Bechuanas,[2] but M'Kenzie's account, to which he refers, is somewhat obscure, and at any rate imperfect. It is only said that when the head wife of a man who has been dead for some years gives birth to a son, he is held to be the heir, even if there were male descendants by the other wives. McLennan does not seem to be acquainted with Livingstone's much more instructive report. The latter writer states that Skeletu, according to the Bechuana custom, became the owner of his father's wives, and took two of them for his own ; but in such cases the children of these women were termed his brothers. When the elder brother died, the same thing occurred with his wives; the next brother took them, in accordance with the Jewish practice, and the children were held to be children of the dead brother, to whom he had raised up seed.[3] Neither Spencer nor McLennan can account for this fact; the former, because in this case we have not to do with a childless widow, and the latter because in the polyandry of Thibet it is only decreed that the son's children by the widow should

---

[1] Spiegel, vol. iii. p. 678.　　[2] McLennan, *Patr. Theor.*, p. 328.
[3] Livingstone, *Miss. Trav.*, p. 185.　Appendix XXXV.

be regarded as his brethren and sisters, because the legal possession of the wife is altogether from the husband's point of view, not from that of the begetting father. It is precisely this mode of looking at things which McLennan has failed to recognize.

It is equally difficult to reconcile the Bechuana Levirate with the assumption that there was a prior female line, since the Levir-son is indeed the son of the dead man's wife, whose children are not brethren to the begetting father on the maternal side, since the son never had intercourse with his own mother. On the other hand, these strange conditions of kinship are altogether in agreement with the conditions of inheritance which we have described above. When only legal considerations prevail, posthumous children are placed on an equality with those born in their father's lifetime, because the mother served as the bond of union to the children while the father lived; they all belonged to the circle which was defined by her. This circle was not broken by the husband's death, although the connection between the wives was changed, and thus it was that even when years had elapsed since the husband's death, the children born to his wife still belonged to the circle of the dead man's children, and to the fraternal circle of the other children.

Haxthausen writes of the Ossetes of Transcaucasia that every child born in wedlock, even if its mother's adultery be proved, is entitled to the family name, succession, and right of inheritance. A married woman who has borne children cannot marry out of the family after her husband's death; she has been bought, and becomes a family possession. The father or brother of the dead man may marry her, and this, indeed, is regarded as a duty and honour. But, in accordance with the Ossetes' ideas of law, this is only a continuation of the first, sole, and perpetual marriage, to which the children of this fresh marriage are still ascribed, and they inherit the name and property of the dead man, in conjunction with those who are really his children. But this conception is still further enlarged. If the dead man leaves no father nor brother, and the widow is consequently obliged to remain unmarried, yet there is nothing to prevent her from living with other men, and the children which she bears to them are held to be just as legitimate as those born of the marriage which was dissolved by death. On the other hand, a childless widow may marry again, but her new husband must repay to the family which she then forsakes half of the purchase money which had been paid for her. And if a child be born within the year of her husband's death, it will still belong to his family.[1] After they have borne children, or when they have been married for four years, the women live unchastely, although up to that time they are chastity personified.

In like manner, a widow in Assam does not marry again, and yet the children which she may possibly bring forth are held to be legitimate.[2]

We learn from Wilkes that among the Iakali on the Fraser River the priest can inspire any person he chooses with the soul of a dead man, whose name he then adds to his own.[3] According to Waitz's version of the fact, the first child born after his father's death receives his soul, and assumes his name and rank.[4]

[1] Haxthausen, vol. ii. pp. 24, 25.   [2] Cooper, p. 102.
[3] Wilkes, vol. iv. p. 453.
[4] Waitz, vol. iii. p. 195. We cite the analogous case in which the new husband assumes the skin of the dead : " Whenever a distinguished warrior falls in battle, or otherwise, it is considered a great privilege to marry his squaw ; and whoever does, is obliged to assume the name of her former husband, and to sustain, as far as possible, his reputation and character. This custom of continuing families is indulged to a considerable extent ; sometimes the brother of the deceased becomes the husband ; but the most frequent source of continuance is from the prisoners taken in battle ; who, but for this kind of preferment, are generally condemned to suffer tortures and death " (Hunter, pp. 245, 255. See Adair, p. 189, for a less clear account). "Married by jujur, his brother, the eldest in preference, may succeed to his bed. If no brother chooses it, they may give the woman

According to the Levirate, children were raised up to
the dead man, that is, to a man who was no longer able
to beget children. But this also occurred in all cases in
which a man obtained children which were quite certainly not begotten by him, whether because he, like
the Arabs we have mentioned, was temporarily separated
from his wife, or because, on account of impotence, he
had recourse to the Niyoga, or because he had not
attained to the age of puberty. It was in this way that
among the Ossetes and the Russians a man would marry
a son of six years old to a girl of fourteen, and would
himself have intercourse with his daughter-in-law and
beget children, which were, nevertheless, reckoned to
belong to her childish and lawful husband.[1] This custom
is also found among the Reddies, only in this case the
wife has intercourse with one of her own kinsfolk.[2]

In addition to the juridical character of fatherhood,
of which we have now given so many proofs, we must
adduce instances in which the wife also becomes the
mother of a child born of another woman. These instances
are strongly in favour of the opinion that the juridical
character of fatherhood was in no way due to the fact that
the female line became predominant on account of uncertainty with respect to the actual paternity.

" Among the Chinese, marriage with only one wife is
ordained, and any further connection is simply concubinage. Only one wife is authorized and lawful, and
the children belong to her ; she and the children inherit
the husband's property together, to the exclusion of all the
concubines, whose lot in their subordinate position is a

in marriage to any relation on the father's side, without adat or purchase
money, the person who marries her replacing the deceased. If no relation
takes her, and she is given in marriage to a stranger, he may be either
adopted into the family, to replace the deceased, without adat, or he may
pay her jujur, or take her by semando, as her relations please " (Marsden,
p. 228).
[1] Haxthausen, vol. ii. p. 23. Klemm, *Culturgeschichte*, vol. x p. 59.
[2] Lubbock, *Origin of Civ.*, p. 80.

very sad one. Bought for a small sum of money, they are treated like household slaves, and are not only subject to the man, but to his lawful wife, who in this way again appears as the authorized housewife. They are exposed to all sorts of ill-usage and oppression; they may be sold again at a higher price, and the children they bring forth are not even regarded as their own. The children themselves regard the lawful wife as their mother, and treat the woman who bore them with contempt."[1] McLennan quotes the story of Sarah:[2] "And Sarai said unto Abram, Behold now, the Lord hath restrained me from bearing: I pray thee, go in unto my maid; it may be that I may obtain children by her." Hagar's subsequent behaviour, however, makes this story somewhat obscure, and the story of Jacob, Leah, and Rachel is clearer and more instructive. Rachel was childless, and said, "Behold my maid Bilhah, go in unto her; and she shall bear upon my knees, that I may also have children by her. And she gave him Bilhah her handmaid to wife: and Jacob went in unto her. And Bilhah conceived, and bare Jacob a son. And Rachel said, God hath judged me, and hath also heard my voice, and hath given me a son: therefore called she his name Dan. And Bilhah Rachel's maid conceived again, and bare Jacob a second son. And Rachel said, With great wrestlings have I wrestled with my sister, and I have prevailed: and she called his name Naphtali. When Leah saw that she had left bearing, she took Zilpah her maid, and gave her Jacob to wife. And Zilpah Leah's maid bare Jacob a son. And Leah said, A troop cometh: and she called his name Gad. And Zilpah Leah's maid bare Jacob a second son. And Leah said, Happy am I, for the daughters will call me blessed: and she called his name Asher."[3]

[1] Unger, p. 17.
[2] McLennan, *Patr. Theor.*, p. 273. Gen. xvi. 2.
[3] Gen. xxx. 3-13.

CHAPTER IV.

INHERITANCE BY BROTHERS, AND OTHER SUPPOSED
PROOFS OF POLYANDRY.

Iuheritance of rank and property—Personal and family property—Partition and stewardship of property—Suitability of inheritance by brothers—Right of firstborn—Polyandry and female line—Inheritance by widow—Marriage between widow and brother—Aryan polyandry.

TAKEN alone, there is nothing in the Levirate which can be referred to polyandry. The ideas that the Levir son might be substituted for an actual son, and that the brother of the deceased was bound to act as Levir, were disconnected both with each other and with polyandry. We cannot suppose that the Levir obligation differed from the other duties which the conceptions of primitive men imposed upon the surviving brother, and especially since this duty presents itself as the simple consequence of the survivor's succession to the position of the deceased. As we have already remarked, it may be difficult to connect the development of the Levirate, which excluded the brother from the inheritance, with the custom of inheritance by brothers ; yet this difficulty must not be overestimated. We have to do with the joint family group, within which personal property played a quite insignificant part; the management of the property devolved upon the Levir-brother as guardian, and among primitive peoples guardianship can hardly be distinguished from ownership; it usually continued, not up to the time when the child was of full age, but to that of the guardian's death.

The possible origin of the Levirate has been shown above; the obligation was founded upon the ardent desire of having heirs to offer sacrifice, although, as Spencer suggests, the obligation sometimes arose from the inheritance of the property by the father's brother, and the protection he afforded to it. In primitive times it was, undoubtedly, one and the same thing to inherit and to marry the widow, and the children afterwards born from the widow were, as in the case of the Bechuanas and the Ossetes, held to belong to the deceased. We could, however, dispense with this surmise; we only assert it to be probable that it was in this atmosphere that most of the Levir phenomena arose. There was a close external bond between the Levirate and inheritance by brothers, to which McLennan ascribes so much significance that he asserts that the brother's inheritance both of the widow and property only occurs where polyandry had been previously practised.[1] We must consequently distinguish between the inheritance of property and that of the widow, and we shall begin by considering the former.

We may take it as a type of the order of inheritance that the father's property devolved upon the sons in common, while the chief dignity, which was not divisible, and could not be held in common, fell to the eldest. It is our present object to inquire into the ideas which transformed this order, and produced very different rules of inheritance.

McLennan connects the inheritance of property with that of dignity under the same original rules; he is of opinion that the evolution of the family subsequently transformed the former rule in many ways, but left the latter untouched. Hence came the inheritance of the

[1] McLennan, *Studies*, p. 163; *Patr. Theor.*, p. 90.

dignity of chief by the brother, while the sons inherit the property; this is of frequent occurrence, but the converse order is never found.[1] The family organization in which the inheritance by brothers necessarily takes place is that of the polyandry of Thibet.[2] As we have already said, however, we are disposed to seek for the reasons of this mode of inheritance, not in polyandry, but in the joint family group from which polyandry sprang.

The conditions of inheritance among the Nairs are accurately described by McLennan as a primitive stage of the polyandrous family order; the movable property falls to the sister's children of the deceased, while the land is managed by the eldest male member of the family.[3] McLennan does not inquire further into this distinction between movable and immovable property, which is the more remarkable since it generally occurs in uterine families. We only find one instance of unconditional inheritance by the brother in a uterine family, namely, in Du Chaillu's account of Ashango.[4]

Movable and immovable property is to some extent defined by the contrast between a man's own acquisitions and that which he has inherited, a contrast which is only gradually developed. And even if we do not take this contrast into consideration, McLennan's hypothesis does not embrace all the facts. In Kunawar, where polyandry is practised by all the inhabitants, a son of full age succeeds to the *patria potestas* on his father's death; if he is a minor, the father's brother becomes the heir; it is ordained that sometimes the uncle, sometimes the nephew, should take precedence, but the most capable is usually preferred.[5] Among the Todas, who also live in polyandry, the sons inherit that which is the only heritable property, namely, the cattle, from the fathers, to whom

---

[1] McLennan, *Patr. Theor.*, note to ch. vii.   [2] *Ibid.*, p. 90.
[3] McLennan, *Studies*, p, 150.
[4] Du Chaillu, *Journey*, p. 429.
[5] Cunningham, *Journ. Asiat. Soc. of Bengal*, 1844, vol. xiii. pp. 1, 203.

they were assigned in the mode described above; the land is the common property of the village.[1]

Among the Hindus, as long as the family held together there was in primitive times no private property for its individual members. In later times, however, the individual had the right of disposing of the movable property he had acquired for himself, and in some cases also of that which was immovable.[2] When the goods of the family were divided, it was done in accordance with the lines of descent; the undivided property of the first ancestor was distributed in equal portions among his sons, and each of these portions was again subdivided among the owner's descendants, and so on.[3] In primitive times the son was not entitled to demand the partition; he could only claim the right of maintenance;[4] and the brother's right to share the inheritance was originally, as it appears, only in force after the death of both parents.[5] We cannot fail to recognize the fundamental idea of this order of succession to property, which was so widely diffused that it may almost be termed universal. All brothers had an equal right to inherit from their father; a right which was by no means forfeited, even if the partition did not take place. But the question arose who should preside over the management of the undivided property; whether it should be the eldest brother, followed by his eldest son, so that the succession should continue in the hands of the eldest line, or if it should devolve on the eldest male member of the family.

This question is concerned with the order of succession to dignities, and since in the joint family group there is no property, exclusive of the government, the rules which are made for the latter also decide the inheritance of property. We are compelled to differ from McLennan, and to assert that wherever the inheritance of property

[1] Spencer, *Des. Soc.*   [2] J. D. Mayne, pp. 207, 209, 309.
[3] *Ibid.*, p. 231.   [4] *Ibid.*, p. 211.   [5] *Ibid.*, p. 213.

by brothers occurs, it must be referred to their inheritance of rank, and not conversely. Sir Henry Maine
starts from a primitive line of descent, from father to
son, which also refers to rank. The considerations of
fitness which are presented by the widespread reverence
for old age, made it desirable, however, to entrust the
management of the common interests of the family to
the eldest and most experienced of its members, and this
has produced the collateral line, or inheritance by brothers.
McLennan strongly protests against the attempt to
explain social phenomena by showing that they arose
to serve useful ends.[1] Sir Henry Maine himself strictly
limits such an explanation, saying that no legislation
arises simply from a sense of fitness. This sense of fitness is always preceded by previously existing ideas, and
is only able to influence these, and bring them into fresh
connections.[2]

Maine holds that the actual basis upon which Tanis-
try, or the order that, not the eldest son, but the eldest
of the male kinsfolk should succeed, was founded upon
the preference given to the eldest son in the direct line
of descent.[3] And this right of the firstborn was derived
from the order followed in the succession to dignity,
while property was divided equally among all the sons
(Gavelkind). No idea of disinheriting the other children
in favour of one of them is involved in the privileges of
primogeniture.[4] Subsequently, indeed, the property was
inherited by the firstborn, as was the case in feudal
Europe; but this only occurred because the ordinances of
the primitive community were subject to a foreign interpretation, namely, to the later Roman jurisprudence,
according to which the unlimited right of disposing of
the property was involved in its possession.[5] Maine
considers that the right of primogeniture constituted the

[1] McLennan, *Patr. Theor.*, p. 90.
[2] Maine, *Anc. Law*, p. 233.
[3] *Ibid.*, pp. 236, 239.
[4] *Ibid.*, p. 236.
[5] *Ibid.*, p. 238.

simplest rule for the order of succession to dignities, but whenever political as well as civil dignities were in question, a difficulty arose, especially in communities which hung somewhat loosely together. The chief might survive his eldest son, and die when his grandchild was still quite young; in well-ordered communities this state of things was remedied by the appointment of a guardian, but in those which were still uncivilized, the eldest of the male kinsfolk became the heir.[1]

We feel no doubt that considerations of fitness led to the preference of the eldest as heir; in every primitive community age is a source of reverence and influence. Yet it is precisely this fact which leads us to doubt whether the right of primogeniture was primitive. In proportion to the connection of the dignity of chief with property would be the adoption of similar rules of inheritance. We have already seen that in South America the sons became the heirs as soon as the dignity of chief was combined with the possession of property.[2] The tribe was so readily divided that it was possible for all the sons to be promoted to the Cazikat at the same time, and there was as little question of the right of primogeniture as of the inheritance of property. We find that in Africa the son becomes his father's successor, while his uncles live in remote villages as subordinate chiefs; that is, it is only where the chief's power extends over a definite locality that the eldest son succeeds, instead of the eldest surviving brother, since it is the son and not the brother who inherits the dwelling-place of the deceased.

This fact becomes most apparent in the case of the joint family group. As soon as it becomes enlarged into a village community, the rights of precedence which

[1] Maine, *Anc. Law*, p. 239. Freycinet, vol. ii. pt. i. pp. 134, 475. Caillié, vol. i. p. 145. Raffenel, p. 280. Skene, vol. i. p. 160. Morgan, *Systems*; " Fiji " Quest. iv.–vi. p. 582.

[2] Falkner, p. 150. Comp. Merovingians, Ynglinges, and the Polish nobles.

belonged to the eldest man are gradually transformed into the dignity of a chief, as it befits the eldest member of a definite family, and as soon as such a chief extends his authority over several villages, the eldest son of the eldest line, which is in possession of the place of government, succeeds to the dignity. This is just what occurs on the dissolution of an isolated family group. Their forefather's property is equally divided among his sons, some of whom may have predeceased him, and it is again subdivided among his grandsons. Whatever may have been assigned to a line of descendants by this real or fictitious partition cannot be taken from it as long as that line continues to exist.[1]

I readily admit that I have adduced no proof which completely justifies my opinion that the right of the firstborn to inherit dignities was of later origin than the right of brothers to do so. Yet I doubt whether it will ever be possible to come much nearer to the point. When we consider that in communities of the lowest type with which we are acquainted, the strongest, bravest, wisest, and oldest man enjoys the most influence, it will certainly correspond to the natural course of development that whenever the question of inheritance comes in, the brother should at first take precedence of the son. However this may be, we believe that we have indisputably shown that there is not the slightest connection between the inheritance by brothers and polyandry, or the female line.

We have still to explain why the brother inherited the widow of the deceased.[2] The inheriting of wives

---

[1] The Sumatra brother sometimes receives a portion of the inheritance, when the property comes through the father.

[2] In addition to the Hebrews, Ossetes, Kejangs, and Bechuanas, we may mention the Brazilians (Von Martius, p. 117), the Warruas (Schomburgk, vol. ii. p. 447), Californians (Venegas, vol. i. p. 82), Samoa, Fiji and New Zealand (Waitz, vol. vi. pp. 129, 634. Fison and Howitt, p. 153), New Holland (*Ibid.*, p. 204; Grey, vol. ii. p. 230), Kirghiz (Wood, p. 340), Arabs (Burkhardt, vol. i. p. 112), Abyssinians (Lobo), Kakhyäns (Anderson, *Mandalay to Momien*, pp. 132, 142), Damaras (Anderson,

has usually been placed in the same category as the inheritance of property. On the one side, McLennan has proposed to explain the latter by the former, while referring back to the polyandrous family. On the other side, Spencer simply regards the inheriting of wives as one involved in the succession to the property, and he holds that the same principle applies to the inheritance of the wives by sons as to that by brothers.

I do not think that any proof is necessary to show that when sons divide among themselves such of their fathers' wives as are not their own mothers, the wives were held to be part of the property. But in other cases the matter is somewhat more complex. Almost everywhere the widow has a right, or, at any rate, a claim, to subsistence out of what her husband leaves behind him, and hence she usually lives on with her children. This does not imply that she constitutes part of their inheritance, which only occurs when sons marry their fathers' widows, and in no case does a son take his own mother in this way. The mother has a claim to be supported by her son—a claim which is usually satisfied by making no partition of the paternal inheritance during the mother's lifetime, so that the sons fulfil their obligations to her in common. We can easily see that the performance of this duty may lead to many different arrangements which we need not examine more closely, since they do not concern our present purpose.

These claims of the mother are, if I am not mistaken, connected with the custom which included her in her brother-in-law's inheritance, and this naturally occurs as soon as the family is transformed into a joint family group. Burkhardt expressly mentions that the Arabs think the connection between the widow and brother-in-law desirable, since the family property is thereby kept

Ngami, p. 176), Congo (Du Chaillu, *Journey*, p. 429), Muskohgi (Adair, p. 189), Araucanians (Charlevoix, vol. vi. p. 147), Bellabollah and Vera Paz (Spencer, *Fortnightly Rev.*, 1877, p. 896), Caribs (Gili, p. 346), and Mongols (Du Halde, vol. iv. p. 487).

together. And Morgan makes a similar remark with respect to the Fijians.[1] The Kurnai of New Holland also defend the custom in question on these grounds.[2] Since in the joint family group the brother succeeds to the headship of the community, and its interests and general protection are committed to his care, so also the widow and her young children are committed to him, and under primitive conditions these relations take the form of marriage. In proportion to the importance of the property of the deceased is the difficulty of allowing the widow to return to her own family. It is altogether irrational to seek for the causes of the connection between the widow and her brother-in-law in polyandry. That the brother-in-law had exerted marital rights in the husband's lifetime would only become a necessary condition if carnal considerations formed the corner-stone of the development of the family; but all we know of the life and habits of primitive men clearly shows that this was not the case. Carnal pleasures certainly took the most prominent place in primitive life, but they were also the most easily obtained, and therefore customs were not formed under the influence of considerations with respect to the means of sensual enjoyment.

Before concluding this series of researches, we must briefly mention McLennan's attempt to trace the existence of polyandry in the ancient Aryan race. We do not think that our conclusions would be invalidated, even if our forefathers lived in polyandry; this practice is, indeed, so often found in connection with the development of the family group, that it is quite possible that it was also practised by the Aryans. It thus becomes simply an historical question.

McLennan directs our attention to the following

---

[1] Morgan, *Systems*, p. 583. See, above, the encroachments of uncles among the Sioux and Columbians.

[2] Fison and Howitt, p. 204.

passage from Manu :—" If among several brothers of the whole blood, one have a son born, Menu pronounces them all fathers of a male child by means of that son, so that if such nephew would be the heir the uncles have no power to adopt sons."[1] McLennan does not, however, depend upon this text, since Draupadi's narrative makes it unnecessary by directly mentioning the fact of polyandry. But in his latest work he again refers to the passage, in connection with the conditions which exist in Thibet. He does not admit that the constitution of the father's brother into the father was founded on a fiction. He asserts that it was altogether contrary to the Hindu custom to hinder a man from obtaining sons of his own by fictitious and artificial regulations, and we have seen above that adoption by the uncle was prohibited. It was the chief and most persistent effort of Hindu government to promote the increase of heirs, that is, of separate households, and with these of the centres of religious worship.[2] The prohibition of adoption contained in the text must, he thinks, have had its origin in some very ancient institution.

This view must be rejected as altogether unfounded. J. D. Mayne has shown that religious interests aimed at the dissolution of the joint family groups, and it was on religious grounds that the Brahmans advocated such a dissolution. The head of the family was himself its high priest. As long as the Brahman influence was still slight, the claim of the family group to maintain an heir who might offer sacrifice for them only reached the stage at which we find it in Manu's text, and subsequently, when this influence was fully developed, each brother desired to have a son of his own. The prohibition contained in Manu is merely that which has in all times and all places been the fundamental thought of men, namely, that only in cases in which the existence of the

[1] McLennan, "The Levirate and Polyandry," *Fortnightly Rev.*, 1877, p. 698.   [2] McLennan, *Patr. Theor.*, p. 336.

group was in danger of perishing for lack of legitimate heirs, whether that group consisted of the simple family, the joint family group, or the clan, it was permitted to have recourse to adoption. If, however, one of the brothers in a joint family group had a son, a legitimate heir was not wanted.[1] McLennan also quotes the following passage from Apastamba :—" A husband shall not make over his wife, who occupies the position of a *gentilis* to others than to his *gentiles*, in order to cause children to be begot for himself. For they declare that a bride is given to the family of her husband, and not to the husband alone. That is at present forbidden on account of the weakness of men's senses."[2] Here again McLennan finds a custom similar to that of Thibetan polyandry, based upon a polyandrous theory.[3] J. D. Mayne, however, seems to us to be nearer the truth when he regards this text as a limitation of the Niyoga, which originally included any man whatsoever, and which was now restricted to the Sapinda or Samanodoco.[4] The expression, " A bride is given to the family," does not imply that she is given as a wife common to the family; the statement merely corresponds with Manu's previous statement, which revealed the ideas entertained in the joint family group.

If, in conclusion, we turn to the Draupadi myth, it is evident that the Pandava brothers, distributed into Draupadi, do not justify us in forming any general conclusion. They are ancestors of the Kshatry tribe, which came into India from one of the Kashmir valleys of the Himalayas; and the account only allows us to infer that polyandry occurred locally in an isolated Aryan tribe. Even this conclusion does not appear to me to be completely established, since the myth affords scanty in-

---

[1] J. D. Mayne, p. 211.
[2] McLennan, *Patr. Theor.*, p. 304. See also H. Zimmer, p. 325, who does not admit the existence of polyandry.
[3] McLennan, *Patr. Theor.*, p. 305.
[4] J. D. Mayne, pp. 48, 63.

formation with respect to the reasons which led to Draupadi's connection with the five Pandavas, and also with respect to the ideas which justified this marriage.[1]

[1] Lenormant, vol. iii. p. 497. McLennan, *Fortnightly Rev.*, 1877, p. 699. Bachofen, *Das Mutterrecht*, §§ 94, 195. Wilkes, vol. i. p. 54. J. D. Mayne, p. 57.

CHAPTER V.

NOMENCLATURES.

THE readiness with which a husband in the primitive
community permitted other men to hold sexual intercourse with his wife, was closely connected with the
slight importance which he ascribed to the actual descent
of his children. The idea is historically untenable that,
even in the case of the primitive man, the chastity of
his wife was an indispensable condition of marriage, and
that lascivious customs consequently pointed to a time
when promiscuous intercourse prevailed, and there was
no tie of marriage. McLennan seeks to confirm the
existence of such conditions by means of polyandry, an
attempt which we have shown to be wholly unsuccessful.
We must now turn to other writers, such as Morgan,

Bachofen, and Lubbock, who have had recourse to another
category of facts to establish the already tottering hypothesis of a primitive state of promiscuous intercourse.
Such a state seems to them to have been produced, not
so much by jealousy and conflicting lusts, as by a privilege conferred on all by all, which was prompted by
tribal feeling and religious ideas. We do not, however,
lay much stress on the difference between this theory
and that of McLennan; since, if clear and definite conceptions of rights and duties are not supposed to be
innate in primitive man, we must start from a state of
things in which men strove with each other, and only
after many conflicts found peace in a condition of promiscuous intercourse. It is certain that man was not
originally addicted to promiscuous intercourse, either
from inclination or from sense of duty. In later times,
when this condition had been accepted, it may have
become so firmly established by custom that the ideas of
men might instinctively start from it, as from a fixed
point; and I think that it is only this mode of thought
which is advocated by Lubbock. When, therefore,
McLennan finds fault with this writer for speaking of the
rights of all men, since such rights do not exist in a state of
promiscuous intercourse, he takes the word too literally.[1]
Subsequently, as social relations were further developed,
the time might come for the occurrence of new desires,
to which the old customs were opposed. Wherever there
was this sense of conflict, the sense of rights would arise.

Morgan believes that in nomenclatures, that is, in
the systems of names which define the degrees and stages
of the kinship of primitive men, we may clearly trace
the existence of promiscuous relations within larger or
smaller circles, consisting in a common right to sexual
intercourse between given groups of men and women.
Nomenclatures do not follow the same principle throughout the world, and Morgan makes a distinction between

[1] McLennan, *Studies*, p. 426.

that which is descriptive and that which is classifying. The systems of relative kinship serve to organize families into groups of kinsfolk allied in blood, and as such it possesses great vitality. The descriptive form, as it is found among the Aryan, Semitic, and Uralian families, is a numerical form, and it describes the collateral kinsfolk by a combination of the first and second terms of kinship. On the other hand, the classifying form, in use among the Turanians, the American Indians, and the Malays, is unacquainted with descriptive names, and applies the same name to all those who belong to a class of kinsfolk of which the limits are apparently quite arbitrary.[1]

Morgan makes an attempt to solve various ethnological questions by these nomenclatures, since he is of opinion that when the same form occurs in different races, it points to their common origin. He also proposes to solve by its aid the great question of the origin and development of the family. He holds that a nomenclature was neither introduced nor abandoned from arbitrary motives; it therefore shows us the way in which definite causes influenced a given community at a given time, and also how they were gradually modified in a definite way. The nomenclature was due to custom, and not to legal constraint, and the motive for its alteration must therefore be as universal as the custom itself.[2] On this point we quite agree with Morgan, but we doubt whether it is likely that the important features of a system of nomenclature could long be maintained under a social order which was no longer in agreement with it, since there is nothing to show that the social order changes more quickly and easily than the nomenclature.

No special difficulty is presented by the descriptive

[1] Morgan, *Systeme*, pp. vi. 11, 12, 468.
[2] *Ibid.*, p. 15. See Giraud-Teulon, p. 100. Lubbock, *Origin of Civ.*, p. 161.

nomenclature; it agrees with the natural line of descent, influenced by the marriage of individual pairs.[1] Morgan believes that juridical considerations prompt the definitions of the degrees of kinship, and he believes that this becomes possible, owing to the form of marriage. It is only where marriage between individual pairs prevails that the degrees of kinship can be defined with descriptive accuracy; and the order of inheritance supplies the desire to regulate the motive for this definition.[2] There is greater difficulty in the classifying system, which cannot be explained on the theory of descent, as it is understood by civilized races. It might, perhaps, be possible to bring it into agreement with descent under other conditions of marriage, and Morgan takes this view, without, however, showing that no other solution is possible.

Two causes in particular may have influenced the development of the classifying system: the sexual relations due to the necessity of mutual protection, and tribal organization.[3] The classifying system is marked by the endeavour to prevent the destruction of the tie of blood, while the descriptive system allows us to lose sight of a tie which has always tended to become more remote.[4] The interests of the clan also aim at keeping together the most distant kinsfolk, yet this will not enable us to explain the classifying system, for the cohesive tendency of the clan is not helped by any special plan of the degrees of kinship, and it is therefore the cause, rather than the consequence of the system.[5] It is equally useless to try to explain this system from tribal organization. When the American form regards the children of different sisters as brothers and sisters, it agrees with the definition of the clan, which in this particular follows the female line; the husband's brother's son is, however, held to be his son,

---

[1] Morgan, *Systems*, p. 473.   [2] *Ibid.*, p. 14.
[3] *Ibid.*, p. 474.   [4] *Ibid.*, p. 13.   [5] *Ibid.*, p. 475.

while his sister's son is only his nephew, and yet the latter, and not the former, belongs to his clan.[1] The organization of the clan is not, therefore, in exact corre-spondence with the system, which demands some other explanation.

When Morgan turns to the question of descent, it is at once evident that the classifying system does not agree with the order of descent which is given by poly-gamy, and particularly by marriage with several sisters, and by polyandry.[2] These do not explain why the mother's brother is called uncle, the father's sister is called aunt, while the children of these two are the husband's cousins, and only his sister's son is his nephew. Morgan also thinks that the marriage forms in question occur too rarely to afford an explanation of the whole system of nomenclature, an assertion which is the more surprising since he goes on to seek an explanation in the marriage groups, which are, if they are to be found at all, certainly less common than the marriage of sisters and polyandry.

Morgan merely seeks to show that the nomenclature must be explained from descent, that is, from the marriage form, and starting from the simplest plan of the classify-ing system, he undertakes to construct a form of marriage which shall cause the system to correspond with the descent. He finds this simplest form among the Malays, and beginning from this, the others are to be explained as influenced by the tendency of marriage to assume higher and purer forms.

In the Malay nomenclature, all kinsfolk of the same generation are designated without distinction by like-sounding names, whether the kinship is more or less remote.[3] Morgan holds that this form expresses a con-

[1] Morgan, *Systems*, p. 476.   [2] *Ibid.*, p. 478.
[3] Table I. gives the nomenclature for the speaker's generation, that is, of brothers and sisters. In Morgan's Tables there are accents on the Malay words to indicate different sounds. The accents are very irregular,

sciousness of the descent, if we start from a condition of promiscuous intercourse and see the first stage of development in the communistic family group, in which all the brothers live in common with all the sisters. Morgan's scheme gives, as the second definition in the Malay nomenclature, the Hawaiian custom or the Punalua family, according to which the brothers are the common husbands of several sisters, but not of their own.[1] I do not, however, understand why Morgan should assume the existence of such a custom, since he afterwards positively declares that it is by no means needed to explain the origin of the Malay system.[2] He only makes use of it in order to point out the mode of transition from the Malay to the Turanian system. Perhaps the Punalua family is mentioned in the passage in question in order to account for the distinction between the kinsfolk by birth and kinsfolk by marriage, which occurs in the Malay nomenclature (Table II.). For when a distinction is made between the brother and the husband, it must be supposed that they are two distinct persons, and we should agree with McLennan in rejecting the supposition that the Malays carefully distinguished between the brother and the husband, when they had to do only with the different functions of one and the same person.[3]

It appears to be Morgan's opinion that these peculiar names were included in the Malay nomenclature at a

and as I am unable to understand the principle of variation, I am inclined to regard them as errors of the press, unavoidable in such a work, and do not, therefore, take them into account.

[1] Morgan, *Systems*, p. 480 ; *Anc. Soc.*, pp. 384, 500.
[2] Morgan, *Systems*, p. 489 ; *Anc. Soc.*, p. 386.
[3] McLennan, *Studies*, p. 348 : "While the communal family lasted, the different descriptions of persons referred to, several of which would have been then coincident in a single person, were distinguished in idea the one from the other ; so that when the communal family passed away, the nomenclature, which had applied to those sets of persons while they were yet coincident and ideally distinguished merely, readily extended to them when they became distinct. It is incredible that in the sort of family contemplated, brothers should come to regard each other not only as brothers, but as brothers-in-law."

later period, when the custom of marriage between brothers and sisters and the Punalua family had already begun to decline. But it is more than doubtful whether such marriages and the Punalua family ever prevailed among the Polynesian peoples, at any rate in the Sandwich Islands, from which the nomenclature is taken.

Morgan's Tables, in addition to the Hawaiian custom, give the tribal organization and exogamy as joint causes of the transition from the Malayan to the Turanian form.[1] I am unable to see any clear distinction between these two things, since Morgan holds that the members of the clan originally regarded themselves as brothers and sisters, and the clans must have been formed by creating distinctions between these groups of brothers and sisters. This fact has sometimes been overlooked. The transition to the Turanian form occurred in the following manner. The distribution into exogamous tribes, or groups of brothers and sisters, necessarily made a distinction between the father's and mother's brother, between the mother's and father's sister, between the husband's children and those of his brother on the one side, and the sister's children on the other; that is, children and brother's children were both ascribed to the husband, while sister's children were nephews and nieces, and, conversely, the wife regarded her sister's children as her own, while her brother's children were nephews and nieces.[2] In like manner the children of several brothers could no longer hold the children of their father's sister to be their own brothers and sisters; they were now called cousins.

Morgan mentions as a noteworthy distinction between the Turanian and the Ganowanian nomenclatures, that the Turanians hold the children of the male cousin to be nephews and nieces of the husband, while those of the female cousin are nephews and nieces of the wife, and it is precisely the reverse in the Ganowanian

[1] Morgan, *Anc. Soc.*, p. 433. [2] Morgan, *Systems*, p. 484.

17

nomenclature. Morgan finds that the latter is in more logical agreement with the principles of the system, and he thinks it is difficult to give a satisfactory explanation of the Turanian variation.[1] He goes on to say that it is unintelligible, except as a matter of custom, why a man should be permitted to live with his female cousins, and forbidden to have intercourse with the wives of his male cousin; he dismisses the Ganowanian form, which allows the marriage of cousins, as "a slight variation upon the privilege of barbarism."[2] The two forms, however, find their explanation in the Punalua family, and Morgan makes use of other facts to construct his description of the development of the latter into the civilized family which is monogamous and agnatistic.

The female line produced clans in the Punalua family, with the several sisters as its ancestral mothers. The exogamy of the clans made it difficult, and often quite impossible, for the groups to unite, and in this way the syndyasmistic family arose, in which distinct pairs were united and again parted, and several of such pairs lived together in a communistic household, which did not, however, include sexual intercourse.[3] Morgan admits that the nomenclature only reveals scanty traces of this form of family; in a few instances the degrees of kinship between married persons seem to be changed, while in others the old nomenclature, which is no longer accurate, persists. The syndyasmistic form of a family had indeed long prevailed, but Morgan finds in the absence of monogamy a sufficient explanation of the fact that it had failed to suppress the old nomenclature.[4] There is much in this theory to which we might take exception, if we were not unwilling to interrupt its exposition. For an inquirer has rarely had the courage to solve the most difficult questions by means of so many postulates which are without solid basis. We think it better,

[1] Morgan, *Systems*, p. 391. [2] *Ibid.*, p. 486.
[3] *Ibid.*, p. 490; *Anc. Soc.*, p. 433. [4] *Ibid.*, p. 461.

however, simply to continue our account of Morgan's theory.

Morgan considers that the ever-increasing difficulty of obtaining wives, which arose from the prohibitive decrees of the clan, led to the acquisition of women by violence or by purchase. This increased their value, and they were now jealously watched.[1] Marriage became a more permanent bond, and the syndyasmistic family increased in strength, so that it was able to emancipate itself from the communistic household, and to stand alone. In this way the patriarchal family arose, with the father as ruler, and the father's wish to have children of his own as heirs suppressed the female line, and established agnation.[2] At the same time the wife's position was altered for the worse, and she became a slave. Monogamy, which had hitherto only expressed the inability to procure several wives, became the rule, since it involved the increase of property, and the desire to leave it to the children.[3] A change of nomenclature at once ensued, and although it is only passive, yielding in a radical way to the radical changes in the family, it reveals the historical fate of the latter.[4]

The scarcity of terms of kinship in their present systems seems to Morgan to show that the Aryan, Semitic, and Uralian peoples had previously adopted a classifying system; with such a scanty nomenclature they would never have been able to attain to the exalted heights of monogamy.[5] In any case, more terms would have been handed down to us, and the lack of them is to be explained by the exchange of the Turanian for the descriptive nomenclature. The strong pressure exerted by monogamy may have the more readily led to this exchange, since the generalizations which now came into use were only new in their application to blood kinship, but had long been current among men. We implore our

[1] Morgan, *Anc. Soc.*, p. 458.   [2] *Ibid.*, p. 470.
[3] *Ibid.*, pp. 477, 505.   [4] *Ibid.*, pp. 481, 435.   [5] *Ibid.*, p. 481.

readers to give special attention to the singular conclusion of Morgan's theory. He asserts that if any one
belonging to the races who use the Turanian nomenclature is asked about the relative kinship of two
persons, he describes it in the descriptive terms which
are current among ourselves. A descriptive system
exactly similar to that of the Aryans was co-existent
with the Turanian and Malayan systems, not as a system
of blood kinship, but as the means of establishing the
relations of kinsfolk to each other.[1]

Morgan's theories, and especially his estimate of the
systems of nomenclature, have been accepted by some
writers and strongly opposed by others. Fison and Howitt,
Giraud-Teulon, Engels, and Post are in the former category, while McLennan takes the foremost place among
his opponents. This writer asserts that it is impossible
to regard nomenclature as a system which defines the tie
of blood, since the child calls its mother's sister "mother;'
Morgan hardly gives due attention to this fact, since the
plurality of mothers cannot be explained by the same
ideas as a plurality of fathers.[2] We need not exonerate
Morgan from the reproach of having said that a child
might believe that it had several mothers, since he does
not hold that the word "mother" expressed a tie of blood,
but only a marriage tie.[3] The mother's sister may be
compared to a stepmother. But it must be admitted
that his theories are undermined by this distinction,
since it arouses the suspicion that the terms are, taken
as a whole, prompted by juridical relations. We have
repeatedly called attention to the difficulties which arise
as soon as the attempt is made to distinguish between
these two points; namely, the juridical character of the
relations between persons united by the legally ordained
institution of marriage, and the blood relations which

---

[1] Morgan, *Anc. Soc.*, p. 484.   Appendix XXXVI.
[2] McLennan, *Studies*, p. 345.
[3] Morgan, *Anc. Soc.*, p. 520; *Systems*, p. 478.   See Lubbock, *Orig. of Civ.*, p. 173.

arise between persons who have entered through marriage into sexual connection. This distinction is in no way clearly accepted by Morgan, but the attempt to define it is made by McLennan, and his analysis is intended to supply a new foundation for his theory of polyandry.

The degrees of kinship given by the classifying system are, as McLennan believes, without significance, except as a system of courtly and ceremonial appellations in social intercourse. The system merely regulates the forms of mutual greeting.[1] He, like Morgan, regards the Malayan system as the basis of the whole nomenclature, and he likewise traces its origin to the primitive forms of marriage.[2] A system of greeting would be more readily detached from rights and obligations than a system of kinship, so that these systems would gradually diverge, although they were at first closely connected.[3] Peschel strongly opposes this theory. He writes, " It is impossible that nomenclatures should refer to the facts of sexual origin. We may add that in the eighty North American dialects studied by Morgan, there are, with only two exceptions, special terms in which the wife designates her husband's brother and her sister's husband as brother-in-law, whence it follows that there was no community of wives between brothers, and no community of husbands between sisters. We must also note that in all the languages in which the terms ' father,' ' brother,' and ' son ' are applied to members of the family, as soon as they trace their descent from a common ancestor in a higher, equal, or more remote degree, the elder and younger brother, or father's brother, the elder and younger sister, or father's sister, are distinguished by special names, so that it is clear that it is not the degree of nearness in blood, but the order of generations and the rank within the family which is described; these degrees are of great consequence in domestic life, since

[1] McLennan, *Studies*, p. 366. [2] *Ibid.*, p. 366. [3] *Ibid.*, p. 372.

they affect the reverence for parents, and, which is still more probable, the greater or less obligation to become the avenger of blood." [1]

The difference between Peschel and McLennan is to be sought in the fact that the latter only traces the first shock to the development of nomenclature in the circumstances he mentions, and otherwise assumes that this development was altogether formal, so that the designations were transformed into mere forms of courtesy. Peschel's suggestion is contradicted by the fact that the clan formed a group with exclusive rights, and the nomenclature is not concerned with the clan.[2] When we consider the altogether formal way in which titles of honour are used by civilized peoples, it seems very possible that primitive men, whose mutual intercourse was much more ceremonious than ours, on account of their ever vigilant and lurking fears, should have created an elaborate system of the use of forms of address.[3] Morgan's contemptuous criticism therefore misses its mark;[4] the formal development of nomenclature from the system afforded by the primitive organization of the family may have been uniform throughout. A satisfactory estimate of McLennan's hypothesis can only be made by special research into the history of the several terms; a general observation of the matter would be insufficient.

But in another respect we must show that McLennan's theory is obscure. He writes that when we consider that most of the tribes in which this nomenclature is in use observe the female line of descent, it must surprise us to find two different systems in use among these tribes; where the nomenclature is applied to the blood-kinship, it also contains terms for kinsfolk on the father's side. Hence it is certain that blood-kinship, and not the classifying system, always regulated the succession to dignities and property.[5] But surely the nomenclature must at

[1] Peschel, pp. 241, 242.   [2] McLennan, *Studies*, p. 366.
[3] J. B. Eyre, vol. ii. p. 214.   Williams and Calvert, p. 129.
[4] Morgan, *Anc. Soc.*, p. 518.   [5] McLennan, *Studies*, p. 363.

first have been adapted to the prevailing ideas of blood-kinship. This is asserted by McLennan himself, when he sees no other way of explaining the names for father which occur in the Malayan system; but when some other explanation seems possible, he sets aside the ideas which were from the first connected with the name of father in order to urge them afresh when the female line has disappeared. Then, indeed, nothing is said of the twofold system of blood-kinship. Morgan infers from the names which are used for father that the paternal kinship was recognized in primitive times as well as that of the mother; only the doubtful paternity caused the name to be given to several persons instead of to one individual.[1]

We must now turn to the closer consideration of McLennan's hypothesis. Starting from the ₁Malayan nomenclature, the following terms for the different generations occur: Kupuna, the generation of grandparents; Makua, that of parents; Kaiku, the speaker's own generation; Kaikee, that of his children; Moopuna, that of his grandchildren. In the case of a Nair family these terms would not originally describe the sexual relations between individuals.[2] In such a family nothing is to be said of the father as the begetter among the Makua, only of the mother's brother, mother, and mother's sister. We need not inquire with Morgan how the word "father" came to be used for father's brother and mother's brother, but rather how the original term for the mother's brother became applicable to the actual father and to his brothers. In the Thibetan family the needful extension takes place. Even among the Nairs the terms we have mentioned are sometimes applied to persons living in different houses; we have already seen that a brother occasionally separates himself from his family and establishes a household of his own under the guidance of his favourite sister.[3] According to the Thibetan order, the

---

[1] Morgan, *Anc. Soc.*, p. 515.   [2] McLennan, *Studies*, p. 373.
[3] *Ibid.*, p. 383.

father and his kinsfolk are placed in the same group of
terms; the father and his brothers and sisters become
Makua to the children, like the mother and her brother
and sisters. The latter, who were the mother's Kaiku
in her former home, become by an altogether formal
process of thought Makua for her children. New terms
are only applied to those who are married, because these
are not connected with the family by birth, but annexed
to it in riper age.[1] The fact that McLennan is not
acquainted with the nomenclatures of the Nairs and
Thibetans throws doubts upon his theory, as Morgan has
already remarked,[2] and we are the more inclined to
insist on this fact, since the Dravida tribes and Mongolian
peoples make use of the Turanian nomenclature. If
the Nairs do not possess the Malayan nomenclature,
McLennan's hypothesis becomes untenable. Moreover, it
is quite evident that the hypothesis in no way affects
the polyandry of the Nairs and Thibetans, but merely
the joint family group. We shall presently see the
bearing of this remark.

If we look more closely at the names given to married
persons (Table II.), we shall find that the husband of a
wife's sister and the wife of a husband's brother are
designated by them by the special name of Punalua, of
which "intimate companion" is given as the English
equivalent. According to Morgan's theory, these persons
would be called brother and sister, and he gives no
explanation of the special names. These doubtful titles
tend to show that not only the husbands of several
sisters are not held to be brothers to each other, but
that usually there is no kinship between them, any
more than among the brothers' wives. McLennan's
Thibetan family might explain the first of these special
names, but not the last. As a rule, indeed, each Thibetan
family has only one wife, so that the sisters must marry
into different families; that is, the husband of a wife's

---

[1] McLennan, *Studies*, pp. 385-389.   [2] Morgan, *Anc. Soc.*, p. 517.

sister does not therefore become her husband's brother. On the other hand, the Thibetan does not recognize the idea of the husband's brother's wife, and even when the brothers happen to separate, and each takes a wife for himself, yet this rare exception can scarcely have had any considerable influence on the nomenclature. It may be further observed that the brother's wife of a man's own wife is also said to be his own wife, which may be explained from the position of the family from which the wife came, but it does not necessarily imply polyandry. No name is given for the husband of the husband's sister, which is the more to be regretted since he is the one who usually gives the name of wife to his real wife's brother's wife.

McLennan holds that the Turanian and Ganowanian nomenclatures arose in the polyandrous family under the pressure of exogamy.[1] This attempted explanation resembles in principle the one which is suggested by Morgan for the prohibition of marriage between brothers and sisters; but McLennan gives it a somewhat different turn. Morgan states that as soon as it seemed impossible for the mother's brother to be the father, the special names arose of uncle and aunt, subsequently of nephew and niece, and finally of male and female cousins. McLennan, on the other hand, supposes that these latter names were the first to arise under exogamy; while the other names did not necessarily follow.[2] Brothers, for example, are of one blood with the sisters' children; they do not thereby necessarily cease to be Makua kana, or fathers, to these; or if they do so cease, it is only owing to the principle of reciprocity, because sisters are no longer Makua waheena, or mothers, to their brothers' children. Reciprocity may also have the converse effect, and sisters do not cease to be Makua waheena to the brothers' children, because brothers are still the Makua kana of their sisters' children.[3] In this way McLennan

<hr />

[1] McLennan, *Studies*, p. 304. [2] *Ibid.*, p. 397. [3] *Ibid.*, p. 396.

seeks to account for the variation in the use of the names of uncle, aunt, nephew, and niece, which occurs in many tribes.

McLennan explains the difference between the Turanian and Ganowanian forms in a way which again reminds us of Morgan. He traces the origin of the Turanian custom of reckoning the children of a female cousin as children of the male cousin to the fact that marriage between male and female cousins was customary among the Turanian peoples in early times.[1] After an attack upon Morgan, which we scarcely suppose to be serious,[2] he mentions the Ganowanian custom of reckoning the children of the female cousin to be the nephews of the male cousin, while a man regards the children of his male cousin as his own ; and he explains this custom by saying that the female line of descent did not permit of any change in the successive names for the degrees of kinship, or at any rate did not demand such a change.[3]

Some of McLennan's suggestions are undoubtedly well-founded, but, taken as a whole, his hypotheses are untenable. In the first place, there is nothing to show that nomenclature has its beginnings in polyandrous institutions ; secondly, some North American tribes still exist whose usages altogether contradict the assertion of the absolute necessity of cousinhood, since they do not recognize the relationship ; and, thirdly, it appears to be doubtful whether the marriage of cousins can explain the Turanian custom of regarding the children of the female cousin as children of the male cousin ; not to mention that such an explanation is hardly in accordance with McLennan's train of thought, since it appeals to ideas of blood-kinship, and not, as he has urged elsewhere, merely to a formal development of the Malayan nomenclature. The value of his suggestions consists in his emphatic assertion that nomenclature is in no way

[1] McLennan, *Studies*, p. 403.   [2] *Ibid.*, p. 359.   [3] *Ibid.*, p. 400

founded on the facts of procreation, and that its development is due to the altogether formal principle of reciprocity. We propose to show that these points are not justly estimated by McLennan, but that he is right with respect to this formal principle.

Table III. shows that the Micmac tribe calls the father's sister "aunt," and the mother's brother "uncle," while the children of the uncle and aunt are termed "brothers and sisters." This is also the case with the Ahahnelin, Munsee, Slave-Lake, Red Knives, Louchieux, and Spokane tribes.[1] There is, without exception, a special name for the mother's brother, while the father's sister is sometimes called "mother."[2] There is a very irregular use of the terms "nephew" and "niece." Lubbock is justified in his belief that the differentiation of nomenclature began in the special name for the mother's brother, and the reason for this special name is evident; the mother's brother belongs neither to the family circle nor to the clan.[3] The Minnitaree and Crow tribes call the mother's brother the "elder brother," which seems to indicate that the special name was an expression of reverence for him; in this way the name was used as a title of honour throughout whole tribes.[4] The same tendency is indicated by the usage that the younger must always address the elder man by the term of kinship, while the elder may do as he likes with respect to his junior.[5] Yet it would be rash to conclude that the female line and the predominance of the mother's brother originally prevailed in the North American tribes; we may rather infer the contrary from the usage of having no name for the mother's brother within the immediate

[1] In Morgan's *Systems*, Tables, Nos. 56, 63, 64, 66, 67, 69.
[2] *Ibid.*, Nos. 2, 3, 4, 5, 7, 27, 34, 35, 36, 62; also No. 25, when a woman is speaking.
[3] Lubbock, *Orig. of Civil.*, p. 183. The father's clan is here meant.
[4] Morgan's Tables, Nos. 26, 27. See Labat, vol. ii. p. 110. Waitz, vol. iii. p. 22.
[5] Morgan, *Systems*, p. 396.

family.   Moreover, as we have before remarked, the recognition of special relations between the nephew and the mother's brother by no means implies the existence of a female line.   It can only be confidently inferred from the nomenclature that the mother's brother was closely connected with his nephew through his sister, but that he was distinguished from the father.   ·

It appears to me that the whole series of special names may readily be deduced from the special name for the mother's brother, which differs in different tribes, one tribe being influenced by certain considerations, another by other considerations.   Some tribes lay most stress on the generation of the person who speaks, another on that of his parents; others again regard all the descendants of the mother's brother as uncles and mothers.[1]   Table IV. affords a catalogue of the terms for "son" and "daughter," "nephew" and "niece," in which we can trace the same principle which underlies the terms for "uncle."

When the Seneca and some other tribes reckon among a husband's children those of his brother and male cousin, while the children of his sister and female cousin are nephews and nieces, this is simply the result of the formal position of the mother's brother.   He stands in a peculiar relation to his sisters children, but not to his brother's children; that is, the children which are connected with his generation through the other sex are not regarded as his own, and therefore bear another name.   It follows that the children of the male cousin are children to the husband and nephews to the wife, and conversely in the case of the children of the female cousin.

McLennan explains the different custom of the Turanians by the marriage of cousins, but various facts are opposed to this hypothesis.   Table V. gives the special names for the married cousins, and the mere existence of

---

[1] In Morgan's *Systems*, Tables, Nos. 18-21, 46-55.

these special names throws doubt upon the hypothesis, since it seems strange that the wife should designate her married cousin with a different name from that of her other cousins, and yet be so indifferent to more natural distinctions, that she makes no distinction between her mother and mother's sister, her father and father's brother, her own children and those of her sister and cousin. It is certainly possible to regard the special names of married people as due to the ceremonial character of marriage, yet this by no means agrees with McLennan's estimate of marriage. The hypothesis is contradicted by the fact that all the designations of the Tamil system, with the exception of some trifling variations, are in agreement with the marriage of cousins, and that none of these designations are found in the Seneca and Wyandot tribes. We also know that the marriage of cousins was by no means rare among Turanian peoples, and that such a marriage was occasionally regarded as a duty, or at any rate as very desirable. The Karens, by whom the intermarriage of cousins is highly esteemed, call the children of their female cousins " nephews " and " nieces."

A closer examination of the Fijian nomenclature throws further doubt on the explanation suggested by the marriage of cousins. Of this we give the following scheme :—

Sister's husband	*corresponds to*
The husband says : my cousin.	The wife's brother = male cousin.
The wife says : my staff.	The wife's sister = my staff.
Brother's wife	*corresponds to*
The husband says : my staff.	The husband's brother = my spouse.
The wife says : my cousin.	The husband's sister = my cousin.

Again, the wife simply addresses as " wife "—(1) the wife of her husband's brother, (2) the wife of her father's sister's son, (3) the wife of her mother's brother's son. So likewise the husband addresses as " husband "—(1) the man married to his wife's sister, (2) the man married

18

to his father's sister's daughter, (3) the man married to his mother's brother's daughter. We cannot avoid inferring from these designations that the persons in question believed that they were closely connected with each other, and it is a strange fact that husbands should give the name of "sister" to the wife of the father's sister's son, and to the wife of the mother's brother's son, while the wives gave the name of "brother" to the husband of the father's sister's daughter, and to the husband of the mother's brother's daughter. The children of a man's father's sister become his male and female cousins, and so also do the children of the mother's brother, while their children, again, may be either nephews or children. It is also the case that the man calls the wife of his male cousin "sister," but he does not call the husband of his female cousin "brother." The marriage of cousins will not account for this state of things, and some other explanation must be sought for it.

We have seen above that the Fijian brother-in-law becomes at once a guardian and second husband to the widow, and a father to the child of his deceased brother. The wife has, therefore, no other name for her brother-in-law than that which she used for her husband, who was his brother. This name does not prove the brother-in-law's right to hold sexual intercourse with the wife during her husband's lifetime, but only his position as protector and guardian. It is in agreement with this fact that the brother-in-law chooses a special name for his sister-in-law—"my staff," or support. The brother's wife and the wife's sister stand in much the same relation to the husband, so that the same name is applied to both, and it is also used by the wife's sister in addressing him. As soon as these names are introduced, it is no longer possible for the husband to call his wife's sister's husband "brother," for the wife addresses the husband's brother as "my husband," but the sister's husband as "my staff." This does not, however, explain why the wife will not call her husband's brother's wife "sister," for the husband uses the same name for his wife's sister and his brother's wife—"my staff." We are here simply referred to the formula that the wife's sister's husband and the husband's brother's wife are correlative persons.

We are told that Fijian husbands never make use of the names " brother " and "female cousin " in the case of married people, and the wives never use the names of "sister " and " male cousin," with the single exception that the husband's sister's husband is addressed as " cousin." This order is not at all consistent with the marriage of cousins. If we turn to consider those who are really the children of brothers and sisters, we find the names of "male and female cousins" are only applied to persons whose kinship is through parents of different sexes, that is, to the children of a brother and sister. This follows from the practice of regarding all the children of brothers as children, and all the children of sisters as children; where the two sexes are concerned, they become nephews and nieces. When we consider how vitally the fate of the individual is affected by sex, and especially in the primitive community, it becomes easy to understand that the ideas which dictated the terms of nomenclature were mainly due to sexual considerations.

The course taken in formulating the idea may be traced in two ways. On the one side we may take as the starting-point that the speaker calls his brother's child his own, as being of the same sex; in this way we establish the principle that the children of kinsfolk of the same sex and generation are all the speaker's children. This gives the Ganowanian form, which includes the children of the male cousin among the husband's children, and the children of the female cousin among the wife's children, while the former become nephews and nieces to the wife, and the latter are nephews and nieces to the husband. On the other hand, the dawning differentiation between the brothers and sisters and their children may be taken as the starting-point. The cousin is now not connected with the cousin of his own sex, but he traces his descent from the same grandparents and through another sex. In this way the significance of the name of " cousin " is more exactly esti-mated, that is, a cousin is a man who is not the speaker's brother. Hence the children of cousins do not bear the same name as the children of brothers. This process of thought gives us the Turanian form, according to which the husband calls his brother's children " children," and his cousin's children "nephews," but the converse is done by the wife. This also applies to the mode of naming the children of sisters and of female cousins. As soon, however, as the man has called his cousin's children "nephews," the cousin's wife—that is, the mother of these nephews—formally becomes his sister; on the other hand, when the cousin's children rank as children, as in the Ganowanian system, the cousin's wife obtains no defini-tion of kinship; this may be seen in Table V.

It appears from Table IV. that in Tamil and Fiji the Ganowanian system of nomenclature is adopted for the children of the granddaughter of the grandfather's sister, and for the children of the great-granddaughter of the great-grandfather's sister; but the Telegu in these cases make use of the correct Turanian terms. We see, again, from Table VI., that while the Tamil and Fijian rightly call the father's sister " aunt," they nevertheless give the name of " mother " to the daughter of their grandfather's sister, and to the granddaughter of the great-grandfather's sister; and we learn from Table VII. that the children of these persons are regarded as their brothers and sisters. In this case, also, the Telegu practice differs from theirs. Morgan adds an interrogative mark to these designations, but they may easily be explained by the formal nature of the principle. A Turanian husband, indeed, logically calls the children of his father's sister's daughter—that is, his female cousin's children—simply "children," while the children of his father's sister's son, that is, children of his male cousin, are "nephews." But the children of his grandfather's sister's daughter are the same as the children of his father's female cousin, that is, they are called "children" by his father; they are consequently his own brothers and sisters, and their mother is as a mother to himself. Hence it follows that the children of these so-called brothers and sisters, in accordance with the Turanian system of nomenclature, would receive precisely the same names as those afforded by the Ganowanian form.

In the latter form we trace a tendency to make the nomenclature for women less ample than that for men.[1] We find the starting-point for this nomenclature in the special name for the mother's brother, and in correspondence with this, the principle of reciprocity brought with it the names for the father's sister, nephew and niece, male and female cousin. The Cayuga women, and those of the Two Mountains tribe, and others dependent on it, do not distinguish between children and nephews, and the father's sister bears the same name as the mother. We cannot be mistaken in assuming that these facts are in connection. On the other hand, there is a special name for the male cousin; but this involves a special name for the mother's brother, although it cannot be said that it always occurs when we find the latter. The Micmac and Two Mountains tribes, for instance, do not possess names for cousins. The name for "nephew" may also be limited in its application. Thus the Tuscarora women only regard the brother's children and those in the same degree as nephews and nieces, but not the children of cousins.

In the Cayuga tribe, and the tribes which follow them, the men call the children of the female cousin

[1] Morgan, *Systems*, p. 235.

"nephews," while the grandchildren of the father's female cousin are "children;" their children, again, are usually called "nephews." There is nothing absurd in this variation, which is the legitimate result of the considerations which relate to the preceding generation. It seems that it is useless to show that the persons in question should be regarded as the grandchildren of the speaker's father; for since they are children of his father's daughter—that is, children of the speaker's sister—they must be called "nephews." It is, however, the fact that the speaker knows that they are not the children of his father's daughter, although they are his grandchildren; they must, therefore, be distinguished from his sister's children, and are not to be called "nephews," and hence no name but that of "children" can be given to them. In other tribes, they are, out of excessive formalism, called "grandchildren," not because they are really such to the speaker, but because they are grandchildren of the man from whom the successive generations of the speaker are counted.[1] We might expect that the great-grandchildren of the grandfather's female cousin would be held to be children, but to them, again, the names of "nephew" and "niece" are applied. The following scheme shows that this is correct:—

(1) The children of female cousins are, in accordance with the difference of sex in the speaker's generation, nephews and nieces to the man.

(2) The grandchildren of the grandfather's female cousin are reckoned as children to the man, because they are children of the father's niece, that is, not his own sister's children, so that they cannot be called his nephews and nieces.

(3) The man calls the great-grandchildren of his grandfather's female cousin "nephews" and "nieces;" they are the children of the grandfather's niece's daughter, which, in accordance with the second clause, is the same

[1] Morgan's *Systems*, Tables, Nos. 18-24, 46-55.

as if they were the children of the father's daughter. They therefore become sister's children to the speaker, that is, they are his nephews and nieces.

The formal principle, so far as it has been carried out, begins with the distinction between the father's and the mother's brother. When we consider that the name of "uncle," occurs without the name of "nephew," but not the converse fact, it seems the more probable assumption that the differentiation began in the younger generation, and then extended to the elder generation, since the reverence felt for the latter was the moving cause. The difference between the father's and mother's brother has been remarked before, and nothing further is needed to explain the nomenclature. The special names for the mother's brother would only lead us to infer the existence of the female line, if the nomenclature expressed predominance of the mother's brother, which, however, it does not do; whichever is the superior, the formal expressions remain the same. In one respect only would it be possible for the nomenclature to express the way in which the power was distributed—that is, if the distinctions between the kinsfolk of the dominant line were given in greater detail. We also find that the tribes which have only a single designation for the mother's brother and all his descendants follow the male line, but those tribes which call the father's sister "mother" and "grandmother" observe the female line. The first of these groups of nomenclatures is, however, the least elaborate, and we are therefore justified in our conclusion, with respect to the line of kinship, that the male, rather than the female line, was the more primitive.

If we revert to the Turanian nomenclature, it also affords facts which undoubtedly point to the formal principle we have just stated. Tables VIII. and IX. give the Tonganese nomenclature. It is, unfortunately, so fragmentary that we are unable to ascertain whether the mother's brother's special name was given to any one

else.   We may, perhaps, infer that it was exclusively
applied to the mother's brother, since we find that the
special name of father's sister was given to no other person.
It appears that the name of " cousin " is in close connection
with these designations, since he is given as the uncle's
son, or the aunt's son.   There are no definite designations for the children of male and female cousins, and
the other members of the generation of a man's children
are named after a noteworthy fashion.   The names " son "
and "daughter" are given to a man's brother's children, to
those of his father's brother's son, and to those of his
mother's sister's son.   The women, on the other hand,
never apply these names to any but their own children.
They address their brother's children as the men address
their sister's children, the children of the father's brother's
daughter, and the children of the mother's sister's daughter; and the women use the names *tama* and *tahine* for
sister's children, as well as for the grandchildren of the
father's brother and of the mother's sister.

We must point out the first characteristic of this
nomenclature : it is, almost throughout, restricted within
the limit of the lines marked out by the parents, the
brothers and sisters of the parents, and their children,
their own brothers and sisters, and their children.   The
second characteristic consists in the strict isolation of the
children through their mothers, while the action of the
fathers is merely formal.   The formal principle is also
shown in the fact that the son of the father's elder
brother is himself called the " elder brother," even although
he is younger than the speaker; and it is still more
apparent in the fact that the daughter of the father's
father's sister is, quite irrationally, called " father," and
the son of the mother's mother's sister is likewise called
" mother."   We are here again presented with the process
of thought which, in the case of the Punka and some
other tribes, gives the name of "uncle" to all the posterity of the mother's brother.   We may also trace this

distinction and the equality of the sexes in the order in which the different members of the family are ranked; this distinction and the formal mode of placing the sexes on an equality appear in the fact that men regard as equal, on the one side, the children, brother's children, children of the father's brother's and of the mother's sister's son, and, on the other side, the sister's children, and the children of the father's brother's and of the mother's sister's daughter. The women, again, distinguish their own children and their brother's children from all others. When the married pair are of equal birth, the husband takes the first place, then come the wife, the eldest son, the eldest daughter, the next son, the next daughter, and so on; if there are no children, the husband's brother and sister are next in rank. But the wife's family takes precedence if she is of nobler birth.[1]

A peculiar light is thrown upon the Tonganese nomenclature by the following circumstance. It is not used in daily life; not even the nearest kinsfolk are addressed by the names of kinship; a child, for instance, never says "father," but prattles his father's name.[2] Yet we are told by Wilkes that the Tonganese form of government so far resembles a family that the officials address each other by the names of "father," "son," "uncle," and "grandfather," without the slightest reference to their mutual kinship.[3] This makes all the irregularities of the system quite intelligible, since it is precisely the daily use which modifies the nomenclature and causes it to be infused with the formal principle. The most varied considerations will influence the system when this influence is not impeded by its everyday use, by the mother's unwillingness, for instance, to put the children of other people on a level with her own.

The same fate, of not coming into everyday use, for the most part applies to the descriptive nomenclatures.

[1] Rienzi, vol. iii. p. 45.   [2] Morgan, *Systems*, p. 580.
[3] Wilkes, vol. iii. p. 17.

Since we have seen that among the Tonganese, descriptive names are given to the male and female cousins, the suspicion arises that a connection exists between the descriptive character of the terms and the fact that they are not employed in daily intercourse. The descriptive nomenclature merely consists in writing down the ideas which, as Morgan has told us above,[1] are entertained by those people who have also a classifying nomenclature. But Morgan is mistaken in ascribing the descriptive nomenclature to the Aryan, Semitic, and Uralian peoples, as if they were acquainted with no other system. Some categories of descriptive nomenclature, such as " father," " mother," " uncle," " aunt," and in some instances "brother," " sister," " son," " daughter," " nephew," " niece," " male and female cousin," are in everyday use ; and, as we have already observed, in speaking of the use of classifying nomenclature, the four first terms, which are used by the younger generation in addressing their elders, are generally adopted. The others, and particularly the terms used by the elder generation in addressing the younger, are only employed instead of the proper name in an exceptional and quite irregular way. In everyday use these names are much more inclusive than they appear to be from the Tables. Instead of the descriptive names, of which the meaning is difficult to grasp, the terms " uncle," " aunt," " cousin," etc., are employed. The names of more limited application, such as " father," " mother," " brother," and " son," are less freely used, although they also come into use where only the character of the relationship, but not the descent, is in agreement with the ordinary meaning of the name.[2] We cannot avoid regarding Morgan's classification of the nomenclature as quite erroneous. The descriptive and classifying nomen-

---

[1] Morgan, *Anc. Soc.*, p. 484.

[2] In East Africa, a "son" signifies the inhabitant of the same village, and "brother" an inhabitant of the same district (Burton, *Zanzibar*, p. 421). In Poland, the tribes which use the same arms called each other " brother " (Caro, vol. ii. p. 519).

clatures are respectively employed, the latter for everyday use, the former not; that is, the first becomes most
prominent where the legal relations are parallel to those
of kinship; the second is of most weight where individuals do not stand in legal relations to other individuals, but where such legal relations are established
between groups, sometimes clans, sometimes joint family
groups, sometimes a mixture of both. We may mention
as instructive instances the Eskimo and Karen nomenclatures.

The Karens differ from the Tamil race in important
points. They call the father's brother "uncle," the
mother's sister "aunt;" the children of these are
"cousins," and their children, again, are "nephews" and
"nieces." This is also the case with the Eskimos. Lubbock expresses surprise that two peoples, dwelling so
far apart, and under such different conditions, should
possess the same nomenclature, and, moreover, a nomenclature which is not in harmony with their social state.
This cannot be an accident, but must be regarded as a
development which took place in accordance with the
principle they had in common. Lubbock observes that
the nomenclature in question differs from ours in three
particulars, and it is precisely in these particulars that
it is not in agreement with itself. The children of
cousins are called "nephews," which, as a matter of fact,
they are not; the children of nephews are called "grandchildren," and the grandfather's brothers and sisters are
"grandfathers" and "grandmothers." [1] Lubbock considers that these names date from a time when parents'
brothers and sisters were held to be parents, and the
children of brothers and sisters were held to be brothers
and sisters. · Yet it is at once apparent that we ourselves
run the risk of such irregularities of speech as soon
as our descriptive nomenclature becomes the mode of
address. We have the word "great-uncle" for the grand-

[1] Lubbock, *Orig. of Civ.*, p. 199.

father's brother, but we have no special term for the children of a cousin or nephew—a sure sign that in daily intercourse the names belonging to other degrees of kinship would be employed. The mode in which both peoples live—in distinct patriarchal families—is in complete agreement with the use of a special name for the father's brother; the necessity for such a special name is wanting in the joint family group, as the Turanian nomenclature shows.

In no instance do Morgan's explanations appear more forced than when he attempts to account for the difference between the typical Turanian system, as it is found among the Tamil, Telegu, and Canarese peoples, and its variants among the Hindus and Chinese. He applies to the Hindu system a loose and altogether groundless fancy with respect to the possible effect of a conflict between races, one of which was settled in the country and possessed the Turanian nomenclature, while the other, the Sanscrit people which made a victorious entry into the land, doubtless brought with them a nomenclature which was descriptive in its main features. Among the Sanscrit races, indeed, the marriage of distinct pairs took place, and their nomenclature was consequently of a descriptive character. Morgan finds the strongest confirmation of the tenacious power of resistance possessed by the fundamental ideas on which the Turanian nomenclature relies, in the fact that the Sanscrit peoples, in the course of the conflict, renounced the nomenclature which was in harmony with their manners and customs.[1]

If, however, Table X. is more closely examined, it must be admitted that the characteristic features of the Turanian nomenclature are considerably suppressed, so that it becomes a question whether the Hindu nomenclature is altogether Turanian. Not only the mother's brother receives the special name of "uncle," but the

[1] Morgan, *Systems*, p. 408.

mother's sister is called "aunt." All the children of brothers and sisters are "nephews" and "nieces," and no distinction is made between the children of male and female cousins, but both are called "nephews" and "nieces." The characteristic name for "cousin" does not occur. Either the name of "brother" or "sister" is used, or an altogether descriptive term defines the exact degree of kinship—such as "brother" or "sister" —through the paternal or maternal uncle or aunt. Such a nomenclature is quite in harmony with the social relation of the Hindus; religion unites father and child with special bonds, and teaches them to distinguish this from any other connection; on the other hand, the living together in a joint family group makes the distinction between the brothers and sons of the father's brothers unimportant, so that all the cousins are declared to be Sapinda, as if they were brothers.

Morgan has taken much trouble to show that the Chinese nomenclature is intermediate between the Malayan and Turanian nomenclatures,[1] and I am compelled to inflict upon the reader a somewhat lengthy account of his views. As we see from Table X., the word *chih* is used for the brother's descendants, as distinguished from those of the speaker. Morgan finds it difficult to give a fitting definition of the *chih* category.[2] It is used for the posterity of the brother and of the speaker's collateral brother. The term "class" is adopted by Hart, and although it does not fully represent the idea, it is preferable to "branch" or "degree." These and other similar categories are best interpreted by their mode of use. In the closest degree of kinship *ir* and *neu* define the family relationship; *ir-tsze*, or "boy-child," is a son, and *neu-ir*, or "maiden-child," is a daughter; *ir* is therefore the term for kinship, while *tsze* and *neu* only appear to indicate the sex. Morgan is unable to decide how far the two latter words, when the *ir* is omitted, still

[1] Morgan, *Systems*, p. 415.   [2] *Ibid.*, p. 416.

19

signify "son" and "daughter," or if the unexpressed *ir* is
to be understood.   The reciprocal relations of kinship in
the cases in question appear to be those of father and
son, father and daughter, grandfather and grandchild.
If this were so, the Chinese possessed the first characteristic feature of the Turanian system.   In spite of the
distinction made by the word *chih* between the brother's
posterity and those of the speaker, yet this branch of the
first collateral line flows into the direct line through the
categories of kinship which characterize both the Malayan
and Turanian systems.

Morgan goes on to say that the man calls his sister's
son *waesung*, which Hart translates as "outside nephew."
Wae signifies outside, and *sung*, originally signifying "the
daughter's child," acquires the meaning of "sister's son"
when preceded by *wae*.   "Outside child" would, perhaps,
be a more correct translation.   The sister's daughter is
called *wae-sung-neu*, translated by Hart as "daughter of
the *wae-sung* class."   As we have said above, this might
be translated as "outside female child," or niece.   This
latter form is preferable, since it is the correlative of the
uncle's degree of kinship.   The son of the sister's child is
called *wae-sung-sun*, and his daughter is *wae-sung-sun-
neu*, that is, "grandchildren of the *wae-sung* class."   These
translations are only valuable so far as they show that
the Chinese possess the third characteristic feature of
the Turanian system—that is, that a man's brother's
children rank as his own, while his sister's children are
nephews and nieces.   Morgan proposes to show that this
feature does not so completely penetrate the system as
in the typical Turanian form.

On the other hand, the woman calls her brother's son
wae-chih, "outside nephew," or, if *ir* is implied, "child of
the *wae-chih* class;" she calls her brother's daughter *wae-
chih-neu*, "outside niece," or "child of the *wae-chih* class."
The woman regards the children of these nephews or
nieces as grandchildren of the same class.   The correla-

tive degrees of kinship are, in the first place, "aunt-mother," and sometimes "aunt." If this implies the relative kinship between aunt and nephew, we observe another of the characteristic features of the Turanian system; but if *ir* is understood, the brother's children are held to be children, in virtue of the categories of kinship, and are only to be distinguished from these by specific expressions which are found in no other system. Hence it appears that the Chinese form is in process of transition from the Malayan to the Turanian system.

The woman calls her sister's son *e-sung*, to which no translation is subjoined. Hart observes that the particle *e* is combined from two words, one of which signifies "woman" and the other "stranger." It recurs in the word for "mother's sister," *e-ma*. *Sung* has been given above. This branch of the first collateral line is the same, whether the speaker be man or woman, except that in the former case the prefix *wae*, in the latter case the prefix *e*, is used. The sister's children, therefore, stand in the same relation to the female as to the male kins-folk, except that the kinship is held to be more or less remote in accordance with the ideas expressed by the particles *e* and *wae*.

The explanation given by Morgan in the foregoing passage cannot be accepted, since it undertakes, without any good reason, to set aside the class-words applied to the nearest degrees of kinship, and at the same time regards the termination by which the expression is qualified as the only one which is decisive. Take, for example, his explanation of the word *wae-sung*. *Wae* is said to mean "outside," and *sung*, of which the original meaning is "daughter's child," signifies "sister's son" when the prefix *wae* is added. Morgan, as we saw, pro-poses to translate "outside child" as equivalent to nephew. It must, however, at once be evident to the unprejudiced reader that the difficulty which we have to solve consists in the fact that a word, of which the.

original sense is "outside daughter's son," should come to mean "sister's child," and, indeed, "sister's son," and should cease to indicate the speaker's grandchild. Morgan is intent on providing the nephew with the same designation as the child, and in his eagerness he overlooks the point in question. However great the difficulty may be, it is solved by the periphrasis of using the word "father's daughter" instead of "sister." *Wae*, or "outside" then signifies that the mother of the child in question is not the speaker's daughter, but the daughter of the speaker's father—that is, she springs from the generation outside of that of the speaker.

The Table shows that *wae-sung* ascribes the children of the father's brother's daughter to the class *tang;* these are, however, the children of the grandfather's son's daughter. *Wae-sung*, of the class *peaon-chih*, stands for the children of the father's sister's daughter, that is, for the children of the grandfather's granddaughter. But the word *sung* never occurs to designate the children of the mother's brother's daughter, that is, for the children of the son's daughter of the mother's father; nor, again, for the children of the mother's sister's daughter, that is, for the children of the mother's father's granddaughter. All these persons are entitled *wae-peaon-chih* and *wae-e-peaon-chih*. In this way the meaning of these expressions no longer presents any difficulty. The Table teaches us that the children of full brothers and sisters are designated in two ways, according to the speaker's sex, but that these twofold expressions are only used in this degree of kinship. The word *wae* only occurs in these twofold expressions in speaking of the children of brothers or sisters of a different sex from that of the speaker, and the word only occurs in the other categories when the daughter's children of one of the brothers and sisters of the speaker's parents are in question.

Starting from this fact, it may seem to be an irregularity that women should use *wae* in speaking of their brother's children. But the twofold expressions applied to these degrees show that it is due to considerations of the different sex of the brothers and sisters in this first generation. The position of individuals within the patriarchal family is the same or different, in accordance with the fact that they are of the same or of another sex; on the other hand, their relation to their grandfather's generation does not depend upon the sex of the individuals, but upon the fact that they are connected with that generation through the father or mother. This shows that all the expressions in question are influenced by the same idea, namely, that the children of the father's house are aliens to their mother, and belong to their father's family.

In this way we have a simple explanation of the use of the particle, of which the meaning has been given above as " stranger woman." The degrees of kinship which are thus designated are all connected with the mother's sister, either as her children, grandchildren, or great-grandchildren. No bond unites the families to which the children of two married sisters belong, while both are united with the family of these sisters' brother, who represents their original family. Only the children of the speaker's mother's sister, not those of his mother's brother, are of such remote kinship as to be designated by the particle *e*. There is only a single case which throws doubt upon this usage. The woman calls her sister's children *e-sung*, but the man calls them *wae-sung*. Morgan, as we saw above, holds that *e* and *wae* are used in the same sense, but he does not explain how it is that the sister's children in this case obtain a designation which is in other instances reserved for the family of the mother's sister. It is only needful to refer to the conditions of kinship to see that a male speaker is mother's brother to his sister's children, while the female speaker is the mother's sister. There is therefore a strongly marked difference between *e* and *wae,* which is due to the legal connection of the two families, and it is quite logical that the woman should place her sister's children in the category of *e.*

The word *tang* is used when the generations are connected through brothers, of whom the speaker is not one. The word *peaon* is used when the brothers or sisters are of a different sex from that of the speaker.

The principle dominating the Chinese nomenclature is therefore the same as that which prevails in the Turanian, and in some cases in the Ganowanian systems; namely, that the position of the individual is decided by his parents' generation and not by his own.

In the whole nomenclature the word *chih* presents the only difficulty. It does not occur in the designations for sisters' children, and for the daughter's children of the father's brother. This may lead us to surmise that its meaning became superfluous owing to the use of *wae-sung* or *e-sung;* but the two words are used in connection for the daughter's children of the father's sister. This is perhaps because *peaon-chih,* which always occurred together, had been almost fused into one word, so that the expression *peaon-chih-wae-sung* for the daughter's child of the father's sister merely includes a superfluous definition.

If we are to define the character of the Chinese nomenclature, we should say that it resembles our own; that it is a classifying, descriptive nomenclature, which has been polished by frequent use in daily intercourse. The great power exerted by groups of kinship and the life of a community partly founded on economical considerations, decide the selection of the classifying categories which are employed. As Morgan observes, the posterity of a married pair does not in theory go beyond the class of brothers, and hence there arises a recognized connection of kinsfolk which never becomes extinct, although practically it is not considered beyond the fifth degree. If the father dies intestate, the property is usually not divided during the widow's lifetime, but it remains under the control of the eldest brother. After the widow's death, the eldest son divides the property between himself and his brothers, and the portion of the younger brothers is altogether dependent on the will of the elder.[1]

A consideration of the whole series of our researches into nomenclature will show that it affords no warrant for the far-reaching conclusions of Morgan, McLennan, Lubbock, and others. The nomenclature was in every respect the faithful reflection of the juridical relations which arose between the nearest kinsfolk of each tribe. Individuals who were, according to the legal point of view, on the same level with the speaker, received the same designation. The other categories of kinship were formally developed out of this standpoint. The writers in question hold that the correct understanding of nomenclatures must be found in considerations of the circumstances of marriage and descent which are concealed in the categories of nomenclature, but the assertion is altogether unproved. We must, however, admit that the correct interpretation which we now flatter ourselves to have given, diminishes the significance of nomenclatures as a contribution to the means of historical research to such an extent that it ceases to possess the interest which would entitle us to dwell further on the subject. Lubbock, in his remarks on Morgan's book, states that while he does not accept his most important conclusions, yet he cannot avoid declaring that Morgan's work is one of the most important contributions to ethnological science which has appeared for many years.[2] With all respect for Morgan's diligence as a collector of facts, I am more disposed to agree with McLennan that his work is altogether unscientific, and that his hypotheses are a wild dream, if not the

[1] Morgan, *Systems*, p. 424; Appendix ix., p. 425; Appendix xvi.
[2] Lubbock, *Orig. of Civ.*, p. 157.

delirium of fever.[1]   His statements throughout are based on such vague analysis and such irrational psychology, that they can only confuse the question, unless they are altogether ignored.

[1] McLennan, *Studies.* p. 360

CHAPTER VI.

EXOGAMY AND ENDOGAMY.

Conception of exogamy and endogamy—Their relation to incest —Modern
ideas of incest—Immorality and incest—Various explanations of
exogamy—Symbol of rape—Its bearing—Causes of rape of women
—Symbol of rape and modesty—Criminal ties—Desire of trophies—
Clanless tribe endogamous—Exogamy and incest —Australian legend
—Crime and punishment—Marriage and sexual intercourse—Marriage of royal brother and sister—Breach of privilege and marriage
—King and his sister—Legal character of marriage—Endogamy—
Arabs—Castes and classes—Karens—Kookas—Ceremonial intercourse of parents and children-in-law—Ceremonial and marriage
by violence — Modesty of Bechuanas and Beni-Amirs—Reverence
of Caribs—Symbol of rape.

In the preceding pages we have repeatedly had to consider exogamy, and also some of the facts of endogamy.
We need only remind our readers that exogamy signifies
the prohibition to contract marriages within the group,
while endogamy forbids marriage outside the group. It
is not too daring to hope that a closer examination of
these two customs may enlighten us with respect to the
ideas which underlie primitive man's view of marriage,
whether these ideas agree with our own, or display the
same difference between barbarism and civilization as
we find to exist in the relations between parents and
children.

The strong moral force which characterizes these prohibitions, the inexorable strictness with which they
are obeyed, and the deep abhorrence with which a

transgressor is regarded, are sufficient reasons for venturing to place these prohibitions on a level with those which in our own case define the limits of a lawful contract of marriage. There is little which has to do with endogamy now extant in our communities, but at any rate class-prejudices assert themselves to a degree which is almost as stringent as express prohibitions; exogamy, on the other hand, is confidently believed to actuate our ideas of incest. If this belief is correct, the ideas of incest must originally have had a different scope from those which prevail with us, for primitive men often permit the marriage of persons who are, according to our ideas, too nearly akin, while, on the other hand, persons whom we reckon to stand in very remote kinship to each other are, according to primitive ideas, unconditionally forbidden to intermarry. The different conceptions of kinship entertained by ourselves and by primitive communities compel us to infer a like difference in the ideas which actuate a possibility of entering into a contract of marriage; and this difference may detract from the interest with which we consider the conditions of kinship which regulate all the circumstances of life so rigidly that they are almost a religion. If this view is not confirmed, and the ideas of incest are shown to arise from a common source, the justice of the theory we have put forward may be called in question. We must, in the first place, consider the basis on which our moral estimate of incestuous connections is founded.

If the idea of marriage is defined to be a bond which unites souls as well as, and even more truly than, bodies, it would immediately appear that no better conditions of marriage could be devised than that between brother and sister, father and daughter, mother and son. In the two latter cases, indeed, the disparity in age would as a rule be so great that there would be less probability of a perfect marriage, with spiritual interests in common. But as marriage between persons of different ages was allowed in other instances, this circumstance could not have been the reason of the prohibition. The moral aversion which we entertain in the case of marriage between near kinsfolk may, I think, be indirectly explained, for there cannot be a more valid objection to such marriages than the fact that the offspring of such marriages are so often idiotic, or at any rate in some respect deficient. Whatever may have been the origin of these prohibitions, they obtained a character of moral sanctity from the fact that they have so long been part of the moral code which is based upon religion. The moral aversion to incest must for the most part be traced to this historical source, and it is certainly in general agreement with the ideas of primitive men. But what we are now anxious to ascertain is whether incest ought to be condemned for the same reasons as theft and murder. Except for the undesirable character of such connections which we have mentioned above, it hardly seems possible to find a single valid reason for the vehement condemnation of these marriages.

It must also be remembered that when incest is in question among ourselves, we always have to do with an immoral connection, since the law does not recognize a marriage between kinsfolk who are within the prohibited degrees. While such immorality is in all cases held to be blameworthy, it is naturally still more severely condemned when it occurs between persons who are ordinarily supposed to stand in a peculiar relation to each other. We cannot precisely estimate how far this circumstance influences our abhorrence of incest, but it is certainly not insignificant. The historical basis for the prohibition of marriage between near kinsfolk also involves the abhorrence of any sexual connection between them, since its legalization by marriage thereby becomes impossible. I maintain that the prohibition should be observed if it can be proved by facts that the connection of kinsfolk is injurious to their offspring, since it is morally culpable to bring sickly children into the world. But in a community in which marriage takes place between consumptive and syphilitic persons, and those affected by hereditary disease, without being condemned by public opinion, and still less by the law, it cannot be said that the condemnation of incest is founded on our regard for posterity. The explanation should rather be sought in its historical origin, and here, as we have said, we are confronted with exogamy. But it by no means follows that the same ideas which originally produced these prohibitions underlie the various prohibited degrees of marriage which are now in force.

Speaking generally, we may say that the unmarried woman of barbarous peoples enjoyed full liberty in all sexual matters. But the prevailing custom of marriage between quite young children had the effect of subjecting a girl to the same restrictions as a married woman of mature age. Whatever other causes may have been at work to produce the demand for chastity in unmarried girls, I believe that its chief source is to be found in these early marriages, and in the consequent habit of desiring and enforcing discreet behaviour in young girls. Long before this demand for chastity was established, however, we meet with exogamy, or a prohibition of marriage between certain persons. Two conflicting explanations of this fact have been given. The first, which is put forward by Mc Lennan, Spencer, and Lubbock, refers exogamy, as the express prohibition of certain marriages, to certain customs which had nothing to do with any abhorrence of incest. The other explanation, by Morgan, regards exogamy as the desire to prevent connections between too near kinsfolk. We will first consider McLennan's view.

A symbol exists among the wedding ceremonies of most peoples which in some way or other illustrates the forcible capture of the bride by the bridegroom, as, for instance, in the well-known Roman custom, for which an explanation was invented in the tale of the rape of the Sabines.[1] In order to understand this symbol of rape, McLennan suggests the following basis for further inquiries. Wherever we find symbolic forms, we are justified in the conclusion that the actual facts of the extinct life of the people were in correspondence with them ; and when we find such actual customs in the mode of life of primitive peoples, which have, owing to a growing culture and civilization, naturally passed into mere forms, we cannot hesitate to infer that the people which now use the symbol at one time lived after the manner of these primitive men.[2] The symbol of rape, therefore, points to a time when the people obtained their women by violence.

To this we reply, in the first place, that the greatest caution should be used in identifying a given symbol with a definite previous practice ; especially since, in the case we are considering, the conclusion that we have to do with a symbol of rape is somewhat too hasty, since there is only the faintest display of force on the part of the husband. The fact that the man carries his bride into the house on his back does not, without further evidence, appear to us to be one of the symbols of rape ; nor, again, that the bride apparently or in reality runs away and conceals herself from the bridegroom, who is compelled to find and seize her. And, secondly, McLennan's assertion does not seem to be altogether intelligible. In order to refer a symbol to an extinct fact, it is not enough to invent customs which might naturally have faded into such forms ; it must also be shown that the forms in question can be explained in no other way. McLennan has so completely accepted his own theory that he does not consider this. It is not true that there is always an actual fact in correspondence with the

---

[1] It is not difficult to find instances. I may refer to ch. ii. of McLennan's *Studies ;* Lubbock, *Orig. of Civ.,* p. 106 ; and Dargun, p. 78.
[2] McLennan, *Studies,* p. 6.

symbol, even when it is added that it is an image of an extinct fact. In many places there is a wedding custom that the bride should prepare a meal for the bridegroom; this custom cannot be an image of an actual fact, but it simply represents a definite process of thought. At any rate, we should not in the outset set aside the possibility of interpreting the symbol of rape in a similar way. After these parenthetical remarks, we return to our statement of McLennan's theory.

The symbol of rape is not only a survival of the sad reality of primitive times, it is also an important ceremony. Hence McLennan finds it impossible to understand how the simple lawlessness of savages should have been consecrated into a legal symbol, or that a like symbol should not occur in transactions which have to do with other kinds of property.[1] If the custom of obtaining wives by fraud or capture had not been so general as to prevail almost without exception, it would be difficult to understand how the association between rape and marriage became so close in the popular mind that the one was not valid without the other. The rape of women must have been systematic in the tribe, and it was of necessity women of another tribe which were taken by violence.[2] If this view is accepted, it becomes possible to see a proof of exogamy in the symbol of rape; that is, the murder of female infants led to the custom of obtaining the women of another tribe by capture; and this custom, again, created a prejudice against marriage with women of the same tribe, which, as so readily occurs with all prejudices which refer to marriages, acquired the strength of a religious principle.[3] McLennan thinks any other view unreasonable, since he is of opinion that the facts of primitive life, and the disappearance of exogamy as communities become more

[1] Lubbock, *Orig. of Civ.* (p. 105), assigns as a reason for this fact that the wife is not transmitted to her owner with his other property.
[2] McLennan, *Studies*, p. 112.   [3] *Ibid.*, p. 112.

developed, exclude the supposition that the law arose from an innate or original abhorrence of marriage between kinsfolk. Primitive men had, indeed, no such prejudice, and if not strictly endogamous—which involves the prohibition of marriage with any but kinsfolk—they were more addicted to connection with the latter than with strangers.[1]

Spencer may be mentioned as the first of McLennan's opponents, and then Lubbock. In the *Fortnightly Review* (1877), McLennan has disputed the truth of Spencer's explanation of the ideas of exogamy and endogamy, but he has done it in a way to which no importance can be attached. He says that Spencer speaks of communities which are at once exogamous and endogamous; and it must be admitted that, according to the strict meaning of the terms, this is a contradiction. But if we are to agree with McLennan in regarding exogamy as arising from a custom which was only gradually developed, no objection can be made to Spencer's assertion that the custom in question was not yet fully established. With respect to Lubbock, we may mention in passing that he misunderstands the question in a way to which the reader's special attention must be drawn. He writes that McLennan declares marriage by capture to have arisen from exogamy, whereas it might be more justly inferred that exogamy resulted from marriage by capture.[2] Lubbock in this case does not distinguish between two wholly different things—marriage by capture, and the symbol of rape at the wedding feast. McLennan traces the origin of exogamy to marriage by capture, while he holds that the former—that is, the transformation of marriage by capture into a system—caused the symbol of rape to become a wedding ceremony.

If McLennan's explanation is correct, it implies that the scarcity of women was the reason for obtaining them by capture. Spencer denies the possibility of this

[1] McLennan, *Studies*, pp. 112, 116.   [2] Lubbock, *Orig. of Civ.*, p. 105.

assumption, since the tribes which obtained their wives by capture were as a rule polygamous.[1] This objection appears to me to be unanswerable; but Spencer's other objection is less happy, namely, that some polyandrous tribes, such as the Eskimos and Todas, do not take women by force. Even if polyandry indicated a scarcity of women—which, however, is not the case—the practice of these tribes would show that the attempt to supply a scarcity of women was not always made, but not that they would not make use of the expedient of obtaining them by force if the desire to do so arose. We need not, however, lay any stress upon this point, since we are not concerned to know whether they usually had recourse to the rape of women as the means of supplying a scarcity, but whether the scarcity of women was the universal cause of such rape. We think that Spencer is justified in rejecting the latter hypothesis, and hence it becomes necessary for him to supply another explanation for the one he has rejected, and to indicate what was the general cause of the rape of women.

Spencer asserts that this custom was at first the result of success in war; the captive woman had a double value, since she not only served as a slave, like the tribal wife, but she also served as a trophy of victory. Hence marriage with women of other tribes was held to be more honourable, and rising ambition, especially in the most warlike tribes, ultimately produced the imperative demand that the wife should come from another tribe.[2] Spencer's explanation goes a step further than his theory will warrant. He undertakes to explain exogamy, and not the occurrence of the symbol of rape among the wedding ceremonies. McLennan is convinced that it is only the general practice of obtaining women by capture which explains the existence of the symbol, and that it is therefore the evident sign of exogamy. Spencer only agrees with McLennan in regarding exogamy as a custom

[1] Spencer, *Princ. of Soc.*, p. 647.   [2] *Ibid.*, p. 650.

changed into law, but he does not accept the symbol of rape as its evident sign, since it may owe its origin to the violent seizure of tribal women, instead of to the capture of those of other tribes.[1] But if the rape of women can be practised within the tribe, it need no longer be assumed that a young man's ambition impels him to take a wife from another tribe, and therefore we say that Spencer's conclusion has exceeded the limits of his own theory.

Spencer goes on to say that the symbol of rape may have this meaning among others—that it symbolizes the resistance which the woman opposes to her seizure, and she can reckon on the aid both of her female and male kinsfolk for this resistance. While Lubbock will not admit that the woman's modesty can be the cause of the symbol of rape, Spencer quotes some instances which seem to him opposed to Lubbock's opinion.[2] Of these we will only cite one. Among the Arabs of Mount Sinai, the bride defends herself by throwing stones, and often wounds the young man, even when her wooer is not displeasing to her; for according to their customs her fame is increased by the vehemence with which she resists, bites, pinches, screams, and struggles. Even during the procession to her husband's bed, modesty enjoins her not to cease from screaming and sobbing.[3] Spencer's quotation does not mention that this stone-throwing takes place when the bridegroom and his comrades fall upon the bride as she is returning with the flocks from pasture. This circumstance is, I think, not insignificant, since it seems to constitute the whole incident into a symbol of rape; both during the conflict and after the bridegroom's victory, the bride plays the part of being distracted by

[1] Spencer, *Princ. of Soc.*, p. 653.
[2] Lubbock, *Orig. of Civ.*, p. 106. See McLennan, *Studies*, pp. 15, 16.
[3] Burkhardt, vol. i. p. 263. With respect to the Araucanians, see Smith, p. 215; to the Pampas, M'Cann, p. 128; to the Malays, Earl, p. 244; to the Assamese, Butler, p. 226; to the Druses, Chasseaud, pp. 148, 165.

the dread of actual violence. Yet it is not possible to discover any symbol of rape when the whole ceremony consists in the weeping and wailing of the bride as she is being taken to her new home. Spencer remarks that there is at any rate a motive for the bride's resistance, since the savage is harsh to his wife, and uses her as his slave.[1] Although the extent of her husband's brutality is doubtful, and the daughter's lot may not appear to be much milder than that of the married woman, so that such a cause for weeping may not exist, yet this remark shows the direction in which the' true explanation lies. It symbolizes the sorrow of the bride on leaving her former home; her close dependence on her family is expressed by her lamentation. We cannot be surprised to find such symbols in communities of which the family bond is the alpha and omega.

Among the Samojedes, when the bride sews the seams of her husband's tent, her kinsfolk stand in a row and exclaim, " Why do you bend over it ? Stand upright; your father lives, your mother lives."[2] The plaintive song of the Druse bride, the words of consolation addressed to the Fijian bride, etc., all indicate the same tendency.[3] The grief of seeing the old bonds relaxed or broken is expressed in the bride's lament, and it can find no more fitting symbol than in the resistance offered by her kinsfolk ; if this basis is conceded, it is easy to account for all the symbols of rape with which we are acquainted. We shall presently pursue this train of thought, but in the meantime we return to Spencer.

The question with which we are immediately concerned, is whether Spencer's interpretation of exogamy is valid, as far as it is concerned with the symbol of rape. Without going further, it must be admitted that whatever has originally been held to be peculiarly honourable may gradually be transformed into that which is only

---

[1] Spencer, *Princ. of Soc.*, p. 654.   [2] Klaproth, p. 90.
[3] Chasseaud, p. 165.   Williams and Calvert, p. 145.

customary, and which it would be disgraceful to omit.
But the abhorrence with which exogamous tribes regard
endogamous connections seems to imply something more
than this. Thus, among the Australians, those kinsfolk
who intermarry are persecuted to death; only if they
have been able to avoid such persecution for a long
period, it ceases, and the whole story is forgotten and
forgiven. Even the children which are born of this
criminal connection run the risk of being put to death.[1]
Although marriage with women of other tribes, which
was originally an honourable distinction, may become so
general as to cease to be meritorious, while marriage
with tribal women, which was originally the most usual,
has now become contemptible, yet we can hardly accept
the suggestion that this contempt was simply transformed
into an abhorrence which regarded such a marriage as a
crime, of which the guilt was immense and unpardon-
able. So many dishonourable acts met with indulgence
that we must seek for the cause of this passionate emo-
tion. Hardly any explanation can be satisfactory of
which the intelligible basis does not consist in ideas of
the violation of a sacred right; but we cannot see that
this is the case with Spencer's suggestion, although we
are not bold enough to assert that it is absolutely
impossible.

We have another remark to make on Spencer's hypothesis. It does not agree with the fact that there is no
tribe in which the men only marry captive women, nor
indeed in which such marriages are the most common.
When Spencer states that before marriage it was often
necessary to give proof of courage, and that this led to
the symbolizing of the wife as a trophy, we cannot agree
with his opinion, since we believe that the proofs of
courage demanded of a bridegroom must be regarded as
a symbolic warrant of his capacity to provide for and
protect a wife. Moreover, exogamy, or marriage with

[1] Fison and Howitt, pp. 64-67.

none but alien women, cannot have had its origin in a desire for trophies. The love of fame might perhaps impel a man to obtain one wife by force, but it would not excite the desire to obtain them all in this manner, and a man who could only support one wife would certainly not be strong enough to seize and defend her. If marriage with women of the tribe was gradually suppressed by marriage with captive women, these wives would also gradually lose their value, and the tribe would be endangered by the lusts of robbers from other tribes. We have spoken above of the general massacre of female infants which would doubtless have ensued, and which Spencer himself has ceased to ridicule as an absurdity. Exogamy could only become possible when marriages were contracted in a peaceable manner, and in that case the alien wife must have ceased to be a trophy.

Lubbock's explanation is altogether different. He assumes that the relations between the men and women of the same tribe were originally communistic; the warrior might perhaps claim the captive taken in battle as his own, and withdraw her as far as possible from the communistic usages. The captive occupied an exceptional position; the tribe had no claim to her. Her captor, who might have killed her, had spared her life; he had acted independently, and the tribe had no word in the matter.[1] Thus exogamy was the means by which communism gave way to the marriage of individuals, and the advantages which were partly due to such permanent connections and partly to the fusion of different tribes, secured victory to the exogamous tribes in the long-run, and this, again, served to establish exogamy.[2] Lubbock believes that the symbol of rape became such an important part of the wedding ceremonies, because it was the symbol of giving up the woman to become the exclusive possession of one man.[3]

[1] Lubbock, *Orig. of Civ.*, p. 104.   [2] *Ibid.*, p. 124.
[3] McLennan, *Studies*, pp. 444, 446.

Lubbock's explanation of exogamy is so closely interwoven with his communistic hypothesis that it must stand or fall with it. As we have already declared, and shall more clearly show in the sequel, we regard the communistic hypothesis as wholly false, so that there is no reason for closely examining his explanation of exogamy; we may content ourselves with quoting McLennan's incisive criticism. This writer observes that a symbol must represent actual facts. The symbol of rape may, however, represent several acts; either a siege, or a battle, or the forcible entry into a house by a band of men; only occasionally, instances might occur of a capture by one individual. The man's kinsfolk stand on one side, the woman's kinsfolk on the other. If, however, women were usually taken captive by a group of men, acting in common, and enjoying their sexual pleasures in common, I do not see how it would be more easy for a man to take for himself a captive woman, instead of one belonging to his tribe.[1] This criticism is destructive of Lubbock's hypothesis, and only leaves the modest remnant of truth, that whoever in a primitive community wishes to obtain a wife for himself, must generally contend with a rival. It is possible that it occurred to Lubbock to derive the symbol of rape from a conflict within the tribe, since he himself takes credit for the greater merits of his hypothesis as compared to that of McLennan, which is not in agreement with the fact that some endogamous tribes observe the symbol of rape.[2]

When we turn to the second group of the suggested

[1] McLennan, *Studies*, pp. 444, 446.
[2] Lubbock, *Orig. of Civ.*, p. 121. This criticism must be an oversight, since immediately afterwards Lubbock remarks on the important part which this fact plays in McLennan's estimation, as bearing witness to the transition from exogamy to endogamy in the tribe in question: "It is not easy to believe that such a regulation, existing among endogamous tribes, is referable to the feeling that a victorious warrior should have the full disposal of spoils of war; it is much more likely that it was a relic of a time when the tribes—or rather, the race from which they sprang—were not endogamous," etc. (McLennan, *Studies*, p. 72).

explanations of exogamy, which assert that it arose from ideas of the hatefulness of incest, we meet with some observations which, if they are correct, overthrow the theories of the writers we have just quoted. Maine writes that he does not consider the ideas of exogamy and endogamy to be directly opposed to each other, since no community can be found which is not at once exogamous and endogamous.[1] Morgan observes in the same sense that it is by no means probable that an exogamous tribe, divided into clans, has existed at any time and in any place. Wherever we find clans, with some few exceptions, marriage within the clan is forbidden. This affords what McLennan calls exogamy. Intermarriage between the clans is, however, ordained; that is, each clan is exogamous, and the tribe is endogamous. The twofold conception, which is only concerned with the one fact that marriage is prohibited within the tribe, then becomes unavailing, since we can no longer regard exogamy and endogamy as a twofold conception, defining social ordinances which are directly opposed to each other.[2] We admit that it is scarcely credible that McLennan, Spencer, and Lubbock should not have observed that exogamy is only concerned with the clan, but not with the tribe, even if McLennan, on whom the other two inquirers rely, had not directly declared that exogamy was merely observed by the subdivisions or clans.[3] Here we agree with Morgan, for this fact has not been duly estimated by any of the writers in question, and they begin by assuming the exogamy of the tribe. The clans must have arisen from the introduction of alien women, whose posterity belonged to their mother's family, or from the fusion of several tribes into one tribe, consisting of several clans.[4] We have

[1] H. S. Maine, *Early Law*, p. 222.
[2] Morgan, *Anc. Soc.*, pp. 512, 514; copied from Giraud-Teulon, p. 106.
[3] McLennan, *Studies*, pp. 113–115. Morgan was aware of this passage, and quotes it in *Anc. Soc.*, pp. 511, 512.
[4] McLennan, *Studies*, pp. 93, 184. Lubbock, *Orig. of Civ.*, p. 109.

seen above that the clan did not always exist, and that tribes in which there are no clans may still be found. The question then arises whether these clanless tribes are to be considered exogamous. Without exception, however, they prove to be endogamous, or at any rate not exogamous, so that there is no positive fact which confirms McLennan's theory. And if it further appears, as Morgan declares, that the tribes subdivided into clans are endogamous for the tribe, the basis of exogamy—if our hypothesis is to rely on a basis of facts, and not on *à priori* axioms—is to be sought in the circle of ideas upon which the clan rests. It is, consequently, incumbent on us to discover which of these ideas are at work to cause the prohibition of marriage between members of the same clan.

The difficulty urged by McLennan, Spencer, and Lubbock, with respect to the source of the profound abhorrence of such marriages, now no longer exists. If it had arisen out of custom, exogamy must make an abrupt transition in order to produce the abhorrence of the marriage of kinsfolk; but we now see that exogamy has its origin in this abhorrence, and in the ideas to which it is due. Morgan traces the source of the abhorrence in question to a reformatory movement, which aimed at the prevention of marriages between brothers and sisters.[1] Maine also regards exogamy as equivalent to a prohibition of incest.[2] The objection to the hypotheses of Morgan and Lubbock is that they are closely connected with theories which we have already shown to be untenable, and they must therefore share the same fate. There is consequently no special reason for considering Morgan's explanation in detail, yet we cannot avoid inquiring whether exogamy is to be placed in the same category with the other prohibitions of the marriage of kinsfolk which are found among primitive men.

[1] Morgan, *Proceedings*, p. 469; *Anc. Soc.*, p. 69.
[2] H. S. Maine, *Early Law*, p. 227.

We do not yet know whether we are entitled to regard the clan as a group of kinsfolk allied by blood, and kept together by the idea of their common descent. If we do so regard it, however, the prohibition to marry within the clan must simply be placed in the same category with the prohibition to marry father, mother, brother, or sister. Another question arises, whether the idea of incest is the cause or consequence of this prohibition. Lubbock observes that exogamy only affords a slight protection against the marriage of kinsfolk, since wherever it is reduced to a system, it still permits the marriage of a half brother and sister.[1] Hence he infers that it is impossible to explain exogamy by means of the ideas of incest. We lay still greater stress on the fact that sexual relations between father and daughter, or mother and son, only occur in tribes in which there is neither exogamy nor a clan. We need say nothing of the marriage of brothers and sisters in cases in which the practice occurs in order to preserve the purity of the royal line : thus it was in Peru and Egypt, and so it is now in many parts of Africa and Hawaii ;[2] so many distinct ideas are at work in such cases that we can no longer say how far they are in conformity with the idea of blood-kinship.

A sexual connection between parents and children, and between brothers and sisters, frequently occurs in Brazil, in the tribes dwelling on the Amazon and on the Rio Negro; among the Chippewyans, and in one section of the Karens. Even the Veddahs, who share our abhorrence for marriage with an elder sister, prefer marriage with a younger sister to all others.[3] It is plain that exogamy, as a simple definition of the clan, cannot forbid a marriage between mother and ·son, when exogamy is

---

[1] Lubbock, *Orig. of Civ.*, p. 133.

[2] Garcilasso, p. 30. Cameron, p. 70. Spencer, *Des. Soc.*, "Island Negroes;" *Princ. of Soc.*, p. 635. Varigny, p. 14. Wilkes, vol. iv. p. 32.

[3] Von Martius, vol. i. p. 116. Spencer, *Princ. of Soc.*, p. 636. Tibbos, Hornemann, vol. i. p. 149. Spencer, *Princ. of Soc.*, p. 637.

in force, nor between father and daughter, where the
uterine line prevails; since, however, such prohibitions
exist, they afford another proof that the definition of
kinship peculiar to the clan does not put an end to all
connection between the child and one of its parents.
If, however, exogamy, as a definition of the clan, cannot
directly produce these prohibitions, which are found
wherever exogamy occurs, and in some instances where
it is absent, we are led to the conclusion that the causes
which produced these prohibitions have some connection
with those from which exogamy arose; the ideas which
prohibit incest in clanless communities may be at any
rate partly the same which lead to exogamy when
applied to a community divided into clans. The only
question we have to consider is, therefore, whether it was
really the idea of incest which led to the prohibition of
marriage between parents and children.

Fison relates an Australian legend, on which Morgan
lays special stress in his Introduction to the book by
Fison and Howitt, because it throws light on the origin
of the division into classes, and on exogamy.[1] According
to this legend, brothers and sisters, and others in the
nearest degree of kinship, intermarried after the creation,
until the evil consequences of these connections became
apparent, and the chiefs assembled in council, in order
to consider the means of averting them. The result of
this council was to appeal to Muramura, the good Spirit.
The Spirit replied that the tribe must be divided into
branches, distinguished from each other by different
names, which were derived from objects of the animate
and inanimate world, such as the dog, mouse, emu,
lizard, rain, etc. Members of the same branch might
no longer intermarry, but this was lawful for members
of different branches. The son of the dog might no
longer marry a daughter of the dog, but they were both
at liberty to form a connection with one of the mouse

---

[1] Fison and Howitt, pp. 4, 24

21

or rat branch. This order is still observed, and the first question asked of a stranger is to what *murdoo* or family he belongs.

This account is especially noteworthy for the great distinctness with which it asserts the evil consequences of the intermarriage of kinsfolk. If we may trust the legend, the Australians dreaded such connections just as the Tonganese, for instance, dreaded that their offspring should be deaf; but it does not tell us what evil consequences were expected to ensue. If the sickliness of their posterity was meant, yet it is not proved that the prohibition arose from a desire to avoid such a result. These men may merely have regarded it as a symbol of something terrible which is not named. The strong reprobation of these prohibited marriages cannot be explained by the dread lest a man's offspring should be sickly or deficient. The crimes for which the tribe or clan inflicts punishment on its own clan are such as are dangerous to the whole tribe, since it is responsible for all its members ; such crimes, for instance, as theft and rape. But, even supposing that the fact that the child of a brother and sister was deficient had attracted the attention of savages, yet they would only regard it as the omen of some calamity threatening to come upon the whole tribe; and such omens, created by fancy, are the more readily accomplished, because their accomplishment is looked for.[1] We must, however, leave it unde-

[1] In a state of nature sickly posterity are extremely rare, so that we can readily understand that any congenital deformity would be interpreted by the superstitious as a mystical intimation of the wrath of the higher powers. If the parents are brothers and sisters, this fact at once gives a definite tendency to the imaginative faculty, which results in the condemnation of such connections. Moreover, it is not yet clearly shown that the marriage of kinsfolk is hurtful. . In many instances no harm seems to follow from the marriage of brothers and sisters; small endogamous tribes are neither mentally nor physically weak. Giraud-Teulon remarks that it has been observed among some negro tribes that the connection between near kinsfolk was far from injuring the excellence of their offspring. Heredity shows that fresh blood is needed to check the defects and faults inherent in every race. Where the growing race,

cided whether considerations of the hurtfulness of such connections had much to do with the abhorrence with which they were regarded; considerations as to descent cannot have played an important part, since in many cases the prohibition did not extend to half-sisters, and in other cases brothers and sisters might intermarry when this was forbidden to parents and children. We therefore think that some other explanation of the prohibition must be found.

It may appear that incest originally consisted in marriage between too near kinsfolk, while sexual intercourse without the sanction of marriage was not forbidden. Thus Schayer writes of the Australians : " The general remark will suffice that sexual intercourse between the nearest kinsfolk was not prohibited, but a man generally chose his peculiar wife from another tribe." [1] In many tribes there were large huts, common to all, in which unmarried girls passed the night and received young men.[2] Among the Marianas, brothers and sisters might have intercourse with each other in such a house.[3] We are told of the ancient Tupinambazan tribe that such intercourse could only occur in a clandestine manner.[4]

These facts afford an indication of the quarter in which an explanation is to be found; the probability that a distinction was made between the prohibition

as among ourselves and our domestic animals, is nourished and guarded with the utmost care, I believe that the weak points of the parents reappear in an aggravated form in their offspring; but in the natural state, when the brutal struggle for existence has to be fought out, the sickly die off before their weak points are fully developed ; in the long-run, only the strong and able persist, and these characteristics are perhaps confirmed by the marriage of kinsfolk, rather than by mixed marriages.

[1] *Monatsbericht der Gesellschaft zur Erdkunde zu Berlin*, 8th year, new series, 1846, vol. iv. p. 227.

[2] Cacharees (*Journ. Asiat. Soc. of Bengal*, vol. xxiv. p. 603); Meekirs (*Ibid.*, p. 610); Kols (*Ibid*, vol. xxxv. p. 175); Mishmee (Cooper, p. 147); Moxos, Guarani, Chiquitos (D'Orbigny, vol. iv. p. 91); Tonga (*Journ. Roy. Geog. Soc.*, vol. iii. p. 194); Tahiti (Cook; Hawkesworth, p. 244).

[3] Freycinet, vol. ii. p. 368.   [4] Von Martius, vol. i. p. 116.

of marriage and of sexual intercourse is increased by
the fact that communities exist in which the marriage
of near kinsfolk is altogether forbidden, while in certain
cases sexual connection is allowed. If such intercourse
were held to be blameworthy in itself, it becomes unintelligible that the king should be bound to marry his
own sister. The ideas which place restrictions on the
connections of the common people must be of a kind
which can give way to other ideas, and these make the
connections which are otherwise prohibited desirable.
If, however, the sexual connection with one of the same
blood was dreaded, it might seem probable that this
dread would increase with the importance of the individual; it would be absurd to regard that connection as
expedient for the man of highest position which was
abhorred in the case of all others. If the king takes a
sister as his wife, in order to maintain the purity of
blood in his race, a similar wish might influence other
men of noble birth. The king is, indeed, in this case
assigned to his sister, since he is the only one of the tribe
who has no equals; but this is not the main question.
There is an external conflict between the dread of any
mixture of blood which leads to state endogamy and the
dread of incest which prevails in the people, and which
is based upon the idea that there should be no connection between those of the same blood. The question of
state-endogamy does not affect our position with respect
to the prohibited marriages, and may therefore be set
aside for the present. The prohibitions of marriage now
in existence only display a superficial connection with
incest, as we ourselves understand it, and a thorough
examination of the idea shows it to be involved in inex-
tricable absurdities. We cannot, for instance, explain
the Veddah prohibition by the ideas of incest current
among ourselves. A man may not marry his elder sister,
but marriage with his younger sister is to be preferred
to any other connection. We must at any rate make

the attempt to explain such facts by the ideas of primitive life with which we are acquainted.

The husband is in all cases the lord of his wife. Even when the child belongs to his mother's clan, and she has the management of the household property, she is in sexual subjection to her husband. We have seen that among most rude peoples, and even among the Australian savages, the mother exerts great influence over her son, who regards her with considerable reverence. This is also the relation of the sister to her younger brother, although in a minor degree. In like manner, as Bachofen tells us, the Nairs respect their elder sisters, who stand in the place of a mother to them. They never remain in the same room with their younger sisters; they do not touch or even enter into conversation with them, since it might, as they say, give rise to some sinful act, as the girls are young and inconsiderate, while respect for their elder sisters puts an end to any such thought.[1] A marriage between a mother and son, or between a brother and elder sister, would altogether transform their relations, and the breach in the respect due to their elders, the confusions and contradictions which would ensue, would be quite enough to produce an aversion to such marriages. This aversion would be increased by the fact that it was generally impossible to contract such marriages, since the son possesses nothing which he could offer to the father as purchase-money. To enter the paternal house by force, in order to carry off the wife or daughter, would be an unheard-of crime among savages, and would certainly call forth the same anger on the perpetrator as that which punishes the slayer of a clansman with death. The connection between a father and daughter is not affected by these circumstances, but it rarely occurs, since a father is unwilling to renounce the advantages of bestowing his daughter in marriage. Even among the Australians, a son-in-law

[1] Bachofen, *Ant. Briefe*, vol. i. p. 237.

is bound to give a considerable part of the prey obtained in hunting to his parents-in-law.[1]

If in this way the impression arises that there is something unusual and incompatible with other ideas in marriage between such persons, an occasional calamity which befalls any of them will be enough to excite the imaginative faculty in the highest degree; and if no prohibition previously existed, the absolute condemnation of such marriages would then be pronounced. The intermarriage of individuals of the same family implies that persons who have no legal right to dispose of themselves and their property, nevertheless agree upon such legal disposition, an encroachment which would certainly be violently opposed by primitive men.

Wherever we find that the marriage of near kinsfolk is allowed, as in the instances quoted above of marriage between a king and his sister, or, as among the Persians, between a mother and a son,[2] it may always be shown that these ideas of encroachment could have no place. In communities which are under a despotic rule, we may find that a chief marries his sister, and in such communities there is a prevalent idea that the king cannot contract a true marriage with his subjects, who can only become his concubines. The legal relation which exists between man and wife, and, at a later period, between mother and son, might appear to the human consciousness, although not indeed in every case, to be only possible between persons in the same legal position; in the king's case there is no one on this legal equality, except his sister, nor can the latter be subordinate to any one

---

[1] Fison and Howitt, Appendix D., p. 261.

[2] " Nomen autem hominis, quem Nimrod constituit sacrum Ignis ministratorem, erat Andshan cui Diabolus e medio Ignis hisce usus est verbis; Nemo hominum potis est rite Igni ministrare nec mea sacra callere, nisi commisceatur cum matre sua et sorore sua et filia sua. Fecit itaque Andshan juxta quod dixerat ei Diabolus. Et ab eo tempore qui sacerdotio apud Magos functi sunt, commisceri solebant cum matribus, et sororibus suis, et filiabus suis. Et Andshan hic primus erat, qui hunc morem incepit" (Selden, p. 625).

but to her royal brother. Since they are thus thrown upon each other by their peculiar conditions, a marriage between them may readily occur. We shall see the effect of these ideas when we come to consider endogamy. The conditions in Persia stand alone in being produced by religious ideas; but even there they may be explained by the endogamy of the state.

We can understand why the prohibition of marriage between brothers and sisters did not extend to those of half blood, since, in the primitive family, children, as we have seen above, belonged to the mother's kindred, and, therefore, particularly in all questions relating to property, their legal position with respect to each other was independent.

The clan, like the family, is a legal group, and the groups were kept together by legal bonds long before the ties of blood had any binding power. The same ideas which impelled a man to look for a wife outside his family also impelled him to look for her outside the clan.

We quite admit that those who maintain the current ideas with respect to the marriage of primitive men will be unwilling to accept this explanation of exogamy, since they regard primitive marriage as simply a sexual relation. But it is the essential point of our explanation that sexual considerations were not the basis of marriage. The final chapter of this section will be devoted to this point of view, and I trust that the last difficulties which beset our path will then disappear.

The explanation of exogamy which we have just given may also explain other regulations of marriage. Marsden tells us that the Rejangs of Sumatra forbid the intermarriage of brothers' children, nor may a brother's son marry a sister's daughter. The sister's son may, however, take to wife a brother's daughter.[1] In like manner we find that among the Tulawayan Buntars, a

[1] Marsden, p. 227.

man is bound to marry the daughter of his mother's brother.[1] This is also done by the Ghonds, and it is expressly stated that it is less incumbent on him to marry the daughter of his father's sister.[2] The connection between the sister's son and the brother's daughter is therefore the one preferred. Primitive men are fond of doing over again that which has been done before; the new generation acts like the former one, and this is merely what occurs when a young man becomes a wooer in the house of his mother's brother—he goes where his father was a suitor before him. If, however, the brother's son marries the sister's daughter, the bride returns to her mother's house and becomes a wife where the mother was only a daughter. In Brazil, as a substitute for the purchase-money of a wife, the firstborn daughter was surrendered to the mother's father, and was legally assigned to the mother's brother as his wife. In this case, therefore, we find that the brother's son marries the sister's daughter, but this is due to the idea that an equivalent for the bride must be given.[3] If the explanation of these ordinances is sought in the ideas of blood kinship, we should be hard pressed to find it, for it is a strange view of blood kinship which forbids a man to marry the daughter of his father's sister, while it permits and indeed enjoins him to take to wife the daughter of his mother's brother.

We must interpret in like manner the Eskimo's unwillingness to marry into the family to which he belongs, as well as the fact that the Macusis—who, it will be remembered, observe the female line—and the Mundrucus are forbidden to marry the brother's daughter. In these cases the legal position which would be established by marriage cannot be reconciled with that which

---

[1] Buchanan, vol. iii. p. 16.
[2] Spencer, *Desc. Soc.*, p. 8. See the narrative of Isaac and Jacob.
[3] The mother's brother is bound, in order to support her, to marry his niece if she can find no other husband.

the members of the same family hold with respect to each other.[1]

The correctness of our explanation of exogamy is also confirmed by the fact that its reconciliation with endogamy thereby becomes possible. Exogamy prohibits marriage between persons who are so nearly related that they have no legal independence of each other; endogamy prohibits the marriage of persons whose legal status is too remote from each other.

The most common form of endogamy is that a man may not take a wife from another tribe; if, however, he wishes to do so, she must be incorporated into her husband's tribe by adoption. As a rule, captive women are thereby received into the clan, although it is a question how far the connection with them is regarded as a valid marriage, or merely as concubinage; in Brazil it is considered disgraceful to marry a captive.[2] Speaking generally, I doubt whether endogamy can be termed a prohibition to marry outside the clan; the restriction is no more than a custom, which is itself limited, both by the readiness with which alien women are adopted by the clan, and by the disinclination to surrender women to alien husbands, since they are thereby lost to the tribe. Just as the family constrains a suitor to join his bride's household, so the tribe will not give to an alien one of their maidens to wife, except on condition that he transfers himself to her tribe. We have mentioned this custom above in speaking of the Columbians and of the New Zealanders; Strabo tells us of the Arabs that they had intercourse with their own mothers, while

[1] A marriage ordinance which points to the same idea of the legal equality of the members of one household, is found in the custom that a man marries all the sisters of his bride, as well as herself. Morgan, *Systems*, p. 447; *Anc. Soc.*, p. 160. Fison and Howitt (Australians), p. 202; Schomburgk (Macusis), vol. ii. p. 318; Lafitau (America), vol. i. p. 560; Labat (Brazil), vol. ii. p. 125; Du Tertre (Brazilians and Karibs), vol. ii. p. 377; Baegert (Californians), p. 368; Spencer, *Desc. Soc.*, (Todas).

[2] Von Martius, vol. i. p. 71.

adultery was punished with death, and a connection with one of another family was adulterous. Burton also states that the national life is preserved by systematic intermarriage. The savage does not withhold his daughter from a foreigner, but the son-in-law must take up his abode among them.[1]

The Arabs afford a legitimate example of a race which adopted endogamy after having been originally in the state of exogamy.[2] Wilken, whose attempt to show a prior observance of the female line of descent has been mentioned above, seeks a proof of his hypothesis in the custom which entitled a man to marry the daughter of his father's brother; not that he was bound to marry her, but she might not marry another man without his consent. The female cousin was therefore called by courtesy *bint-amm*, or wife.[3] Wilken goes on to say that this custom was directly opposed to the aversion with which they otherwise regarded the marriage of near kinsfolk; and since, as he believes, this aversion clearly points to a prior exogamy, and the observance of the female line absolves a marriage with the daughter of the father's brother from any incestuous character, he feels justified in assuming the previous existence of the female line.[4] On this point we are unable to agree with him. In the first place, an aversion to marriage between near kinsfolk does not indicate a clan-exogamy, which we have found to be of later origin; and in the second place, Strabo's account at any rate makes it doubtful whether this aversion existed before Mahomet's time. We may add that the male cousin's right springs from the same process of ideas as that which founded endogamy. The brothers, indeed, no longer remain in joint family groups, yet they still hold together as united against strangers. Just as a man marries his brother's widow in order to

---

[1] Burton, *A Pilgrimage*, vol. iii. p. 40.   [2] McLennan, *Studies*, p. 207.
[3] Burkhardt, vol. i. pp. 113, 272. Burton, *A Pilgrimage*, vol. iii. p. 41.
[4] Wilken, pp. 57–59.

keep the family property, so the son of one brother may be enjoined to purchase the daughter of another, so that a stranger may not profit by the purchase-money. We have here a duty rather than a right, but the border-line between these ideas is effaced, since the duty was not unconditional, and the bride's father was bound to surrender his daughter to his nephew at a lower price than he would have given for a wife elsewhere.

We have already stated that tribal endogamy was not as a rule of a strictly exclusive character, and that it might rather be termed a disinclination for marriage with strangers than an express prohibition to contract such marriages. It is only when the tribes become castes, as in India, that the lines of endogamy are more sharply drawn, and all marriages between members of different castes are strictly forbidden. It is easy to discover the cause of these strongly-marked distinctions, and their legal character has been explained by McLennan.[1] The higher caste would be degraded by according to the lower a position of equal legal rights; the first and most powerful expression of an equality in legal rights consisted in the rights of marriage, which was therefore strictly forbidden when such legal rights were withheld. In like manner ranks and classes of men separated from each other; the greater the cleft between them, the greater the impossibility of intermarriage, and the more each class resembled a clan, except in the fact that the clan put forward exogamy as its distinctive mark. The prejudice was at first entertained by the superior class, since they and not their inferiors would be degraded by intermarriage; it was subsequently dreaded by the inferior class, as a means of still further protecting the rights of the great.

We are told that the intermarriage of cousins takes place among the Karens, but that their kinship is held to make the connection undesirable. Marriage with the

[1] McLennan, *Studies*, p. 202.

children of second cousins is considered the most suitable; that of cousins in the third degree is permitted but the kinship is considered to be somewhat too remote. Beyond this degree, marriages are unconditionally forbidden.[1] We know that the Karens are an unruly people, and there is no village which is not at strife with another. They have no castes, and their numerous tribes and clans seem originally to have been formed by the dispersion of families and villages.[2] The disputes which arise among them are usually due to questions of property; such disputes are very frequent when wealth which had been held in common has to be divided among several heirs. Among the Karens the largest share goes to the elder member of the family, and sometimes the youngest have a rather larger share than those who are midway in the family.[3] It is easy to understand the causes of strife which arise when, after a lapse of some generations, the family group becomes distributed into villages. When we consider that in the case of most peoples the joint family group falls to pieces in the seventh degree of kinship—that is, the descendants of a common great-grandfather—we are struck by the fact that the second cousins, whom the Karens marry by preference, are the last to remain in the joint family group; the severance is begun by their children.[4] We cannot be mistaken in regarding the Karen village as resembling the joint family group; and its endogamy represents the legal exclusiveness of the village. In the village, each has a share in the soil, although the near kinsfolk sometimes live together,[5] and this agrees with the fact that they prefer to marry in the more distant degree of second cousins, since in this degree legal independence waxes with the waning kinship.

[1] *Journal Asiat. Soc. of Bengal,* 1866, vol. xxxv. p. 18.
[2] *Ibid.,* 1868, vol. xxxvii. p. 130.
[3] *Ibid.,* vol. xxxvii. p. 142.   [4] Hearn, p. 181.
[5] *Journal Asiat. Soc. of Bengal,* 1868, vol. xxxvii. pp. 126, 127.

EXOGAMY AND ENDOGAMY. 237

Among the Kookas the clans are endogamous. No marriage can be contracted between kinsfolk up to the degree of first cousins; the clans are indeed permitted to intermarry, but they rarely do so, and such marriages are condemned by public opinion.[1] This endogamy of the clan becomes intelligible when we learn that the Kooka clans of North Cachar differ widely in customs and interests, and are often hotly at war.[2] This clan-endogamy is therefore only a form of the customary endogamy of the tribe.

There is a small group of facts, in connection with those we have already stated, which we cannot pass over, although they are not of great importance. It is not uncommon to forbid parents and children-in-law to associate freely with each other. Tylor mentions this custom in his "Early History of Mankind," and quotes many instances of it, to which others might easily be added. Tylor connects the custom with *Tabu*—a very vague and indefinite explanation, since we have still to find the reason of *Tabu*. Lubbock regards the custom as an expression of displeasure on the part of the bride's parents, which it would be easy to understand at a time when the marriage still took place by capture, and it would therefore be a further proof of such a mode of marriage.[3] We do not think it possible to give a single interpretation of the collective forms of the custom in question; they certainly have their origin in different ideas.

In some cases the prohibition extends to both parents-in-law, both as regards the son- and-daughter-in-law, while in other cases it is only partially applicable. At one time a son-in-law may not address his mother-in-law, at another the daughter-in-law may not be seen by her father-in-law. The first glance makes it doubtful

---

[1] *Journal Asiat. Soc. of Bengal*, 1855, vol. xxiv. p. 640.
[2] *Ibid.*, p. 617.
[3] Lubbock, *Orig. of Civ.*, p. 123. Instances of the custom, p. 12.

22

how far marriage by capture can explain these regulations, and the doubt increases when we regard the phenomenon more closely.   It is, indeed, quite possible that a custom which has arisen under given circumstances may persist longer than these circumstances, but this explanation can only be accepted, as we have repeatedly said, when no other is possible, and it has some inherent probability, which is here by no means the case.

Alberti tells us that a Bechuana father-in-law may only see his daughter-in-law in the presence of others, and that is also the case with a mother- and son-in-law ; if they should meet accidentally, the son- or daughter-in-law seeks to hide or escape.[1]   Alberti regards this as an expression of their abhorrence of incest, and I know of nothing to contradict this suggestion but the fact that there is no such concealment in the case of parents and children, after the manner in which a Nair seeks to avoid being alone with his younger sister.   This objection, however, has no weight, since a sexual connection between parent and children-in-law is possible before the marriage takes place, which is not the case with kinsfolk by blood ; it is, therefore, not surprising that the restriction which first occurs in mature age should be marked by a special sign.   Münzinger writes of the Beni-Amir : " There is a firm and eternal friendship between the bride and the comrades of the bridegroom, which never fails ; they may no longer see each other, but retain a mutual affection. . . . The woman conceals herself, as the man does from his mother-in-law." [2]   A feeling of enmity cannot account for this state of things, nor will jealousy and the fear of incest help us, since these could not influence the relations of a mother- and daughter-in-law, and, moreover, there is much unchastity among the Beni-Amir

---

[1] Alberti, p. 105.

[2] Münzinger, p. 325.   For Ostjaks and Samojedes, see Pallas, vol. iv. pp. 71, 99, 577 ; Californians, Baegert, *Smithsonian Report*, 1863, p. 368; China, *Astley Collection*, vol. iv. p. 91.

women after marriage.[1] But when we learn that the Bechuana's marriage only becomes valid after the birth of a child, and that among the Basutos, who are of the Bechuana race, the prohibition only extends to the date of the birth of the eldest child,[2] it becomes evident that the prohibition is an expression of the ideas which characterize the transition state, in which the relations of the new kinsfolk are not altogether established. The ideas that sexual intercourse must be avoided arise from the reverence which the sons- and daughters-in-law owe to the parents.

This latter consideration is undoubtedly the only one in some cases. As we saw above, the Karib bridegroom leaves his own house in order to dwell with his father-in-law; his wives, who are sisters and daughters of the house, have free and unrestricted intercourse with all, but this is not the case with the husband, without express permission, unless his wife's kinsfolk are still children, or when they are drunk.[3] We find similar instances among the North American tribes; the Dyak, again, may not call his father-in-law by name; a Mongolian or Kalmuck bride may not speak nor sit down in her father-in-law's presence; a Jakutan wife may not appear in her household garment, "stripped to the waist," before her father-in-law and her husband's elder brother; a Banyai man is forbidden to sit down negligently in the presence of his mother-in-law; a Mishmayan never eats in his father-in-law's house; a Fijian never eats with his wife, his sister, niece, father-, or mother-in-law, and a son may not speak to his father after he has attained his fifteenth year, etc.[4]

Caillié gives an instance of a nature for which Lubbock's explanation would suffice. On the Senegal,

[1] Münzinger, p. 326. [3] Alberti, p. 104.
[2] Du Tertre, vol. ii. p. 378.
[4] Tylor, *Early History.* Livingstone, *Miss. Trav.* p. 622. Cooper, p. 236. Williams and Calvert, p. 117. Among the Veddahs, the father does not speak to his adult son, nor the mother to her adult daughter.

a bridegroom may never see his parents-in-law. He carefully avoids them, and they cover their faces when they see him. If the wooer comes from another encampment, he conceals himself from the bride's fellow-villagers, with the exception of a few friends, with whom he lives. He sometimes migrates to the bride's encampment, in which case he takes his cattle with him, becomes one of its members, and ceases to practise any concealment.[1] It is more doubtful how we are to interpret the Australian prohibition to speak either of the parents- or children-in-law by name,[2] and also that an Australian is displeased, even if his mother-in-law's shadow falls upon his legs.[3] There is a similar prohibition in the case of the Araucanians. But if any one attempts to connect these phenomena with the rape of women, further consideration will show that they can have had no independent influence on the symbol of rape, but must rather have been dependent on it.[4]

[1] Caillié, vol. i. p. 139.　　[2] Eyre, vol. ii. p. 339.
[3] Fison and Howitt, p. 103.　　[4] Smith, p. 217.

CHAPTER VII.

MARRIAGE AND ITS DEVELOPMENT.

Sexual impulse—Civilizing power of religion—Stages of development—
Mother's rights—Father's rights—Bellerophon myth—Perpati myth—
Pele and Tamapua myth—Interpretation of myths—Tsui-goab myth
—Allegories of theory and conception—Customs of civilization—
Jealousy—Object of marriage—Use of fire—Primitive wooing—
Duration of marriage—Birth of child—Marriage—Polygamy—Wed-
ding—Bride's family—Setting aside of polygamy—Tolerant and
intolerant forms of marriage—Chastity in marriage—Paternal love—
Chastity of unmarried girls—The man's obligation of chastity—Love
and marriage—Independence of married women—Emancipation of
women—Education of children—Unmarried women—Moral independence of married women.

WE have now seen that legal considerations for the most
part define the conception of the relations between
parents and chidren, and also the sphere within which
individuals are permitted to intermarry. Exogamy sets
its mark on a given sphere as too restricted for the
establishment within it of the legal ordinance which is
termed marriage; endogamy, on the other hand, pre-
scribes the limits beyond which marriage is no longer
possible. We must therefore regard marriage as a legal
institution, and the sexual intercourse between husband
and wife is only one of the matters with which this
institution has to do; it is by no means its central point
and *raison d'être*. We are in some respects disposed to
under-estimate the great influence which sexual matters
exert on all the concerns of social life, and the attempt

is sometimes made to sever it from moral life, as a matter of which we are constrained to admit the practical existence, although, from the ideal point of view, it ought not to be. On the other hand, its influence on primitive communities has been greatly overrated. The sexual instinct must be counted among the most powerful of human impulses, and is often unbridled in its expression, but it is devoid of the conditions which form the basis of the leading tendencies in which man's struggle for existence must be fought out. Since it is so easily and quickly gratified, and so transient, it is not adapted to support the heavy burden of social order. In societies in which it is less possible to gratify the sexual instinct, it may become the overmastering passion of the individual, and it may dictate ends to him which decide the direction and nature of his life ; but such a state of being will always be opposed to the deepest and most enduring tendencies which render the life of the community vigorous and healthy, and lead it into fresh and higher developments.

Too high an estimate of the sexual impulse has led to the erroneous assertion, which we have disputed above, that the first human community lived in promiscuous intercourse, and that monogamous marriage was gradually developed from this condition by reflections on the sexual relation. We will now attempt to become more accurately acquainted with the process of development through which marriage passed.

Bachofen believes that he can offer a decisive proof of the fact that the spiritual life of primitive men gathered round their sexual relations and the facts of procreation. He asserts that man passed from the state of promiscuous intercourse into a marriage state which was based on the dominating power of women ; that this gynocracy subsequently took the savage form it assumed in the Amazon period, and then gave way to an order of things which was based on the superiority of the man. The authority for Bachofen's statement is sought by him in the observances of the female line, in licentious customs of all kinds, and in polyandry ; but he also lays special stress on the value of religious myths. He makes use of this material in such a disconnected manner, that a critic can scarcely undertake a harder task than to glance superficially at Bachofen's comprehensive work. I feel bound to say that his process of thought can only be satisfactorily given in its main features, since most of its details are hopelessly obscure and confused. We should rather call his "Mutterrecht" the rhapsody of a well-informed poet than the work of a calm and clear-sighted man of science.

Bachofen writes : "Mythical tradition appears to be the faithful expression of the law of life, at a time when the foundations of the historical development of the ancient world were laid ; it reveals the original mode of thought, and we may accept this direct historical revelation as true, from our complete confidence in this source of history." And again, "Every age unconsciously obeys, even in its poetry, the laws of its individual life."[1] A patriarchal age could therefore not have invented the matriarchate, and the myths which describe the latter may be regarded as trustworthy witnesses of its historical existence. It may be taken for granted that the myths did not refer to special persons and occurrences, but only tell us of the social ideas which prevailed, or were endeavouring to prevail in the several communities."[2] With rather obtrusive self-consciousness, Bachofen goes on to say that the development of the community only advanced by means of these religious ideas. "Religion is the only efficient lever of all civilization. Each elevation and depression of human life has its origin in a movement which begins in this supreme department."[3] "We cannot fail to see that of the two forms of gynocracy in question, religious and civil, the former

[1] Bachofen, *Mutterrecht*, p. vii.   [2] *Ibid.*, p. viii.   [3] *Ibid.*, p. xiii.

was the basis of the latter. Ideas connected with
worship came first, and the civil forms of life were their
result and expression."[1] The woman's religious attitude,
in particular, the tendency of her mind towards the
supernatural and the divine, influenced the man, and
robbed him of the position which nature disposed him
to take, in virtue of his physical superiority.[2] In this
way woman's position was transformed by religious
considerations, until she became in civil life that which
religion had caused her to be. By such a study of
myths, and by the fragmentary accounts of barbarous
peoples which have been handed down to us from ancient
times, Bachofen undertakes to show that man was developed from a state of promiscuous intercourse into the
matriarchate, and the age of Amazons, and then into the
patriarchate; each stage was marked by its peculiar
religious idea, produced by the dissatisfaction with which
the dominating idea of the prior stage was regarded; a
dissatisfaction which led to the disappearance of this
prior condition.

"It was the assertion of fatherhood which delivered
the mind from natural appearances, and when this was
successfully achieved, human existence was raised above
the laws of material life. The principle of motherhood
is common to all the spheres of animal life, but man goes
beyond this tie in giving the pre-eminence to the power
of procreation, and thus becomes conscious of his higher
vocation. . . . In the paternal and spiritual principle he
breaks through the bonds of tellurism and looks upward
to the higher regions of the cosmos. Victorious fatherhood thus becomes as distinctly connected with the
heavenly light as prolific motherhood is with the teeming
earth."[3] "All the stages of sexual life, from aphrodistic
hetairism to the apollinistic purity of fatherhood, have
their corresponding type in the stages of natural life,
from the wild vegetation of the morass, the prototype

[1] Bachofen, *Mutterrecht*, p. xv.   [2] *Ibid.*, p. xiv.   [3] *Ibid.*, p. xxvii.

of conjugal motherhood, to the harmonic law of the Uranian world, to the heavenly light which, as the *flamma non urens*, corresponds to the eternal youth of fatherhood. The connection is so completely in accordance with law, that the form taken by the sexual relations of life may be inferred from the predominance of one or other of these universal substances in worship."[1]

The first state was in all cases that of hetairism. As in the morass, one reed succeeds to another without order or structure, so the sexual life of man was originally devoid of order. Bachofen here inserts the quite unproved remark that the tyranny of the individual is necessarily connected with the community of wives. This rule is based upon the right of procreation; since there is no individual fatherhood, all have only one father—the tyrant whose sons and daughters they all are, and to whom all the property belongs.[2] From this condition, in which the man rules by means of his rude, sexual power, we rise to that of gynocracy, in which there is the dawn of marriage, of which the strict law is at first observed by the woman, not by the man. Weary of always ministering to the lusts of man, the woman raises herself by the recognition of her motherhood. "Just as a child is first disciplined by its mother, so are peoples by their women. The man must serve, before he is allowed to rule. It is only the wife who can control the man's essentially unbridled power, and lead him into the paths of well-doing."[3]

There is an intermediate stage between hetairism and marriage, such as we find among the Massagetes and Troglodytes. "Each man has a wife, but they are all permitted to hold intercourse with the wives of others."[4] Gynocracy may be compared with agriculture. "Thus the connection of law with material motherhood forms

---

[1] Bachofen, *Mutterrecht*, p. xxix.   [2] *Ibid.*, p. 17.
[3] *Ibid.*, p. 19.   [4] *Ibid.*, p. 18.

two stages of life—the lower, of aphrodistic hetairism; the higher, which is cereal and conjugal. The former corresponds to the irregular vegetation of the morass, the latter to organized agriculture. In both stages of culture nature affords a type and measure of human conditions. Nature has taken law into her bosom, and agriculture is the prototype of the conjugal union between man and woman. Earth does not ,imitate woman, but woman imitates the earth. Marriage was regarded of old as an agrarian relationship, and the whole terminology of the law of marriage is taken from agricultural conditions." [1]   While the man went on distant forays, the woman stayed at home, cultivated the ground, and was undisputed mistress of the household. She took arms against her foes, and was gradually transformed into an Amazon. As a rival to the man, the Amazon became hostile to him, and began to withdraw from marriage, and from motherhood. This set limits to the rule of women, and provoked the punishment of heaven and of men.[2]   Thus Jason put an end to the rule of the Amazons in Lemnos; thus Dionysos and Bellerophon strove together, passionately, yet without obtaining any decisive victory, until Apollo with calm superiority finally became the conqueror.[3]

Bachofen's mode of applying the mythical tales has no scientific method, and is carried on in a quite arbitrary manner, prompted by a poetic inspiration, which snatches at every kind of allegory. His method recalls that which was followed by Schilling in his work on the deities of Samothracia, and on the philosophy of mythology; it seeks in myths the abstract ideas to which the religious opinions of civilized men are due; and the search is rarely fruitless, since the opinions which have gradually created these myths are the same as those which would be based on these ideas, as the object of

---

[1] Bachofen, *Mutterrecht*, pp. 9, 73, 142.   [2] *Ibid.*, p. 85.
[3] *Ibid.*, p. 85.

conscious reflection. We will give some instances of these interpretations of myths. The myth tells us that when Bellerophon was living with King Proteus, unchaste overtures were made to him by the king's wife, Sthenobœa. When they were rejected by him, the queen complained to her husband that he had tried to seduce her; Proteus therefore sent him to his father-in-law, Jobates, in Lydia, that he might be there put to death. Jobates charged Bellerophon to slay the monster Chimæra, which he was able to do by the aid of Pegasus. He likewise vanquished the Amazons, but as his services were not rewarded, he besought Poseidon to lay waste the land. It was completely flooded by the sea, until the women implored Bellerophon for mercy; he yielded out of shame, and Poseidon granted his petition that he should desist from laying waste the land. Bellerophon married Jobates' daughter Philomæa, and received a rich dowry of land. On his death, the inheritance devolved on his daughter's son, Sarpedon, not on his son's son, Glaucus.

According to Bachofen's interpretation of this myth, it expresses the dawning reverence for fatherhood; Bellerophon's conflict with the declining power of woman is marked by his refusal to commit adultery, and by his victory over the Amazons. The unbridled violence of dawning fatherhood appears in Bellerophon's alliance with Poseidon, the rudest expression of fatherhood, in contrast to Apollo, who expresses it in its noblest form; Bellerophon cannot overcome the lofty ideas of the gynocracy, and yields to the matron's supplication. The preference of Sarpedon to Glaucus, shows how long the female line was observed in Lydia, and its religious significance appears in the submission of the men to Sarpedon; they lay their arrows in a ring fastened on the child's breast, which points him out to be a mother's son, since the ring is the symbol of feminine κτείς.

Such an interpretation connects features which by

no means necessarily arise from one process of thought. There is nothing to show that Bellerophon's chastity, his victory over the Amazons, his alliance with Poseidon, and his yielding to the matrons are to be explained in the same philosophical connection. The myth becomes more intelligible if we compare it with others, with whose origin we are acquainted.

Newbold tells us that in Menangkabowe the female line is explained by the following myth : " Perpati Sabatang built a magnificent vessel, which he loaded with gold and precious stones so heavily that it got aground on the sands at the foot of the fiery mountain, and resisted the efforts of all the men to it her off. The sages were consulted, and declared all attempts would be vain until the vessel had passed over the body of a pregnant princess. It happened that the Rajah's own daughter was in the condition desired; she was called upon to immolate herself for the sake of her country, but refused. At this juncture the pregnant sister of the Rajah boldly stepped forward, and cast herself beneath the prow of the vessel, which instantly put itself in motion, and again floated on the waves without injury to the princess. The Rajah disinherited the offspring of his disobedient daughter in favour of that of the sister, and caused this to be enrolled in the records of the empire as the law of succession in time to come." [1] Bachofen makes the following remarks on this myth : " The legend is the product of a time when the customary right in question threatened to yield to contact with peoples who observed other customs, and under the influence of progressive ideas and conditions ; recourse was had to legendary motives, and to a reference to the authority of a lawgiver. It is therefore certain that it has no historical value. . . . But the matter has another aspect . . . it is the mutual affection of brothers and sisters which is expressed in the conditions of inheritance between a mother's brother and a nephew. The

[1] Newbold, vol. ii. p. 221.

immediate succession was set aside, because the regard felt between man and wife could not be compared with the closeness of the connection between brother and sister; it was not the wife but the sister who was capable of sacrificing everything for the man. This popular idea was based on the condition of the people."[1]

This legend is undoubtedly a poetical explanation of the female line. But Bachofen is mistaken in the assertion that the ideas which, at a later period, appeared to the popular consciousness to explain the female line, were the same as those in which it had its origin. The myth shows that the female line appeared to the popular consciousness to be somewhat abnormal and absurd, but it tells hardly anything about its origin, and the king's sister's act of self-sacrifice only appears to be a reason given at a subsequent time for the persistence of a custom, not a symbol of the sisterly affection which was universally active. This act was a concrete, individual occurrence, for which we are not justified in substituting the abstract idea.

The same may be said of the Bellerophon myth. An explanation was to be found for the Lydian observance of the female line, and the act performed by the women was consequently invented, since it would explain the preference given to them. The country owed its deliverance to them, and they might therefore assert their special claims.

The remainder of the myth in question is merely the divine personification of natural things which is so common. Man imagines that a passion and a deliberate force like his own lurk behind the phenomena of nature, and he seeks to explain the expression of this passion in accordance with the form which it assumes in man. In Hawaii, worship is given to the goddess Pele, the personification of the volcano Kilauea, and the god Tamapua, the personification of the sea, or rather, of the storm which

[1] Bachofen, *Antiq. Br.*, vol. i. p. 140.

lashes the sea and hurls wave after wave upon the land.
The myth tells us that Tamapua wooed Pele, who rejected
his suit, whereupon he flooded the crater with water, but
Pele drank up the water and drove him back into the
sea. On another occasion Tamapua fought a battle at
Oahu with a king who enclosed him and his men in a
narrow valley; the men climbed upon his back in order
to surmount the rocks, and he himself escaped without
difficulty; the traces of his footsteps may be seen in the
deep clefts worn in the rock by the mountain torrent.
The origin of this myth is perfectly clear, and there is
no reason for treating the Bellerophon myth differently.
Since it was assumed that women must have performed
some act which caused the descent of the child to be
defined through them, Poseidon must have laid waste
the coast, incited thereto by Bellerophon; he himself
was injured by Jobates, at the request of Proteus, etc.
Occurrences were selected and invented by chance in
order to complete the myth, such as Bellerophon's relations with Jobates' daughter, and the opposition offered
by the women to the influx of the sea, or the wrath of
Poseidon. There is no reason to assume that there is
any essential connection between these details. With
respect to the conflict with the Amazons, we need only
observe that Amazon myths exist among many barbarous peoples, although no one has been able to ascertain
that an Amazon state had any real existence. Fancy
loves to invent conditions which are the exact contrary of
the facts with which we are acquainted, such, for instance,
as the narrative of men who can take off their heads
and carry them under their arms, etc. The Amazon races
are undoubtedly the creation of the same kind of fancy.

We have only touched upon the question of the
interpretation of myths in passing, and wish to avoid
dwelling too long upon it. But before absolutely rejecting Bachofen's suggestions, we must have a clear and
distinct idea how myths should be interpreted, so that

it is necessary to bestow a little more consideration upon
the subject.

The principle we have followed above is almost
identical with that which is maintained by Max Müller.
He states that man displays a tendency to personify
natural objects; that, for example, he calls the moon a
carpenter, etc. This does not imply that he forgets the
difference between an actual carpenter and the moon,
but the personifying name exerts a great influence on
his ideas, and the most difficult problem to solve is, not
why a man was inclined to personification, but how
he finally extricated himself from the power of his
inventions. This power, added to the personifications,
may explain myths; the first step was taken in the
form of an allegory, and hence the poetic invention took
a definite form.[1]

One out of many examples may be given. The
Hottentots say that their god Tsui-goab, the god of
heaven, and of the sun, rain, and storm, was some few
generations before a quack doctor with a broken leg.[2]
Max Müller rejects the suggestion that a magician with
a crippled leg had really lived, and was deified after
his death. This explanation follows the principle laid
down by Spencer and Lubbock, on which Tylor's
criticism has been already given. The first element
of this principle is based upon the human personality.
Man's fancy begins to weave inventions round some
given person; if his name is derived from some natural
object, he is identified with that object, which also
begins to be regarded with reverence; myths arise in
the form of tales about the acts of men which are,
owing to the similarity of name, transferred to the objects and forces of nature.[3] Max Müller's principle of

---

[1] Max Müller, *Orig. of Rel.*, p. 193; *Introd.*, p. 210. Appendix
XXXVII.
[2] *Ibid., Introd.*, p. 285.
[3] Spencer, *Princ. of Soc.*, p. 300.

interpretation is much simpler, and the Hottentot myth in question is interpreted by him in a way which affords one of the finest examples of a simple and natural reconstruction of the mode adopted by the creative consciousness, so that all other interpretations appear irrational and forced beside it.[1] Spencer, indeed, tries to avoid Bachofen's erroneous views, and takes care to represent myths as the invention of a deeper consciousness—that is, as the concrete image of an abstract idea. But although this latter allegorical invention must be unconditionally rejected, it by no means follows that the allegories upon which the personification relies should be rejected also. We all speak of "the roaring sea," which arouses the image of a raging animal; of "the lashing storm," which makes us think of a horse-driver, and so on. These are allegories of the intuition, not of the intellect, and are as current among primitive men as those of the latter are unfamiliar to them.

Hesiod tells us that chaos existed before the gods, who first brought order into the world. These are not the ideas of a maker of myths, but an attempt to interpret them, and to collect some scattered myths into a connected form. The dawn of day was reverenced because it chased away the night and its terrors; the

[1] **Max** Müller, *Int. Sc. of Rel.*, p. 295: "*Goa-b* is derived from a root, *goa*, to 'walk, to approach.' From it is formed *goa-b*, meaning, as a verb, 'coming he,' *i.e.* 'he comes,' and as a substantive, 'the comer,' 'the approaching one.' This *goab*, meaning originally 'the goer,' was used for 'knee.' But the same *goab* has a second meaning also, viz. 'the day,' and more particularly, 'the approaching day.' Thus *goara* means, 'the day dawns.' . . . The general meaning of *tsu* is 'sore,' but it can also mean 'bloody,' 'red-coloured.' . . . If there were any doubt as to *tsu* having had the meaning of 'red,' how could we account for *tsu-xu-b*, a name for 'night'? The verb *xu* means 'to go away,' *tsu-xu-b* therefore means 'tsu-gone-away-he.' Here the translation, 'the Sore one is gone away,' would have no meaning at all, while 'the Red one is gone away,' is a perfectly intelligible name of the night." Max Müller might have retained the translation "sore one," since the myth was based upon the meaning of "blood-red." *Tsui-goab*, "the wounded leg," was used of the rosy morning dawn. The first meaning, again, was, "he with the wounded leg," "the limping wanderer," and hence came the myth of reverence for the morning dawn.

god of thunder was reverenced because he smote the black and threatening clouds ; speaking in the abstract, the god of order was reverenced because he put an end to disorder.   If men loved savage and unbridled lawlessness more than a state of law, we should find chaos instead of Zeus.   But man now seeks to tread the path which leads from terror to peace, and in his poetry he therefore puts the terrors of nature first, in order to be able to grasp the blessedness of peace, rising victoriously above them, as the legitimate result of these occurrences. The power of reflecting upon myths marks a step in advance, and the myth that Zeus, the god of heaven, . conquered chaos, must be regarded as the fruit of such reflection, which therefore indicates the advance of culture.   It would, however, be irrational to assert that chaos had at one time been the ideal of man, and that it gave place to other ideals as culture increased.   The progress of civilization merely consists in the establishment of an ordered state of things; greater culture produces the higher intellectual power which enables men to give more individuality to their gods, and by a fusion of the myths which belong to different localities, a theogony is created.

When the myth tells us that Aphrodite yields to Demeter, and that Poseidon was vanquished by Dionysos and Apollo, we cannot accept Bachofen's interpretation that men passed from aphrodistic hetairism into demeterism, and hence into apollinism.   It simply represents the mutual relations of natural phenomena which are personified in the deities.   Demeter subdues Aphrodite, because it was by the labour of man that the rich, but still waste, morass was transformed into a fruitful field. This state of things can be defined by an abstract formula, because, not in this case only, but always and everywhere, man prefers a state of order to a state of disorder.   So it was, that when the human fancy grasped the analogy between the vegetation of the morass and the lawless coupling of animals, and between agriculture and marriage, the moral estimate of the sexual life of man found its fitting form in primitive poetry.

The ordinances of worship are, as we can readily understand, in accordance with the nature of the deity which is to be reverenced. It would, however, be a forced interpretation to infer from these what was the earlier condition of common life. It is difficult to regard the prostitution practised in the worship of Aphrodite as a survival of a licentious age; it is altogether impossible to accept the suggestion that it is a reminiscence of an age when prostitution was regarded as a duty, and marriage, or the restriction of sexual intercourse, was a crime for which expiation must be made.[1] Every Babylonian woman was bound, once in the course of her life, to seat herself at Aphrodite's altar and hold intercourse with strangers.[2] We cannot, however, see anything in this custom except a sacrifice and prayer offered to the generating power. In opposition to Lubbock, who accepts Bachofen's view of the prostitution in the temple and other unchaste customs of the same kind, McLennan offers the valid objection that these customs cannot be regarded as an expiation, because the communistic rights of the tribe were infringed by marriage; since we are never told that the bride and bridegroom belonged to the same group, or that the men to whom they were given up belonged to their group.[3]

We must now turn to the direct testimony which exists with respect to the conception of marriage and of its development. Great stress is laid on the fact that the conflict which arose among men for the possession of women must have been a constant source of danger to the rising community; in order, therefore, that its development might not be checked, it became necessary

---

[1] Bachofen, *Mutterrecht*, pp. xix., 13. Lubbock, *Orig. of Civ.*, p. 125.
[2] Herodotus, bk. i., chap. 199.
[3] McLennan, *Studies*, pp. 425-440.

not to give way to the feeling of jealousy, but to be satisfied with promiscuous intercourse. We have no doubt that disputes about women were of frequent occurrence, but when they occurred in the tribe itself, they were probably fought out between individuals, and they only extended to groups when an appeal was made for the aid of friends and dependents. They were therefore in many cases no source of danger to the tribe; the weaker man was vanquished, and in this, as in other matters, he submitted to the inevitable.[1] These disputes did not, therefore, lead to promiscuous intercourse, but to a change in the woman's master.[2]

Darwin and Maine likewise declare it to be improbable that sexual intercourse was ever perfectly free, since the passion of jealousy is so strong in the whole animal kingdom that it cannot be supposed to have been dormant in primitive communities of men.[3] We have already given innumerable instances of the way in which a man willingly surrenders his wife to others; his jealousy is only aroused when she acts independently in permitting the access of strange men without his will and knowledge. Hence the rule may be laid down that jealousy was only excited when the man was afraid that he should lose his wife. The more or less promiscuous intercourse which we have described above appears to have been developed at a subsequent period, with the growth of tribal feeling, and with the forms so

[1] As soon as one party has decidedly proved itself the strongest, the affair is set at rest, and they live as before, without offering each other any further molestation. Burchell, vol. i. p. 374 (Hottentots).

[2] *Hearn's Diary*, quoted by Sprengel, *Auswahl der besten Nachrichten*, vol. vii. p. 169. In Hudson's Bay the custom is general that men should compete for their wives, and the prize falls to the victor. A weakling can therefore seldom keep a wife who is desired by a stronger man. For whenever the wives of the stronger man are overladen with provisions or furs, he does not hesitate to rob another of his wife, in order that she may carry part of the burden.

[3] Darwin, *Descent*, vol. ii. p. 362. H. S. Maine, *Early Law*, pp. 206, 216.

closely connected with a strengthening sentiment for the clan and family. Promiscuous intercourse was a proof of friendly feeling, backed by the confidence that there was no danger of forfeiting the right of possession. The husband's rights were less protected when the tribal bond was weak, and this makes it improbable that he would neglect the self-defence prompted by jealousy. We do not believe that the structure of communities could have been permanent at a time when all men were inflamed by constant desire for all the women with whom they came in contact. The natural restriction of the sexual impulse, both with respect to its period and its objects, could alone make the formation of the tribe possible; and yet this impulse is at all times so powerful that it might be seriously imperilled if it were the sole basis of that connection between man and woman which we call marriage.

In all the communities with which we are acquainted, there is a distinction between the sexual relations and marriage, nor does it appear that a man wishes to isolate all the women with whom he holds sexual inter- course from time to time in the same way in which he isolates his wives. If marriage were decided by the sexual relations, it would be difficult to understand for what reasons marriages were contracted in those com- munities in which an altogether licentious sexual life is permitted to the unmarried. We are by no means with- out a clue to the motives for obtaining a woman as the absolute property of one individual. The man requires her to work for him and to keep his house.[1] This idea is manifested in many of the ceremonies with which marriage is contracted, such as that by which the bride prepares a meal for her future husband. The betrothal

---

[1] "In fact, when asked why they are anxious to obtain wives, their usual reply is, that they may get wood, water, and food for them, and carry whatever property they possess" (Eyre, vol. ii. p. 321). It would be easy to adduce many other instances.

of children, which occurs almost everywhere, excludes
the supposition that love, as such, is the essential point
of marriage. So far as we are concerned with human
existence, it must be assumed that this claim to the
woman's labour had its value. It is difficult to define
with clearness the border line between man and animals,
since, as we have already said, all forms of transition are
continuous. We are not now interested in the fleeting
phenomena of the transition period, but in the appearance of those communities which are unquestionably
human. We shall meet with no stronger distinction
between animal and human existence than the use of
fire. By its use the way was opened to man to obtain
better nourishment; it then became possible to become a
flesh-eating animal. The necessary preparation of food
which resulted from this fact caused a division of labour
between the sexes, which was unknown in the animal
world. The man then became the regular provider of
food, not, as in the case of animals, only occasionally,
and it was the woman's part to prepare the prey. In
this way she became indispensable to the man, not on
account of an impulse which is suddenly aroused and as
quickly disappears, but on account of a necessity which
endures as long as life itself, namely, the need of food.

Among nearly all primitive peoples, the wife and
young children are not allowed to eat with the father of
the family. The following is a picture of savage life.
When the man returns from hunting, he throws his game
to his wife, and when she has cooked it, he eats until he
is satisfied or surfeited, without caring what may be left
for his wife and children. He is, therefore, not oppressed
by the care of feeding his family. Yet if the game which
he brings home each day is so scanty as only to be enough
for himself, the wife must soon either forsake him or die of
hunger. She may, indeed, sustain life for a while with
roots and berries, or with the fish which she catches for herself, but this state of things can hardly endure. Under such

circumstances the man feels no desire to possess several wives; one is quite enough to do all that he requires.

As the boys grow up, their desire of obtaining a wife is awakened, so that they may not be inferior to their father, but be able to make use of their own game. It is, undoubtedly, impossible to give a description of the primitive mode of wooing a bride which is applicable to all cases. At one time he may have unexpectedly fallen in with a woman of a neighbouring tribe in the forest, and have carried her off by force; at another he, like the Italmanian, may have joined a family in which there was a marriageable woman, and have continued to live with them until something occurs which leads to a separation, and he then goes off with his wife.[1]

These primitive connections were unquestionably monogamous,[2] since the motive for wishing for a plurality of wives was absent. But they were also, although the fact has not been generally noticed, of an enduring nature. As long as the sexual impulse is regarded as the motive and bond of marriage, it would certainly be the more probable assumption that in primitive times separations were very frequent; but as soon as we admit that marriage had its origin in the necessity of establishing a household, a necessity which was felt by both parties, the matter assumes a different aspect. In primitive communities, indeed, the dissolution of marriage depends solely on the wishes of the couple; both man and wife are usually at liberty to put an end to the connection, and the man, at all events, can separate from his wife whenever he chooses. At the same time it appears that although they may and do separate at any moment, such cases are comparatively rare. In the case of the majority of primitive races, we are told that separations very seldom take place where there are children of the marriage; in other

<hr/>

[1] Lesseps, Forster, *Neue Beiträge*, vol. iv. p. 250. See Klemm, *Die Frauen*, vol. i. p. 50.

Spencer, *Princ. of Soc.*, p. 693.

races the marriage is only held to be complete after the birth of a child, and it also appears that the procreation of a child is enough to establish a marriage.[1] Among the Kafirs the parents do not use the milk of the cows which are destined to be the daughter's property until the child is born. At King's Mill, the dowry is not paid before the birth of a child. Among the Abipones, the young couple continue to live with the woman's parents until after the birth of the child. We have a like account of the tribes on Mount Sinai; a Badakschan wife, on the other hand, may not re-enter her parents' tent until her child is born. In the Marean tribe, the wife's relations are bound to pay ten cows to her husband after her first delivery, and these become his private property. The temporary marriages mentioned by Kulischer must be placed in the same category; connections are formed on trial, which are again dissolved if no children are born within a given interval.[2] Cook writes of the loose bonds of the Tahitians, that the man may on his side always make another choice, but if the woman with whom he lives becomes pregnant, he must put the child to death, and afterwards either continue his connection with its mother, or desert her. If, on the other hand, he accepts the child, and permits it to live, the pair are held to have entered into the marriage state, and they usually continue to live together.[3] Herrera states that a Mexican demands the woman who pleases him of her father, but it is not always easy for him to obtain her, since the father may reply that he only desires her in order to beget children. As soon as a son is born, the father requests the young man either to marry the girl

[1] Muskohgi (Bartram's *Reisen*, p. 487); Caribs (Gili, p. 346); Mugearn, Sahara (Forster, *Neue Beiträge*, vol. xiii. p. 162); Cucis (*Ibid.*, p. 248); Hottentots (Le Vaillant, *Voyage*, vol. ii. p. 42); Natches (Lambert, p. 316); Charruas (Azara, vol. ii. p. 23); Tehuelche (Falkner, p. 157).

[2] Alberti, p. 104. Wilkes, vol. v. p. 101. Dobrizhoffer, vol. ii. p. 257. Burkhardt, vol. i. p. 269. See Ploss, *Das Weib*, vol. ii. p. 509; Wood, p. 28; Munzinger, p. 211; *Archiv. für Anthropol.*, vol. xi.

[3] Cook, *Third Voyage*, vol. ii. p. 157.

or to leave her, and if he sends her back to her father, he holds no further intercourse with her.[1]

Among the Scottish Highlanders there was a custom of *handfasting;* that is, two chiefs agreed that the heir of the one should live with the daughter of the other as her husband for a year and a day; if at the end of that time, the woman had become a mother, or, at any rate, if she was pregnant, the marriage was regarded as valid, even if unblest by a priest; but if there was no sign of pregnancy the connection was dissolved, and each party was at liberty to enter into another connection, either by marriage or handfasting.[2]   Evidence of a similar process of thought may be traced in the Kafir custom of fining a man whose children were born out of wedlock; in Kunavan, the father is bound to support such children; in Assam, he is enjoined to marry the mother, and the Muskohgis dislike to see unmarried girls become mothers; although among all these peoples unchastity is not condemned.[3]

This process of thought leads us to infer that the conception of marriage is sharply distinguished from the mere relations of passion. We have seen that a man connects himself with a woman in order that she might keep house for him, and to this may be added a second motive, that of obtaining children.   His ownership of the children does not depend upon the fact that they were begotten by him, but upon the fact that he owns and supports their mother.   In the case of the Italmanians, the wooer attaches himself to the family of the woman of his choice without a word, and assists her in all her labours, and no one asks what his intentions are; only if she becomes pregnant by him, he has to provide for her and the child.   Bagos children are betrothed in their eighth year and live together after their betrothal, but

[1] Herrera, p. 363.   [2] Skene, p. 166.
[3] Klemm, *Die Frauen*, vol. i. p. 64. *Journal Asiat. Soc. of Bengal*, vol xiii. p. 1. Cunningham, p. 204. Cooper, p. 228. Jones, p. 69. Charlevoix, *Nouv. France*, vol. i. p. 195.

the wedding is only celebrated after it appears that the woman has lost her virginity.[1] Thus it is evident that marriage does not imply permanent relations of love, but relations in which the man is the provider and protector.

In primitive communities children are of great service to the father. They add to his importance, which increases with the number of dependants and friends he is able to gather round him. The child which was carried in its mother's bosom belongs to that mother's owner, and we can readily understand that he who wishes to possess the child will not willingly separate from its mother. We have already spoken of the local bond between mother and child, and have sought to estimate the significance of the conflicting interests of the mother's and father's family in deciding to which the child shall belong. The interest felt in children must have exerted its influence on the form of marriage, since it furnishes a motive for polygamy which is not included in the need of a housekeeper. A man will be actuated by this motive in proportion to the number of available women, and to his power of purchasing and providing for them. It follows from the nature of things, and we have so repeatedly dwelt upon the fact that we need not say more about it, that polygamy can never have been the normal condition of a tribe, since it would have involved the existence of twice as many women as men. Polygamy must necessarily have been restricted to the noblest, richest, and bravest members of the tribe. This would, however, furnish a fresh motive for polygamy, since it was held to be a sign of high position. We must, moreover, admit the difficulty of making any clear distinction between polygamy, and monogamy combined with permitted concubinage; concubines are always slaves, and subject to the true wife, but where there are several wives, it is also usual that one should be regarded as the chief. Only one way remains open for us—to

[1] Caillié, vol. i. p. 244.

24

ascertain whether the customary wedding ceremonies are as fully observed in the case of all the wives, or if they are in use at one special wedding.

As we have repeatedly said, the significance of these ceremonies consists in the illustration they afford of the different thoughts which pass through the minds of other members of the family at their complete or partial separation from one of the daughters, which always ensues from marriage. The mind is either occupied with the fact of separation, which furnishes the symbol of rape, or with the duties which the bride has to perform for the bridegroom, whence we have the symbol of preparing food; or, finally, prominence is given to the bridegroom's duties, and this gives us the symbol of a protector and provider, of the wooer's efficiency as a hunter, etc. These ceremonies afford a public and legal declaration that the persons in question are for the future to be regarded as married people; they create the centre of association round which all the ideas which refer to these persons will hence, orward gather. The force exerted on the consciousness by these ceremonies will be great in proportion to their solemnity, and so will be the difficulty of a divorce. Since the marriage was effected by a contract to which the relations and friends gave their assent, that assent will also be required for its dissolution.[1] The sanctity of marriage is thereby increased, and its sacramental meaning begins to be developed. Several reasons arise for only one observance of the complete ceremonial, and consequently the suppression of polygamy as a valid form of marriage followed.

Marriage does not merely affect the bride and bridegroom, but the relative position of their respective families, since they, and especially the kinsfolk of the bride, not only have a voice in the conditions of marriage, but also continue to feel an interest in the married pair. The

[1] Hunter, p. 253. Carver, p. 313. Bartrams, p. 487. Cooper, p. 101. Butler, p. 83.

female line was the strongest assertion of this interest, but there are many other confirmations of its existence. The Californian enjoins his daughter to maintain her conjugal fidelity, but he adds that she must come to him if she has any cause of complaint. The Hassanyah stipulates that if the bride performs her conjugal duties for four days of the week, she must be quite at liberty for the other three.[1] Polygamy may have obtained some support from the interest which the bride's family continued to take in her, since it may be important to the man to be connected with as many distinguished families as possible,[2] and many overtures may be made to a distinguished warrior that he should marry this or that woman. Yet this interest would generally exert a tendency opposed to polygamy, since it is impossible to avoid making a distinction between the several wives of a polygamous family.

Where the man goes to live with the family of his chosen bride in order to woo her, he can do so only on the occasion of his first marriage, and he must therefore endeavour to obtain his subsequent wives in other ways. This must also be the case when members of his family, and especially his father, do the wooing for him, since a man who is already married is too independent for the further continuance of such guardianship. The first wife would, as the first-comer, naturally try to assert her authority over those which come later; and since, moreover, she is usually the only one who has been wooed, we can easily understand that she would not be satisfied with any position but that of mistress of the house. And conversely, the growing dignity of the first wife must be included in the reasons which led to the neglect of ceremonial observances in the case of subsequent connections.[3] Thus the conditions react on each other.

---

[1] Duflos de Mofras, vol. ii. *Descr. Soc.*, No. 5, p. 8.

[2] Thus the Jakute has a wife in each place which he visits in his wanderings. Forster, *Neue Beiträge*, vol. v. Lesseps, p. 85.

[3] Hunter, p. 249. Lafitau, vol. i. p. 555. Von Martius, pp. 104, 108, 109. Burchell, vol. ii. p. 60. Orbigny, vol. iv. p. 226.

Since the eldest or noblest wife is commonly called the chief, a girl's family is unwilling to give her to a man who is already married. This is decidedly the case among the Malays; they refuse to give their daughters to a man of their own class if he is already married. If a man wishes to have more than one wife, he must have recourse to a lower class, and these women are only regarded as concubines, since the ceremonies are observed at the first marriage alone.[1] In Sumatra, polygamy occurs in Djudur marriages, but not in Semando marriages. In Nicaragua, it is forbidden, under pain of death, to make use of ceremonial observances in more than one marriage.[2] The fact that a Marauha who has brothers is forbidden to have more than one wife is probably due to another train of thought, namely, to that which, as we have already seen, leads to polyandry, or to the order that only one of several brothers may marry, which is the case amongst the Malabar Brahmans.[3]

In this way we find that polygamy is threatened on many sides, and since mutual jealousy is an additional obstacle,[4] the facts entitle us to infer that polygamy is based upon motives which only superficially affect the minds of men, instead of being deeply rooted in the conditions under which their social life is developed. Polygamy must disappear as soon as a growing development brings into play permanent motives and fundamental forces. Like primitive monogamy, and most cases of polyandry, polygamy is not a form of marriage which can be regarded as the expression of a marriage law; that is, it is not a form of marriage which is striv-

[1] Freycinet, vol. i. p. 639. Crawfurd, p. 77. Earl, p. 58. Forster and Sprengel, vol. ii. p. 63.

[2] Marsden, p. 270. Herrera, p. 320.

[3] Spix and Martius, vol. iii. p. 1185.

[4] The woman keeps a jealous watch upon her husband. Charruas, Azara, vol. ii. p. 23; New Zealand, Dieffenbach, vol. ii. p. 37; Marianas, Freycinet, vol. i. p. 477; Touaregs, Duveyrier, p. 340; Batlas, Forster and Sprengel, vol. i. p. 15; Moors, Caillié, vol. i. p. 12.

ing for the mastery, and which cannot tolerate other co-existent forms of marriage. On the other hand, the later monogamy, which arises from a distinct condemnation of polygamy, or from a secret aversion to it, is character-ized by self-assertion and seeks to exclude other forms of marriage. We must, however, be cautious about regarding isolated forms of polyandry, and that mono-gamy which is associated with concubinage, as special forms of marriage; these are only phenomena of mono-gamous marriage, which persist until the sexual side of marriage becomes of such importance that married people are pledged to purity of life.

Chastity was, as we have seen, at first imposed upon the married woman, because she was the property of the man, and might only transgress this rule with his know-ledge and permission. We have, therefore, two problems to solve—on the one side, how it was that men discon-tinued these licentious customs after marriage; and on the other, how the sexual freedom of unmarried women gradually gave place to more orderly conditions.

Licentious practices after marriage tend to disappear as soon as the idea of procreative conditions enter into the conception of fatherhood, so that those sons take the seniority which were begotten by the man himself, as we learn from the table of Hindu sonship given above. We have shown that although the idea of procreative conditions did not originally decide the conditions of fatherhood, yet it is well known that these conditions were of great importance to the child. Their greater effect was hindered, on the one side, by the slight reference which they bore to the local ordinances which were in all cases the basis of the ideas of property, and on the other, by the overpowering desire to obtain as many children as possible. Gradually, however, as the association of men's ideas was freed from the direct and material consideration of locality, and the desire to have many children gave place to a desire to have them as good as possible—that is, most capable of offering sacrifices for the dead—the begetting power of fatherhood had greater weight.

Even in primitive times, the character, or soul—the inward, mysterious being—of the father was supposed to decide the character of the child; and the more close and complicated the relations between father and son became, the more evident it seemed that they were one in their inmost being; the associations which were external, palpable, and local, gave place to the inner conceptions of thought. The joy excited by the excellent qualities of a child was first aroused in the breast of a primitive man when that child owed its being to himself, and its excellence was a proof of the excellence of its begetter, that is, of himself. I venture to assert that even now this idea plays the strongest part in what we call the voice of blood, and the difficulty of feeling the same affection for a foster child or step-child as for one who is really a man's own, is owing to the fact that all the tender feelings which the child, as such, arouses can only gather round the child which is really one with its father, and these feelings tend to increase in strength. The connecting idea is that we are ourselves the cause of the child's existence, while the idea of another father will always come in to estrange us from the child which is not our own. Vanity, a sentiment which is often condemned, yet not always blameworthy, finds sustenance in the most trivial occurrences of everyday life from the thought, "Here I trace myself; the child has inherited that tendency from me," etc. If the child was begotten by another, there is only room for vanity in the fact of its nurture. In life, however, there is no clearly defined limit between that which is acquired and that which is innate; whatever a young man is, is reckoned to be his own nature, and the necessary development of his innate qualities. The rude, material instincts of primitive man are not susceptible to the vanity of paternal feeling; but refined mental culture and the development of sentiment provide, in the strength and moral dignity of fatherhood, the bonds which knit together the begetter and his offspring.

The demand for chastity of life on the part of unmarried girls is not always combined with the same demand for chastity in a married woman. To give only one instance, the Ossetes keep a strict watch over unmarried women, while those who are married lead a very unchaste life. The early betrothals have more than anything else to do with the fact that only married women become mothers, and, according to the nature of things, the discountenance of motherhood in the unmarried which we have mentioned above is easily transformed into the discountenance of unchastity in the case of girls. Where such a feeling does not prevail, no attention is paid to the unchastity of the unmarried.

When limits are set to the sexual freedom of the woman, the man cannot retain his sexual liberty, since he is thus deprived of the means of unrestrained sexual intercourse. The condemnation which is directly incurred by the unchaste woman is consequently, although in an attenuated form, incurred by the unchaste man. He is not so much blamed for unchastity, as for having seduced the woman to violate her pledge of chastity, and also because he did not hesitate to overwhelm her with misery. The difficulty of estimating the precise bearing of facts, so as to make a just distribution of guilt and innocence, has up to this time blunted the edge of blame awarded to the men, and, owing to the weakness of human nature, it may perhaps continue to do so. It is so ordered by nature that the reasons for which, as we saw above, unchastity was originally condemned, only applies to the woman.

Although the sexual impulse must be reckoned among the strongest of human impulses, yet it cannot become an element of social development. On the other

hand, the begetting of children is of the highest importance to the social life of man. It is the woman, however,
who brings forth the fruits of love, and the formation of
legal ideas will, in accordance with external, material
facts, consequently be directed only against her. The
man's chastity is an object of the morality of nobler
minds. In human communities there will always be
two kinds of morality; the one displays the highest
development of refined consciousness, but it will never
suppress the other, the morality of the common herd; it
can only place before the latter an ideal to which it may
perhaps eventually attain; but not until ideal morality
has long been exalted into still higher spheres.

When, therefore, the limits set to the sexual freedom
of women had pointed out marriage as the province of
sexual life—at any rate, as far as legal ideas are concerned—a complete transformation of the conception of
sexual conditions took place, while the idea of marriage remained almost unchanged. As the characteristic moment
of conjugal life, the sexual instinct is associated with all
the feelings which are developed among men who live
together, and from which, setting the sexual relation
aside, marriage has so much to fear. Erotic enthusiasm
is closely allied to the sexual impulse, but conjugal love
is derived from another source. We have seen above
that no tender sentiment—at any rate, not what we call
love—inspired man with the desire to marry, and that
primitive marriage, as hard and dry as primitive life
itself, had its origin in the most concrete and prosaic
requirements. Even now it is an unworthy marriage in
which the erotic sentiment predominates in the relations
between the married pair.

The common household, in which each had a given
work to do, and the common interest of obtaining and
rearing children were the foundations upon which marriage was originally built. And from the sympathy which
inevitably springs from the interests which they have in

common, that love is developed which effects a perfect and stable marriage. In primitive communities, the paths of man and wife diverged too widely to further any rapid growth of mutual sympathy. There was a sharp distinction between their household tasks, and the point of contact consisted only in their children. The mother was more valued and esteemed than the mere wife. We have also seen that the mother acted as guardian to her child's share of the inheritance, and as such she had a voice in all which concerned the management of the property. This position was not maintained after the family organization was more firmly established, so that there was less risk of any disturbance in the order of succession. She then relied upon her character as mother of his children in order to assert her position with respect to her husband, unless she received support from her own family. Marriage as such did not entitle her to this support. We have seen the result of the family sentiment in the polyandry of the Nairs and the Semando marriage of the Malays, and the later forms of marriage among the ancient Romans are clear examples of the important influence exerted on marriage by the independent position of the wife. It would be unwise to advocate such an order of things for the future, since we have no reason to think that different consequences would ensue from it. It is incumbent upon us to declare that if legal independence, especially with respect to property, is given to both man and wife, a cause of separation is introduced into marriage which must sooner or later lead to the granting of divorce from arbitrary motives. And a divorce on such grounds degrades marriage into concubinage.

The movement in favour of the greater independence of women which is now so strong, has received its peculiar character from the fact that it is mainly upheld by unmarried women. It was owing to the division of labour which took place in the primitive family, and which assigned to the man the duty of providing sustenance, to the woman that of keeping the house, that the nurture and development of the two sexes were so different. The struggle for existence was chiefly fought by the man, and his mental faculties were consequently stimulated to greater exertions than those of the woman. Owing to the difference of the tasks imposed upon him in everyday life, the wife was deprived of the advantage of any common discussion of his plans and occupation. It was only in the tranquil life of the village communities, in the tilling of the soil, in the rearing of the cattle, which almost exclusively occupied their lives, that women could place themselves on a level with men. When social relations were complicated under the stimulus of the struggle for wealth, which was always becoming more intense, while the growing respect for law made the enjoyment of wealth more certain because it was more protected, the demands made upon the bread-winner increased, while the housewife's position was constantly becoming more easy and tranquil, and the intellectual difference between man and wife gradually increased.

At the same time, the great demand for the education of children could hardly be satisfied by the highest mental culture. The education of the children, as the central point of family life, became the strongest bond of union between man and wife. While the husband's mental capacity exceeded that of his wife, in consequence of his strenuous conflict for subsistence, yet this conflict seemed of less importance to the children in comparison with the woman's quiet influence at home. The female mind gained in this respect what it lost in the sphere of common life, and the slighter exertions demanded by the latter made it possible for the woman to foster the tender germs of childish understanding with constant watchfulness, deep intelligence, and refined feeling. In this way the mother became the noble and esteemed companion of the man, and the greater the duties entrusted to her, the greater became the love and sympathy which united them. The fugitive and erotic sexual impulse fails to harmonize with the nobility of this sentiment, since it is wanting alike in duration and power.

While, therefore, we see no reason to call a woman's lot contemptible, we readily admit that where the uniting and ennobling centre of the child's education is wanting, the inequality of the labour imposed respectively on man and wife may easily make itself felt in a manner disadvantageous to the woman. A childless marriage lacks the best and most natural condition of happiness, and hence it is plain that a childless couple finds it more difficult to attain to that state of content and equanimity without which happiness is unattainable, and which is most easily achieved when the object of our existence is understood to consist in living for others. The childless man is in danger of becoming so absorbed in labour which only concerns material support that he regards his wife as a mere housewife. There is still greater danger that the wife, dissatisfied with mere housewifery and unable to take interest in her husband's occupations, should abandon herself to the life of show to which the faithless mirror of society lends brilliancy and colour, while it holds frivolous sentiments in constant and changeful activity, only that it may stifle all the germs of nobler sentiments.

When we turn from the childless marriage to the unmarried woman, it must be admitted that the inferior development of the female intelligence, for which she is not to blame, has been of great disadvantage to her. Yet we are not disposed to concede that the unmarried woman, when thrown upon her own resources, can without reserve be placed on a level with the man who is a bread-winner. The man generally has to provide for the maintenance of a family, while the unmarried woman has only to provide for herself, and on that account the struggle for existence becomes more easy. Moreover, the human community takes account of sexes and not of individuals; modes of life are formed in accordance with general rules, and those only who conform to them come under the protection of the community. The unmarried, whether man or woman, are and must always remain the exception, and they must accept whatever is arranged for them. It would be impossible for their sakes to imperil all which the experience of a thousand years has shown to be the best means of promoting the development of those aspects of human life which are most productive of happiness. The movement for the emancipation of women has not always been mindful of this general law.

The individual may justly claim such an education as will enable him to be independent of others, if necessary, but the demand does not hold good when he forgets this saving clause. The movement has sprung from the moral sentiment that we are bound to make the lot of the unmarried as tolerable as possible, but it has also overstepped the sacred threshold of marriage, and has advocated the married woman's right to her independent earnings. This assumes a legal right to independent property—a rash assumption, which would be fatal to the bond of marriage. If it is thought that independence of character and the elevation of moral worth are only possible in association with material independence, the real factors of the civilized life of man are not duly estimated. Among primitive peoples, the independent ownership of property is the condition of an independent position. The service which a wife renders to her husband might be performed by any other woman, if her personality is not to be taken into account, and she can therefore only rely on the physical forces of possession. But as soon as the wife's personality comes into play, because her capacity to bring up her children depends upon it, the attempt to base her position upon her legal right to independent property again degrades her to the rudely material standpoint.

The lower classes are often in a position which is most in favour of the woman's material independence. But those of the upper classes who snatch at means which may perhaps effect a temporary improvement in the condition of the common people, act in a short-sighted way. It would be difficult to place a woman of the lower class in a different position from those of the higher, without checking the advance into higher grades, and creating a fatal distinction of classes. To give women a position which is only in harmony with rude conditions, while it threatens the cultured forms of society with destruction, would be irrational and even criminal. If it is supposed that the legal independence of women with respect to property would remain a dead letter in the cultured classes, we may soon have reason to repent of such an error. Independence with respect to the possession of property must inevitably lead to independence with respect to its acquisition, and a woman's life must become the copy, and not the completion of that of man. It must not be forgotten that in the hard struggle for existence to which the woman is now drawn, man has lost the tender refinement of feeling which enables a mother to be the cherisher of childhood. A woman cannot take a man's burden on her shoulders without succumbing to a like fate.

25

CHAPTER VIII.

THE FAMILY, THE CLAN, AND THE TRIBE. CONCLUSION.

Social and political meaning of the institution of the family—Patriarchal theory—Distinction between the family and the clan—The family dissolved into the clan—Conclusion.

WE have now ended our inquiries into the origin of the family, and will only make some brief observations on its bearing and importance with respect to the social and political forms of the State. The family has been shown to be an organization which was formed, not in order to make it easier to earn wealth, but for the better enjoyment of the wealth which was already earned; when once founded, it was maintained and carefully developed, because it offered external advantages to the man, inasmuch as his power was increased as his sons grew to manhood, and his daughters brought him into profitable relations with other families. It was an organization which was not self-contained, but depended on an external world, through which its internal ramifications were in many ways defined and modified. We have seen that the development of the family was not merely advanced by the relations which existed between its members; it was rather the different family relations of the two parents which paved the way for this development. There was, therefore, a constitutional weakness in the family, owing to the difficulty of carrying on an organization which is intended to include wider circles. We have also seen that the family may be enlarged into a family group, but that the structure derived from the family can only maintain its vitality within narrow limits, and that in the course of a few generations it falls again into a group of families.

The conception of the growth of the political community which until lately has been generally accepted, saw in the family the unit out of which the wider organization sprang. It was said that the State consisted either in an association of families, or in an expansion of one primitive family, and the two conceptions run into one. It was inevitable that the theories criticised above, which ignored the primitive existence of the family, sought to overthrow the so-called patriarchal theory, and to assign another origin to the State. This attempt has been very completely carried out by Morgan, and in many respects in a most able manner.

He asserts that the clan cannot have had its origin in the family, since the exogamy of the latter must have hindered its incorporation into a clan. The clan was homogeneous and of a permanent character, and as such, it was the natural basis of the social body. The monogamous family might assert its individuality and power in the clan, and especially in the community; but, nevertheless, the clan did not and could not admit it to be its elementary basis. The same may be said of the modern family and of the modern political community. While its individual character was established by its right of property, and its legal existence was recognized by the law, the family was in no sense the elementary unit of the State. The State was divided into districts, and these into villages, but these were not concerned with the family. The nation recognized its tribes, and the tribes their clans, but the clan, again, is not concerned with the family.[1] Without accepting the erroneous

[1] Morgan, *Anc. Soc.*, p. 227.

theory which Morgan advocates with respect to the family, we think that he is right on this point. The clan does not consist of families, but of individuals.

We must, however, observe, in opposition to Morgan, that the fact that the clan consists of individuals and not of families is not enough to show that it did not have its origin in the family. For if we assume that the clan was an enlarged family, there is no reason why it should not retain its character as a confederation of individuals, even in its enlarged form. There is nothing to show that the enlarged family must necessarily consist of separate families. We cannot, therefore, regard it as proved that the family and clan were of distinct origin, and if we ourselves nevertheless reject the patriarchal theories, we do so for other reasons.

The functions of the family are quite distinct from those of the clan; and the forms of government in both differ in so many respects that we cannot but regard them as fundamentally distinct. This assertion may be received with surprise, since the strongest support of the patriarchal theory has been sought in the assumption that the origin of the chiefship may be traced from the function of the paterfamilias.[1] In this case, however, the indefinite character of primitive ideas has been misleading, and also the intermixture of ideas of descent in the conceptions of primitive clans, and in the strong resemblance in the mode of development or power which is involved in the nature of things. We must go back to the beginnings of paternal authority, and of that of the chief, in order to form a clear idea of the matter.

In some of the later modifications of the tribe, the chief possesses the authority of the father of the family, and in some of the later modifications of the family the paternal authority is degraded to that of a chief; but they were originally distinct, and the primitive

[1] H. S Maine, *Early Law*, p. 239; *Anc. Law*, p. 136; *Early History*, p. 117.

organization of the clan is derived from that of the tribe, and not of the family.   The character both of the primitive clan and of the tribe is that of free association for mutual protection.   It was guided rather than ruled by the most capable and noblest man ; and it is doubtful whether the chief was elective, or if he ruled by mere force of character.   The clan differed from the tribe, as a part from the whole.   The tribe was the unit, with respect to other and hostile tribes, but the clan could only be opposed to other clans.   This opposition did not, however, constitute a complete distinction and thorough independence, such as the distinction between the tribes ; it was an opposition maintained within the sphere of relations which they had in common, and which united several clans into one tribe.

The family, on the other hand, is an altogether independent formation which flourishes within the tribe or clan.   The family is not a group which obeys a leader but a collection of individuals which belong to another man. The father of the family was originally regarded as its owner, and he appealed to the clan, as an association for mutual protection, when his rights as a husband and father were endangered.   Since, however, the family consisted of living men, it was an association of individuals who might perform the same offices as the clan.   And as soon as the family was enlarged into a group, it exceeded its own limits, and approached more nearly to the organization of the clan, in proportion to its endeavour to assume the same functions.   When we assert that the clan was not derived from the family, which may rather be said to have been swallowed up in the clan, the advocates of the patriarchal theory may reply that we have just shown how the family passed into the clan.   This, however, is an error.   The family does not develop into a clan ; the forces which give to it its special character, simply cease to work when the spheres within which they should work become too great, and other forces, quite independent of those which affect the family, in which several individuals make common cause, come into play. No clear conception can be formed of the clan and the family without finding that the difference between the two institutions is expressed in every particular. The clan exists on account of the struggle for existence, the family seeks for the enjoyment of that which they have obtained.

As means and aims are everywhere confounded with each other, so in this case the struggle for existence, at first only regarded as the means of obtaining enjoyment, actually claims the powers and thoughts of men to such an extent that it appears to be the end in view. Only where the means of multiplying, heightening, and ennobling such enjoyment are absent or scanty, man seems to live only for the conflict. In other words, in the infancy of human civilization, the clan may limit and interfere with the family on every side. But as soon as the struggle for existence becomes, not less arduous and severe, but more intellectual and according to rule, means and object again find their relative positions. Pleasure no longer consists in the rude and sensual gratification of the animal instinct, but in the moral aspect of a life which is lived with and for others. The best hours of a cultivated man are lived in the sacred place of home, to which he takes with him no thoughts of self-seeking gain. While the clan, which was of much higher importance in primitive life, has long since been destroyed by the organism of the State, the family is always becoming of fairer and more attractive aspect, since it is now exalted above all the motives which lead men to pass beyond its limits.

APPENDIX.

I. (p. 20). " The divisions were also named, in all clans but one, after the principal locality round which their components were clustered ; and, in that exception, all the divisions but one were named after some man of note " (Fison and Howitt, p. 225).

II. (p. 21). This statement is not altogether correct. There are tribal names for isolated hordes of natives, which are taken from the districts inhabited by them, or which are perhaps the tribal names of an earlier period, which were transferred to the district. I can, indeed, only ascertain the existence of such names among the blacks of Encounter Bay, but the main conditions are the same in the case of all these tribes.

III. (p. 21). " The whole body of the natives are divided into two classes—Erniung and Tem. . . . With respect to the divisions and sub-divisions of tribes, there exists so much intricacy, that it will be long before it can be understood. The classes Erniung and Tem are universal near the Sound ; but the distinctions are general, not tribal. Another division, almost as general, is into Moncalon and Torndirrup ; yet there are a few who are neither. These can scarcely be distin-guished as tribes, and are very much intermingled. The Moncalon, however, is more prevalent to the eastward of our establishment, and the Torndirrup to the westward. They intermarry, and have each again their subdivisional distinctions, some of which are peculiar, and some general ; of these are the Opperheip, Cambien, Mahnur, etc.

" What I, however, consider more correctly as tribes, are those which have a general name and a general district, although they may consist of Torndirrup or Moncalon, separate or commingled. These are, I believe, in some measure named by the kind of game or food found most abundant in the district. The inhabitants of the Sound and its immediate vicinity are called Meananger, probably derived from *mearn*, ' the red root ' . . . and *anger*, ' to eat,' " etc. (Scott Nind, *Journal of Royal Geographical Society*, pp. 37, 42, vol. i., 1832).

IV. (p. 22). " A certain mysterious connection exists between a family and its *kobong*, so that a member of the family will never kill an animal of the species, to which his *kobong* belongs, should he find it asleep; indeed he always kills it reluctantly, and never without affording it a chance to escape " (Grey, *Journals of Two Expeditions of Discovery in North-West and Western Australia*, vol. ii. p. 228).

V. (p. 23). " Yet it is not exclusively his, but others of his family have certain rights over it; so that it may be considered as partly belonging to the tribe. Thus all of them have a right to break down grass-trees, kill bandicoots, lizards, and other animals, and dig up roots; but the presence of the owner of the ground is considered necessary when they fire the country for game " (*Journal of the Royal Geographical Society*, 1832). " A man can dispose of or barter his lands toothers " (Nind, vol. i. p. 28). " If the males of a family become extinct the male children of the daughters inherit their grandfather's land " (Eyre, vol. ii. p. 297). Waitz, vol. vi. p. 792. Grey, vol. ii. p. 326.

VI. (p. 31). " It can be shown with a great degree of probability that the valley of the Columbia was the seedland of the Ganowánian family, from which issued, in past ages, successive streams of migrating bands, until both divisions of the continent were occupied. . . . It seems probable, therefore, that their ancestors possessed the organization into *gantes*, and that it fell into decay and finally disappeared." (Morgan, *Ancient Society*, p. 109).

VII. (p. 31). " Each Indian has his tamanuus, or spirit, which is selected by him at a very early age, and is generally the first object they see in going out to the woods that has animal life. Others create from their imagination one that has never met mortal eyes. The choice of a spirit, however insignificant it may appear, has a great influence on their after-life; for, by its supposed commands, they are directed to good or evil, as they conceive that a nonconformity to its wishes would involve them in a multitude of evils," etc. (Wilkes, *Narrative*, vol. v. p. 118).

VIII. (p. 32). " I have previously had occasion to refer to the fashion among the Indians of carving the faces of animals upon the ends of the large beams which support the roofs of their permanent lodges. In addition, it is very usual to find representations of the same animals painted over the front of the lodge. These crests, which are commonly adopted by all the tribes, consist of the whale, porpoise, eagle, raven, wolf, frog, etc. In connexion with them are some curious and interesting traits of the domestic and social life of the Indians. The relationship between persons of the same crest is considered to be nearer than that of the same tribe; members of the same tribe may, and do, marry—but those of the same crest are not, I believe, under any circumstances allowed to do so. A Whale, therefore, may not marry a Whale, nor a Frog a Frog. The child again always takes the crest of the mother; so that if the mother be a Wolf, all her children will be Wolves. As a rule, also, descent is traced from the mother, not from the father. . . . Whenever or wherever an Indian chooses to exhibit his crest, all individuals bearing the same family-figure are bound to do honour to it by casting property before it, in quantities proportionate to the rank and wealth of the giver" (R. C. Mayne, *Four Years in British Columbia*, p. 257).

IX. (p. 32). "As for clans, there are many, and there are secret badges. All that can be noticed, as to clans, is, that all those that use the same roots for medicines constitute a clan. These clans are secretly formed. It is through the great medicine-dance, that a man or a woman gets initiated into these clans. Although they all join in one general dance, still the use, properties, etc., of the medicine that each clan uses is kept entirely secret from each other." "The medicine-sack of a deceased Indian is given to the nearest relation; this is the only mark of identity. This sack is kept for two or three generations sometimes; but the names of the owners have no affinity to the former family. So all is kept in the memory; and when that fails, all is gone " (H. R. Schoolcraft, *History, Condition, and Prospects of the Indian Tribes of the United States*, vol. ii. p. 171; vol. iii. p. 242).

X. (p. 33). "Every separate body of Indians is divided into bands or tribes; which band or tribe forms a little community with the nation to which it belongs. As the nation has some particular symbol by which it is distinguished from others, so each tribe has a badge from which it is denominated, as that of the eagle, the panther, the tiger, the buffalo, etc. One band of the Naudowissies (Sioux) is represented by a snake, another a tortoise, a third a squirrel, a fourth a wolf, and a fifth a buffalo. Throughout every nation they particularize themselves in the same manner, and the meanest person among them will remember his lineal descent, and distinguish himself by his respective family " (J. Carver, *Travels through Interior Parts of North America*, edit. 1796, p. 164).

XI. (p. 33). "The most influential men in a tribe are the medicine-men" (R. C. Mayne, *Four Years in British Columbia*, p. 260). He speaks further on of other corporations, " which the whites term ' medicine-men ' . . . I may mention that each party has some characteristics peculiar to itself; but, in a more general sense, their divisions are but three—viz. those who eat human bodies, the dog-eaters, and those who have no custom of the kind " (*Ibid.*, p. 286). " I think it is generally supposed that these parties I have described are the doctors of the Red Indians, because their proceedings are called ' medicine work,' and they ' medicine-men;' but I find that the medical profession is altogether a distinct business, and the doctors a distinct class" (*Ibid.*, p. 289).

XII. (p. 34). "In bygone days, these small tribes contended against each other with great bitterness; but by the beneficial influence exercised over them by the Hudson Bay Company, they have been induced to live together in peace, and intermarriages among the tribes now frequently take place ; in which case, it is said, that the husband almost invariably joins the tribe to which his wife belongs, under the idea that among her own family and friends she will be better able to provide for her husband's and children's wants. This also may proceed from the fact of the influence the women possess; for they always assume much authority in their tribe, and are held in high respect. They have charge of the lodge and the stores, and their consent is necessary for the use of them ; for after coming into their possession, these articles are considered the women's own. . . . Polygamy was and is still practised. Where this is the case, or where many families reside in the same lodge, each family or wife has a separate fire " (C. Wilkes, *United States Exploring Expedition*, vol. iv. pp. 447, 457.

XIII. (p. 35). " All that was obtained in hunting belonged of right to the wife's hut, during the first year of marriage. In the ensuing years, the man was compelled to share with his wife, whether she remained in the village or accompanied her husband " (Lafitau, vol. i. p. 579). . . . " As to their (the Seneca-Iroquois') family system when occupying the old long-houses, it is probable that some one clan predominated, the woman taking in husbands, however, from the other clans, and sometimes, for a novelty, some of their sons bringing in their young wives, until they felt brave enough to leave their mothers. Usually, the female portion ruled the house, and were doubtless clannish enough about it. The stores were in common; but woe to the luckless husband or lover who was too shiftless to do his share of the providing. No matter how many children or whatever goods he might have in the house, he might at any time be ordered to pick up his blanket and badge ; and after such orders it would not be healthful for him to attempt to disobey. The house would be too hot for him ; and unless saved by the intercession of some aunt or grandmother, he must retire to his own clan; or, as was often done, go and start a matrimonial alliance in some other." (Comp. Hunter, p. 254.) " The women were the great power among the clans, as everywhere else. They did not hesitate, when occasion required, ' to knock off the horns,' as it was technically called, from the head of a chief, and send him back to the ranks of the warriors. The original nomination of the chiefs also always rested with them " (Morgan, *Ancient Society*, p. 455, App.). " When a young man (among the Knisteneaux) marries, he immediately goes to live with the father and mother of his wife, who treat him, nevertheless, as a perfect stranger, till after the birth of his first child ; he then attaches himself more to them than his own parents ; and his wife no longer gives him any other denomination than that of the father of her child " (A. Mackenzie, *Voyages from Montreal*, p. xcvii.).

XIV. (p. 49). " Names among the Mapuchés were originally given to designate certain traits of character and appearance, or they were derived from particular circumstances, as Eupuelev, ' the winner of two races,' Katri-Lao, ' the red lion ; ' but the necessity of distinguishing

families caused the latter part of the father's name to be transmitted to
the children, with some modifications to distinguish individuals. Thus
arose such family names as Iluens, 'heaven.' Still, though surnames
are becoming more fixed with time, national usage makes it optional
with parents to transmit their own names to their own children or not;
and frequently in a large family no two will be found whose names
bear any relation to each other" (E. R. Smith, *The Araucanians*,
p. 262).

XV. (p. 49). "The idol commanded the priest to tell them that
the chiefs should be divided, each according to his race and family,
that the land should be distributed in four, so arranged that the house
built for the idol's resting-place should be in the middle. . . . When
this separation had been effected, the idol ordained that the gods
should be divided among them, and that each quarter should mark
out other special quarters, in which these gods should be worshipped;
thus each main district included several lesser districts, according to
the number of the gods they were ordered to adore, and these were
termed Calpultutco, that is, district gods " (Antoine d'Herrera, *Histoire
Générale des Voyages et Conquestes*, vol. iii. p. 156).

XVI. (p. 51). "As soon as the change was made (from the female
to the male line) the father would take the place held previously by
the mother, and he, instead of she, would be regarded as the parent.
Hence, on the birth of a child, the father would naturally be very
careful what he did, and what he ate, for fear the child should be
injured. Thus, I believe, arises the curious custom of the Couvade "
(Sir J. Lubbock, *The Origin of Civilisation*, p. 154).

XVII. (p. 52). "The child is no sooner born, washed, and placed in
its bed of cotton, than the women go to work as if nothing had happened
to them, and the husband begins to complain, as if his wife's sufferings
had been transferred to him. He is tended with care; a bed is pre-
pared for him in the upper part of the hut, where he is visited as a sick
man, and is dieted in a manner which might cure the luxurious livers
in France of gout and other maladies. After he has been thus dieted
for forty days, the relations and nearest friends are invited to visit him,
and before sitting down to feast they lacerate the poor wretch's skin
with the teeth of the agouti, and draw blood from all parts of his body,
so that from having fancied himself to be ill, he often becomes so in
reality" (Du Tertre, vol. ii. p. 373). Spix and Martius, *Puris and
Coroados* (vol. i. p. 381): "After a birth has taken place, man and wife
are strictly dieted, and abstain for a given time from the flesh of certain
animals;" *Marauhas* (vol. iii. p. 1185): "After the birth, the mother
washes the child in warm water, lies in a hammock for three weeks,
and may, as well as her husband, only eat gruel of mandioc flour;"
Passés (vol. iii. p. 1186): "The lying-in woman is kept in the dark for
a month after delivery, and may only eat mandioc; this is also the case
with the husband, who dyes himself black, and remains in the hammock

for the same period," *Arayeus* (vol. iii. p. 1190): "The lying-in woman may only eat turtle and fish, not mammals, and the same diet is prescribed to her husband, until the infant can sit up;" *Culinos* (vol. iii. p. 1189): "While the lying-in woman is dieted, the husband eats absolutely nothing for the first five days;" *Cauixanas* (vol. iii. p. 1217): "They, like many other tribes, fast during the time that the wives are in childbed;" *Mundrucus* (vol. iii. p. 1339): "Like the Caribs and the ancient Tupis, the Mundrucu men are accustomed to spend several weeks in the hammock after the birth of a child, and to be nursed by its mother, and to receive neighbourly visits; the child is ascribed to the father only, and the mother's part is compared to that of the soil which receives the seed." Venegas, in speaking of the Californians, says (vol. i. p. 82): "He in the meantime lay in his cave, or stretched at full length under a tree, affecting to be extremely weak and ill; and this farce continued for three or four days." Charlevoix says of the Guaranis (vol. i. p. 295): "As soon as a woman is brought to bed, her husband fasts rigorously for a fortnight, and does not hunt or associate with other men. These Indians are convinced that the child's life depends on the faithful conformity with this usage." Dobrizhoffer says of the Abipones (vol. ii. p. 275): "They comply with this custom with the greater care and readiness because they believe that the father's rest and abstinence have an extraordinary effect on the well-being of new-born infants, and is, indeed, absolutely necessary for them. . . . For they are quite convinced that any unseemly act on the father's part would injuriously affect the child, on account of the sympathetic tie which naturally subsists between them, so that in the event of the child's death, the women all blame the self-indulgence of the father, and find fault with this or that act."

XVIII. (p. 56). "A chief of more than ordinary ability arises and, subduing all his less powerful neighbours, founds a kingdom, which he governs more or less wisely till he dies. His successor not having the talents of the conqueror cannot retain the dominion, and some of the abler under-chiefs set up for themselves, and, in a few years, the remembrance only of the Empire remains. This, which may be considered as the normal state of African society, gives rise to frequent and desolating wars" (D. Livingstone, *Narrative of an Expedition to the Zambesi*, p. 199).

XIX. (p. 57). "The different Bechuana tribes are named after certain animals, showing probably that in former times they were addicted to animal-worship, like the ancient Egyptians. The term Bakatla means 'they of the monkey;' Bakuena, 'they of the alligator;' Batlápi, 'they of the fish;' each tribe having a superstitious dread of the animal after which it is called. They also use the word 'bina,' to dance, in reference to the custom of thus naming themselves, so that, when you wish to ascertain what tribe they belong to, you say, 'What do you dance?' It would seem as if that had been a part of the worship of old. A tribe never eats the animal which is its namesake, using the term 'ila,' hate or dread, in reference to killing it " (D. Livingstone, *Missionary Travels and Researches in South Africa*, p. 13).

XX. (p. 65). "To this his sister—who was also his principal wife—objected, being prompted by the instinct of self-preservation. . . . So, gathering together a strong party, she attempted to surprise and kill him in his hut at night. Rumours of these intentions having reached him, he escaped with a mere handful of men, and his sister proclaimed a brother the ruler in his stead " (V. L. Cameron, *Across Africa*, vol. ii. p. 149).

XXI. (p. 66). "When a young (Banyai) man takes a liking to a girl of another village, and the parents have no objection to the match, he is obliged to sit with his knees in a bent position, as putting out his feet towards the old lady would give her great offence. If he becomes tired of living in this state of vassalage, and wishes to return to his own family, he is obliged to leave all his children behind—they belong to the wife. This is only a more stringent enforcement of the law of 'buying wives' (of allowing) an entire transference of her and her seed into another family. If nothing is given, the family from which she has come can claim the children as part of itself; the payment is made to sever this bond. From the temptations placed here before my men, I have no doubt that some prefer to have their daughters married in that way, as it leads to the increase of their own village " (D. Livingstone, *Missionary Travels and Researches in South Africa*, p. 622).

XXII. (p. 79). "The men are so gallant as to have made over all property to the women, who in return are most industrious, weaving, spinning, brewing, planting, sowing, in a word, doing all work not above their strength. When a woman dies the family property goes to her daughters, and when a man marries he lives with his wife's mother, obeying her and his wife " (Hodgson, *Journal of the Asiatic Society of Bengal*, vol. xviii. p. 707).

XXIII. (p. 81). "The worst feature in the manners of the people . . . is the laxity of their marriages; indeed, divorce is so frequent that their unions can hardly be honoured with the name of marriage. The husband does not take his bride to his own home, but enters her household, or visits it occasionally; he seems merely entertained to continue the family to which his wife belongs " (H. Yule, *Journal of the Asiatic Society of Bengal*, vol. xiii. p. 624).

XXIV. (p. 86). "Among the Limboos (India), a tribe near Darjeeling, the boys become the property of the father on his paying the mother a small sum of money, when the child is named and enters his father's tribe: girls remain with the mother, and belong to her tribe " (Sir J. Lubbock, *The Origin of Civilisation*, p. 149).

XXV. (p. 86). "When it has previously been agreed on, the bride is carried home. The poverty of the bridegroom, however, often renders it necessary for him to remain with his wife's father for some

26

time, to whom he becomes as a slave, until by his work he has redeemed this bride. . . . Children born out of wedlock, and the produce of Limboos and Lepchas, are called 'Koosaba.' Boys become the property of the father on his paying the mother a small sum of money, when the child is named and enters his father's tribe; girls remain with the mother, and belong to her tribe" (A. Campbell, *Journal of Asiatic Society of Bengal*, vol. ix. p. 603).

XXVI. (p. 91). "When rule is strictly followed, the successor of a deceased king is his next brother; failing whom, his own eldest son, or the eldest son of his eldest brother, fills his place. But the rank of mothers and other circumstances often cause a deviation from the rule. I am acquainted with several cases in which the elder brother has yielded his right to the younger, with a reservation as to power and tribute, becoming a man second only to the king " (T. Williams and J. Calvert, *Fiji and the Fijians*, 1870, p. 18).

XXVII. (p. 91). "Rank is hereditary, descending through the female; an arrangement which arises from the great number of wives allowed to a leading chief, among whom is found the widest difference of grade " (*Ibid.*, p. 26).

XXVIII. (p. 92). "Vasus cannot be considered apart from the civil polity of the group, forming as they do one of its integral parts, and supplying the high-pressure power of Fijian despotism. In grasping at dominant influence the chiefs have created a power which, ever and anon, turns round and gripes them with no gentle hand. . . . It is not, however, in his private capacity, but as acting under the direction of the king, that the Vasu's agency tends greatly to modify the political machinery of Fiji, inasmuch as the sovereign employs the Vasu's influence, and shares much of the property thereby acquired. Great Vasus are also Vasus to great places, and, when they visit these at their superior's command, they have a numerous retinue and increased authority. A public reception and great feasts are given them by the inhabitants of the place which they visit; and they return home laden with property, most of which, as tribute, is handed over to the king " (*Ibid.*, p. 28).

XXIX. (p. 98). "Where the common stock (of land) is limited, it is necessary to make rules for its enjoyment; but where all can have as much as they want, no one would take the trouble to make rules, and no one would submit to them if made " (J. D. Mayne, *Treatise on Hindu Law and Usage*, p. 198).

XXX. (p. 103). "On the principle of participation already stated, any bandhu who offers a cake to his maternal ancestors will be the sapinda, not only of those ancestors, but of all other persons whose duty it was to offer cakes to the same ancestors. But the maternal ancestors of A may be the paternal or maternal ancestors of B; and in this manner A will be the bandhu, or bhinna-gotra sapinda of B, both being under an obligation to offer to the same persons " (*Ibid.*, p. 478).

XXXI. (p. 129). " As among other gregarious animals, the unions of the sexes were probably, in the earliest times, loose, transitory, and in some degree promiscuous. . . . The men of a group must either have quarrelled about their women and separated, splitting the horde into hostile sections; or, in the spirit of indifference, indulged in savage promiscuity. That quarrels and divisions were of frequent occurrence cannot be doubted. These were the first wars for women, and they went to form the habits which established exogamy. And whether quarrels arose or not, we are led to contemplate groups indulging in a promiscuity more or less general. The quarrels must have been between sections of the hordes rather than between individuals. No individual at that stage could well carry off a woman, isolate himself, and found a family " (J. F. McLennan, *Studies in Ancient History*, pp. 131–134).

XXXII. (p. 131). "The earliest human groups can have had no idea of kinship. We do not mean to say that there ever was a time when men were not bound together by a feeling of kindred. The filial and fraternal affections may be instinctive. They are obviously independent of any theory of kinship, its origin, or consequences; they are distinct from the perception of the unity of blood upon which kinship depends; and they may have existed long before kinship became an object of thought. . . . Previously individuals had been affiliated not to persons, but to some group. The new idea of blood-relationship would more readily demonstrate the group to be composed of kindred than it would evolve a special system of blood-ties between certain of the individuals in the group. The members of a group would now have become brethren. . . . Once a man has perceived the fact of consanguinity in the simplest case, namely, that he has his mother's blood in his veins, he may quickly see that he is of the same blood with her other children. . . . If the paternity of a child were usually as indisputable as the maternity, we might expect to find kinship through males acknowledged soon after kinship through females " (*Ibid.*, pp. 121–124).

XXXIII. (p. 131). "Heterogeneity as a statical force can only have come into play when a system of kinship led the hordes to look on the children of their foreign women as belonging to the stocks of their mothers; that is, when the sentiments which grew up with the system of kinship became so strong as to overmaster the old filiation to the group (and its stock) of the children born within it " (*Ibid.*, p. 184).

XXXIV. (p. 146). "What is to be done, that the name of the aged or dead man be not put out on earth nor his lot placed in jeopardy beyond the grave ? Now all ancient opinion, religious or legal, is strongly influenced by analogies, and the child born through the Niyoga is very like a real son. Like a real son, he is born of the wife or the widow; and, though he has not in him the blood of the husband, he has in him the blood of the husband's race. The blood of the individual cannot be continued, but the blood of the household flows on.

It seems to me very natural for an ancient authority on customary law to hold that under such circumstances the family was properly continued " (Sir H. S. Maine, *Early Custom and Law*, p. 107).

XXXV. (p. 154). "Sekeletu, according to the system of the Bechuanas, became possessor of his father's wives, and adopted two of them; the children by these women are, however, in these cases, termed brothers. When an elder brother dies, the same thing occurs in respect of his wives; the brother next in age takes them, as among the Jews, and the children that may be born of those women he calls his brothers also. He thus raises up seed to his departed relative " (D. Livingstone, *Missionary Travels in South Africa*, p. 185).

XXXVI. (p. 180). "All the tribes possessing the Turanian system describe their kindred by the same formula, when asked in what manner one person was related to another. A descriptive system precisely like the Aryan always existed both with the Turanian and the Malayan, not as a system of consanguinity, for they had a permanent system, but as a means of tracing relationships " (L. H. Morgan, *Ancient Society*, p. 484).

XXXVII. (p. 251). "Because the moon was called *measurer*, or even carpenter, it does not follow that the earliest framers of languages saw no difference between a moon and a man. Primitive men, no doubt, had their own ideas, very different from our own; but do not let us suppose for one moment that they were idiots, and that, because they saw some similarity between their own acts and the acts of rivers, mountains, the moon, the sun, and the sky, and because they called them by names expressive of those acts, they therefore saw no difference between a man, called a measurer, and the moon, called a measurer, between a real mother, and a river called the mother " (Max Müller, *Origin of Religion*, p. 193). "Our problem is not, how language came to personify, but how it succeeded in dispersonifying " (*Ibid.*, p. 194). "We see how what is called the irrational element in mythology is due to a misunderstanding of ancient names, and how, so far from real events being turned into myths, myths have there, too, been turned into accounts of real events " (Max Müller, *Introduction to the Science of Religion*, p. 280).

TABLE I. (Morgan, *Systems of Consanguinity.* Table III., No. 16. Malay.)

The person addressed.	The man speaks.		The woman speaks.	
	Elder.	Younger.	Elder.	Younger.
Brother	käï'-kŭ-ä-ä'-nä	käï'-käï'-nä	käï'-kŭ-nä'-nä	käï'-kŭ-nä-nä
Sister	käï'-kŭ-wä-heé-nä	käï'-kŭ-wä-heé-nä	käï'-kŭ-ä-ä'-nä	käï'-kŭ-nä-nä
Step-brother	käï'-kŭ'-ä-ä'-nä	käï'-käï'-nä	kŭ-nä'-nä	käï-luï-nä
Step-sister	käï'-kŭ'-wä-beé-nä	käï'-kŭ-wä-beé-nä	kŭ-ä-ä'-nä	
Son of father's brother	käï'-kŭ-ä-nä	käï'-kŭ-nä	käï'-kŭ-ä-nä	käï'-kŭ-nä
Daughter of the same	käï'-kŭ-wä-heé-nä	do.	do.	do.
Son of father's sister	käï'-kŭ-ä-nä	käï'-käï'-nä	käï'-kŭ-ä-ä-nä	käï'-käï'-nä
Daughter of the same	käï'-kŭ-a-ä-nä	käï'-käï-nä	käï'-kŭ-nä-nä	käï'-käï'-nä
Son of mother's brother	käï'-kŭ-wä-hᵉ-é-nä	käï'-kŭ-wä-heé-nä	käï'-kŭ a-ä'-nä	käï'-kŭ-nä'-nä
Daughter of the same	käï'-kŭ-nä'-nä	käï'-käï'-nä	käï'-kŭ-nä'-nä	käï'-kŭ-nä'-nä
Son of mother's sister	käï'-kŭ-w ä-heé-nä		käï'-kŭ-ä-ä'-nä	käï'-käï-nä
Daughter of the same	käï'-kŭ-ä-ä'-nä	käï'-käï-nä		
Son of father's brother's son	käï'-kŭ-ä-ä'-nä			
Son of father's father's sister's daughter	käï'-kŭ-wä-heé-nä			
Daughter of the same	käï'-kŭ-ä-ä-nä			
Son of mother's brother's son				
Daughter of the same				
Daughter of mother's mother's sister's daughter				
Son of father's father's father's brother's son's son			käï'-kŭ-wä-beé-nä	käï'-käï-na
Daughter of father's father's father's sister's daughter's daughter	käï'-kŭ'-ä-ä'-nä		käï'-kŭ-wä-bcé-nä	
Son of mother's mother's mother's brother's son's son	maŭ-käï'-kŭ-wä-beé-nä			
Daughter of mother's mother's mother's sister's daughter's daughter	käï'-kŭ'-ä-ä-nä		käï'-kŭ'-ä-ä-nä	
Brothers		maŭ-käï'-kⁱu-ä-ä'-nä	käï'-kŭ-ä-ä-nä	
Sisters		maŭ-käï'-kⁱu-wä-bcé-nä	maŭ-käï'-käï'-nä	
			maŭ-käï'-ku-wä-beé-nä	

TABLE II. (Morgan, *Systems of Consanguinity.* Table III, No. 16. Malay.)

Kana oder waheena = Husband or wife. Also used for—	Kaikoaka = Brother-in-law or sister-in-law. Also used for—	Punalua = Intimate companion. Also used for—
Husband's brother Sister's husband (woman speaks) Wife's sister Brother's wife (man speaks) Wife of wife's brother Husband of husband's sister (?) Wife of father's brother's son „ „ sister's son „ mother's brother's son „ „ sister's son	Wife's brother Sister's husband (man speaks) Husband's sister Brother's wife (woman speaks) Father's brother's daughter's husband „ sister's daughter's husband Mother's brother's daughter's husband „ sister's daughter's husband	Wife's sister's husband Husband's brother's wife

TABLE III. (Morgan, *Systems of Consanguinity*. Table II, Nos. 1, 7, 2, 59, 26, 27.)

The person addressed.	Seneca (1).	Two-Mountains (7).	Cayuga (2).	Micmac (59).	Minnitaree (26).	Crow (27).
Father's brother............	Father	Father	Father	Father	Father	Father
Father's sister............	Aunt	Mother	Mother	Aunt	Grandmother	Mother
Mother's brother............	Uncle	Uncle	Uncle	Uncle	Elder brother	Elder brother
Mother sister	Mother	Mother	Mother	Mother	Mother	Mother
Father's father's brother's son	Father	Father	Father	Father	Father	Father
Father's father's sister's daughter	Uncle	Mother	Mother	Aunt	Not given.	Not given.
Mother's mother's brother's son......	Mother	Uncle	Uncle	Uncle		
Mother's mother's sister's daughter......	Father	Mother	Mother	Mother		
Son of father's father's brother's son......	Uncle	Father	Father	Father		
Son of mother's mother's mother's brother's son......	Mother	Mother	Mother	Aunt		
Daughter of father's father's father's mother's sister's daughter............	Aunt	Mother	Mother	Uncle	Aunt	Brother's sister
	Uncle	Uncle	Uncle		Uncle	Father, mother
	Mother	Mother	Mother	Mother	Mother	
All the children—						
(1) of the father's brother	Brother's sister	Brother's sister	Brother's sister	Brother's sister	Brother's sister	Brother's sister
(2) of the father's sister............	Male and female cousin	Brother's sister	Male and female cousin	Father's Brother's sister	Father, mother	Father, mother
(3) of the mother's brother............	Male and female cousin	Brother's sister	Male and female cousin	Brother's sister	Son, daughter	Son, daughter
(4) of the mother's sister............	Brother's sister	Brother's sister	Brother's sister	Brother's sister	Brother's sister	Brother's sister

THE VERY DIFFERENT NAMES IN USE AMONG THE OTHER GANOWÁNIANS.

Children of father's brother............	Brother's sister, Nos. 7, 56, 59, 63, 64, 66-68		Man speaks: Step-brother, step-sister, Nos. 41-5, 61, 62 — Woman speaks: Step-brother, Nos. 41, 61, 62. Step-sister, Nos. 41, 44, 45, 61, 62			
Children of father's sister............	Brothers and sisters, Nos. 7, 56, 59, 63, 64, 66, 67, (68), 69, (71)		Man speaks: Nephew } Nos. 18-24, 46-52, 54, 55 — Woman speaks: Child }		Father and aunt, Nos. (28), 32, 33 — Father and grandmother, Nos. (28), 30, 31 — Father and mother, Nos. 26, 27, 29, 34, 35	
Children of mother's brother............	Brothers and sisters, Nos. 7, 56, 59, 63, 64, 66-68		Uncle and mother, Nos. 18-24, 46-52, 54, 55	Step-brothers and sisters, Nos. 61, 62	Children, Nos. 26-35 — Woman speaks { Grandson, No. 30 — Grandchild, No. 31	
Children of mother's sister	Man speaks: Brothers and sisters, Nos. 7, 56, 59, 63, 64, 66-68		Step-brothers and sisters, Nos. 41-45, 61, 62	Nos. 41, 60-63		
Father's sister............	Woman speaks: Mother, Nos. 2-5, 7, 27, 34-36, 62 (and 25, woman speaks)				Grandmother, Nos. 26, 30, 31	Stepmother, Nos. 61
Mother's brother	Elder brother, Nos. 26, 27.					

TABLE V. (Morgan, *Systems*. Table II, Nos. 1, 8. Table III, No. 1. Appendix to Table III.)

The person addressed.	Seneca (II. 1).	Wyandote (II. 8).	Tamil (III. 1).	Fiji (Appendix). Man speaks	Fiji (Appendix). Woman speaks
Brother's wife	Sister-in-law	Sister-in-law	Female cousin	My staff	Female cousin
Sister's husband	Brother-in-law	Brother-in-law	Male cousin	Male cousin	My staff
Husband's brother	Brother-in-law	Brother-in-law	Male cousin	—	Husband
Husband's sister	Sister-in-law	Sister-in-law	Sister-in-law	Male cousin	Female cousin
Wife's brother	Brother-in-law	Brother-in-law	Male cousin	My staff	—
Wife's sister	Sister-in-law	Sister-in-law	Female cousin	—	—
Husband's brother's wife	Not akin	Not akin	Sister-in-law (?)	Sister	A woman
Wife's brother's wife	Not akin	Not akin	Sister	—	—
Husband's sister's husband	Not akin	Not akin	Brother-in-law (?)	A man	Male cousin
Wife's sister's husband	Not akin	Not akin	Brother-in-law (?)	My staff	—
Father's brother's son's wife	Sister-in-law	Sister-in-law	Female cousin	Male cousin	Female cousin
Father's brother's daughter's husband	Brother-in-law	Brother-in-law	Male cousin	My staff	My staff
Father's sister's son's wife	Sister-in-law	Sister-in-law	Younger sister	Sister	A woman
Father's sister's daughter's husband	Brother-in-law	Brother-in-law	Brother	A man	Brother
Mother's brother's son's wife	Sister-in-law	Sister-in-law	Younger sister	Sister	A woman
Mother's brother's daughter's husband	Brother-in-law	Brother-in-law	Brother	A man	Brother
Mother's sister's son's wife	Sister-in-law	Sister-in-law	Female cousin	Not given	Not given
Mother's sister's daughter's husband	Brother-in-law	Brother-in-law	Male cousin	Not given	Not given
Father's brother's wife	Step-mother	Aunt	Mother	Mother	Mother
Father's sister's husband	Step-father	Uncle	Uncle	Uncle	Uncle
Mother's brother's wife	Step-aunt	Aunt	Aunt	Aunt	Aunt
Mother's sister's husband	Step-father	Uncle	Father	Father	Father

The person addressed.	Seneca (II. 1).	Wyandote (II. 8).	Tamil (III. 1). Man speaks.	Tamil (III. 1). Woman speaks.	Fiji. Man speaks	Fiji. Woman speaks
Brother's son's wife	Step-daughter	Step-daughter	Niece	Daughter	Niece	Daughter
Brother's daughter's husband	Step-son	Step-son	Nephew	Son	Nephew	Son
Sister's son's wife	Daughter-in-law	Daughter-in-law	Daughter	Niece	Daughter	Niece
Sister's daughter's husband	Son-in-law	Son-in-law	Son	Son	Son	Nephew

TABLE IV. (Morgan, S

The person addressed.	Seneca (1).		Tuscarora (6).		Two
	Man speaks	Woman speaks.	Man speaks.	Woman speaks.	Ma spea
Brother's children	Children	Nephews	Child	Nephews	
Sister's children	Nephews	Children	Nephews	Child	Neph
Children of father's brother's son....	Children	Nephews	Child	Nephews	
Children of father's brother's daughter	Nephews	Children	Nephews	Child	Neph
Children of father's sister's son	Children	Nephews	Child		
Children of father's sister's daughter	Nephews	Children	Nephews	Child	Neph
Children of mother's brother's son ..	Children	Nephews	Child		
Children of mother's brother's daughter	Nephews	Children	Nephews	Child	Neph
Children of mother's sister's son.....	Children	Nephews	Child		
Children of mother's sister's daughter	Nephews	Children	Nephews	Child	Neph
Children of father's father's brother's son's son	Children	Nephews	Child	Nephews	
Children of father's father's sister's daughter's daughter............	Nephews	Children	Nephews	Child	Neph
Children of mother's mother's brother's son's son	Children	Nephews	Child		
Children of mother's mother's sister's daughter's daughter	Nephews	Children	Nephews	Child	Neph
Children of father's father's father's brother's son's son's son	Children	Not given	Child	Not given	Child
Children of father's father's father's sister's daughter's daughter's daughter	Nephews	Children	Nephews		Neph
Children of mother's mother's mother's brother's son's son's son	Children (?)		Child (?)		C
Children of mother's mother's mother's sister's daughter's daughter's daughter................. ..	Not given	Children	Not given	Child	Not g

wo Mountains (7).		Cayuga (2).		Micmac (59).		Minnitaree (26)	
Man speaks.	Woman speaks.	Man speaks.	Woman speaks.	Man speaks.	Woman speaks.	Man speaks.	Woma
Children		Children		Children	Nephews	Children	Gra
ephews	Children	Nephews	Children	Nephews	Children	Younger brothers and sisters	Ch
Children		Children		Children	Nephews	Children	Gra
ephews	Children	Nephews	Children	Nephews	Children	Younger brothers and sisters	Ch
Children		Children		Children	Nephews	{ Not given	
ephews	Children	Nephews	Children	Nephews	Children		
Children		Children		Children	Nephews	Grandchild	
ephews	Children	Nephews	Children	Nephews	Children	Grandchild	
Children		Children		Children	Nephews	Children	Gra
ephews	Children	Nephews	Children	Nephews	Children	Younger brothers and sisters	Ch
Children		Children		Children	Nephews		
ephews	Children	Children		Nephews	Children		
Children		Children		Children	Nephews		
ephews	Children	Nephews	Children	Nephews	Children	Not given	
hildren	} Not given	Children	} Not given	Children	} Not given		
ephews		Nephews		Nephews			
Children (?)		Children (?)		Children (?)			
ot given	Children	Not given	Children	Not given	Children		

peaks.	Crow (27).		Tamil (III. 1).		Fiji (Appendix).	
	Man speaks.	Woman speaks.	Man speaks	Woman speaks.	Man speaks.	Woman speaks.
ild	Children		Children	Nephews	Children	Nephews
en	Younger brothers and sisters	Children	Nephews	Children	Nephews	Children
ild	Children		Children	Nephews	Children	Nephews
en	Younger brothers and sisters	Children	Nephews	Children	Nephews	Children
	(?)	(?)	Nephews	Children	Nephews	Children
	(?)	(?)	Children	Nephews	Children	Nephews
	Grandchild		Nephews	Children	Nephews	Children
	Grandchild		Children	Nephews	Children	Nephews
hild	Children		Children	Nephews	Children	Nephews
en	Younger brothers and sisters	Children	Nephews	Children	Nephews	Children
			Children	Nephews	Not given	
			Nphws. (?)	Chldrn. (?)	Nephews	
			Nephews	Children	Not given	Not given
	Not given	Not given	Nephews	Children	Nephews	
			Children	Not given	Not given	
			Nephews			
			Nephews (?)			
			Children	Nephews	Nephews	

TABLE VI. (Morgan, *Systems of Consanguinity.* As in our Table V.)

The person addressed.	Seneca (II. 1).	Wyandot (II. 8).	Tamil (III. 1).	Fiji (Appendix).
Father's brother	Father	Father	Father	Father
Father's sister	Aunt	Aunt	Aunt	Aunt
Mother's brother	Uncle	Uncle	Uncle	Uncle
Mother's sister	Mother	Mother	Mother	Mother
Son of father's father's brother	Father	Father	Father	Not given
Daughter of the same	Not given	Not given	Not given	
Son of mother's brother	Uncle	Uncle	Uncle	Uncle
Son of father's father's sister	Not given	Not given	Not given	Mother
Daughter of the same	Aunt	Aunt	Mother	Uncle
Son of mother's mother's sister	Not given	Not given	Not given	Mother
Daughter of the same	Mother	Mother	Mother	
Son of father's father's father's brother's son ...	Father	Father	Father	Not given
Daughter of father's father's father's sister's daughter ...	Aunt	Aunt	Mother	
Son of mother's mother's mother's brother's son ...	Uncle	Uncle	Uncle	
Daughter of mother's mother's mother's sister's daughter ...	Mother	Mother	Mother	Mother

TABLE VII. (Morgan, *Systems of Consanguinity.* As in our Table V.)

The person addressed.	Seneca (II. 1).	Wyandot (II. 8).	Tamil (III. 1).	Fiji (Appendix).
Son of father's brother	Brother	Brother	Brother	Brother
Daughter of the same	Sister	Sister	Sister	Sister
Son of mother's brother	Cousin (male)	Cousin (male)	Cousin (male)	Cousin (male)
Daughter of the same	Cousin (female)	Cousin (female)	Cousin (female)	Cousin (female)
Son of mother's sister	Brother	Brother	Brother	Brother
Daughter of the same	Sister	Sister	Sister	Sister
Son of father's sister	Cousin (male)	Cousin (male)	Cousin (male)	Cousin (male)
Daughter of the same	Cousin (female)	Cousin (female)	Cousin (female)	Cousin (female)
Son of father's father's brother's son	Brother } (man speaks) / Cousin	Brother } (man speaks) / Cousin	Brother } (man speaks) / Brother	Not given
Son of father's father's sister's daughter	Cousin } (man speaks)	Cousin } (man speaks)	Brother } (man speaks)	Brother
Daughter of the same	Cousin (female) } (man speaks)	Cousin } (man speaks)	Sister	Sister } Children of father's sister's son = cousins
Son of mother's mother's brother's son	Cousin (male)	Cousin (male)	Cousin (male)	Not given
Daughter of the same	Cousin (female)	Cousin (female)	Cousin (female)	Children of mother's mother's sister's son = cousins
Daughter of mother's mother's sister's daughter	Sister (woman speaks)	Sister (woman speaks)	Sister (woman speaks)	Sister (woman speaks)
Elder son of father's father's brother's son's son	Brother } (man speaks) / Cousin (female) } (man speaks)	Brother } (man speaks) / Cousin } (man speaks)	Brother } (man speaks) / Sister	Not given
Daughter of father's father's sister's daughter's daughter	Cousin (male)	Cousin (male)	Cousin (male)	
Son of mother's mother's brother's son's son	Cousin (male)	Cousin (male)	Cousin (male)	Not given
Elder daughter of mother's mother's sister's daughter's daughter	Sister (woman speaks)	Sister (woman speaks)	Sister (woman speaks)	Sister (woman speaks)

TABLE VIII. (Morgan, *Systems of Consanguinity*. Appendix to Table III, Table II, No. 80.)

The person addressed.	Tongan (Appendix).	Northumberland Inlet Eskimo (II. 80).
Father's brother	Tamai = Father	Ukka = Uncle
Father's sister	Mehekitaga = Aunt	Achunga = Aunt
Mother's brother	Tuajina = Uncle	Angugga = Uncle
Mother's sister	Fae = Mother	Aigugga = Aunt
Children of father's father's brother	Not given	
Son of father's father's sister	Tamai = Father	
Daughter of the same	Tamai = Father	No designation
Children of mother's mother's brother	Not given	
Son of mother's mother's sister	Fae = Mother	
Daughter of the same	Fae = Mother	
Daughter of mother's mother's sister's daughter	Fae = Mother	
Children of father's sister	Tama amehekitaga = Cousin	(Man speaks) Illunga / Illoa = Cousin; (Woman speaks) Illunga / Illna = Cousin
Son of mother's brother	Tama tuajina = Cousin	Illna / Illoa = Cousin
Daughter of the same	No special name.	Illunga / Illoa = Cousin
All others of this generation	Taokete = Elder brother; Teliua = Younger brother	Illunga / Illoa = Cousin

(If he be the son of my father's elder brother, he is *taokete*; if of my father's younger brother, *tehina*; and this irrespective of our respective ages.)

TABLE IX. (Morgan, *Systems of Consanguinity*. Appendix to Table III, Table II, No. 80, Table III, No. 13.)

The person addressed.	Tongan (Appendix).		Eskimo (II. 80).	Karens (III. 13).	
	Man speaks.	Woman speaks.		Man speaks.	Woman speaks.
Brother's children	Son and daughter	Nephew and niece	Nephew and niece	Nephew and niece	Nephew and niece
Sister's children	Nephew and niece	Boy and girl			
Children of father's brother's son	Son and daughter	Boy and girl			
" father's brother's daughter...	Nephew and niece	Boy and girl			
" father's sister's son.........	No specific term. I being a male, my son will be "*tuatchina*" with my father's sister's son's son				
" mother's brother's son.........	Son and daughter	Boy and girl			
" mother's brother's daughter....	Nephew and niece	Boy and girl			
" mother's sister's son.........	Not given	Not given	No designation	No designation	No designation
" mother's sister's daughter....	Son and daughter	Boy and girl			
" father's brother's son's son...	Not given				
" father's father's sister's daughter's daughter...	Son and daughter	Not given			
" mother's mother's sister's daughter's daughter...	Son and daughter				
" mother's mother's sister's daughter's daughter	Son and daughter				

Appendix to Table IX.   (Morgan, *Systems of Consanguinity.*   Table III, Nos. 1 and 13.)

The person addressed.	Tamil (III. 13). Man speaks.	Tamil (III. 13). Woman speaks.	Karen (III. 13). Man speaks.	Karen (III. 13). Woman speaks.
Brother's children	Son and daughter	Nephew and niece	Nephew and niece	Nephew and niece
Wife of the same	{ Son-in-law, nephew / Daughter-in-law, niece	Son, daughter	Nephew, niece	Nephew, niece
Sister's children	Nephew, niece	Son, daughter	Nephew, niece	Nephew, niece
Wife of the same	Son, daughter	{ Son-in-law, nephew / Daughter-in-law, niece	Nephew, niece	Nephew, niece
Father's brother	Grandfather	Grandfather	Uncle	Uncle
Wife of the same	Mother	Mother	Aunt	Aunt
Mother's sister	Grandmother	Grandmother	Aunt	Aunt
Husband of the same	Father	Father	Uncle	Uncle
Children of father's brother	Brother, sister	Brother, sister	Cousin	Cousin
Husbands of the same	{ Brother-in-law, cousin / Sister-in-law, cousin	Brother in-law, cousin / Sister-in-law, cousin	Cousin	Cousin
Children of mother's sister	Brother, sister	Brother, sister	Cousin	Cousin
Husbands of the same	{ Brother-in-law, cousin / Sister-in-law, cousin	Brother-in-law, cousin / Sister-in-law, cousin	Cousin	Cousin
Husbands of children of father's sister	Brother, sister	Brother, sister	Cousin	Cousin
Wife of children of mother's brother	Brother, sister	Brother, sister	Cousin	Cousin
Children of father's brother's son	Son, daughter	Nephew, niece	Nephew, niece	Nephew, niece
,, mother's sister's son	Son, daughter	Nephew, niece	Nephew, niece	Nephew, niece
,, mother's brother's daughter	Son, daughter	Nephew, niece	Nephew, niece	Nephew, niece
,, father's brother's daughter	Nephew, niece	Son, daughter	Nephew, niece	Nephew, niece
,, father's sister's son	Nephew, niece	Son, daughter	Nephew, niece	Nephew, niece
,, mother's sister's daughter	Nephew, niece	Son, daughter	Nephew, niece	Nephew, niece
,, mother's brother's son	Nephew, niece	Son, daughter	Nephew, niece	Nephew, niece

TABLE X. (Morgan, *Systems of Consanguinity.* Table III., Nos. 4, 8.)

The person addressed.	Hindu (III. 4).	Chinese (III. 8).
Father's brother	Paternal uncle	Wote poh } fu = my senior } father shuh } = my junior } father
Father's sister	Paternal aunt	Wote kumo = my aunt, mother, or Kuseay = my aunt, elder sister
Mother's brother	Maternal uncle	Wote mokew = my maternal uncle
Mother's sister	Maternal aunt	Wote ta } cma = my great } mother leaon } = my little } mother
Son of father's father's brother	Paternal uncle	Wote tang poh (?) = senior father of the *tang*-class
Daughter of father's father's sister	Paternal aunt	Wote peaon ku = aunt-mother of the *peaon*-class
Son of mother's mother's brother	Maternal uncle	Wote peaon poh (?) = senior father of the *peaon*-class
Daughter of mother's mother's sister	Maternal aunt	Wote peaon e = aunt of the *peaon*-class
Son of father's brother	Brother, or brother through paternal uncle	Wote tang heungte = brother of the *tang*-class
Daughter of the same	Sister, or sister through paternal uncle	Wote tang tsze mei = sister of the *tang*-class
Son of father's sister	Brother, or brother through paternal aunt	Wote peaon heungte = brother of the *peaon*-class
Daughter of the same	Sister, or sister through paternal aunt	Wote peaon tsze mei = sister of the *peaon*-class
Son of mother's brother	Brother, or brother through maternal uncle	Wote peaon heungte = brother of the *peaon*-class
Daughter of the same	Sister, or sister through maternal uncle	Wote peaon tsze mei = sister of the *peaon*-class
Son of mother's sister	Brother, or brother through maternal aunt	Wote epeaon heungte = brother of the *epeaon*-class
Daughter of the same	Sister, or sister through paternal aunt	Wote epeaon tsze mei = sister of the *epeaon*-class
Brother's son		{(Man speaks) Wote chih ir {(Woman speaks) Wote wae chih } = son of the *chih*-class
Brother's daughter	Nephew and niece	{(Man speaks) Wote chih neu {(Woman speaks) Wote wae chih neu } = daughter of the *chih*-class
Sister's son		{(Man speaks) Wote wae-ung {(Woman speaks) Wote esung } = son of the *waesung-esung*-class
Sister's daughter		{(Man speaks) Wote waesung neu {(Woman speaks) Wote esung neu } = daughter of the *waesung-esung*-class

TABLE X. (continued.)

The person addressed.	Hindu (III. 4).	Chinese (III. 8).
Son of father's brother's son............		Wote tang chih = Son v. d. *tang*-class, *chih*-branch
Daughter of the same............		Wote tang chih nen = Daughter v. d. *tang*-class, *chih*-branch
Son of father's brother's daughter......		Wote tang waesung = Son v. d. *tang*-class, *waesung*-branch
Daughter of the same............		Wote tang waesung neu = Daughter v. d. *tang*-class, *waesung*-branch
Son of father's sister's son............		Wote peaon chih = Son v. d. *peaon*-class, *chih* branch
Daughter of the same............		Wote peaon chih neu = Daughter v.d. *peaon*-class, *chih*-branch
Son of father's sister's daughter......		Wote peaon chih waesung = Son v. d. *peaon*-class, *chih-waesung*-branch
Daughter of the same............		Wote peaon chih waesung neu = Daugh. v. d. *p.eaon*-cl., *chih-waesung*-branch
Son of mother's brother's son............		Wote peaon chih = Son v. d. *peaon*-class, *chih*-branch
Daughter of the same............		Wote peaon chih neu = Daughter v. d. *peaon*-class, *chih*-branch
Son of mother's brother's daughter......		Wote wae peaon chih = Son v. d. *waepeaon*-class
Daughter of the same............		Wote wae peaon chih neu = Son v. d. *waepeaon*-class
Son of mother's sister's son		Wote epeaon chih = Son v. d. *epeaon*-class, *chih*-branch
Daughter of mother's sister's daughter		Wote epeaon chih neu = Daughter v. d. *epeaon*-class, *chih*-branch
Daughter of the same............	Nephew and niece	Wote wae epeaon chih = Son v. d. *epeaon*-class, *wae*-branch
Children of father's father's brother's son's son............		Wote wae epeaon chih neu = Daughter v. d. *epeaon*-class, *wae*-branch
" father's father's sister's daughter's daughter............		Wote tang chih (neu) = Children v. d. *tang*-class
" mother's mother's brother's son's son............		Wote peaon chih (neu) = Children v. d. *peaon*-class
" mother's mother's sister's daughter's daughter............		Wote peaon chih (neu) = Children v. d. *peaon*-class
Son of father's father's father's brother's son's son's son............		Wote peaon chih (neu) = Children v. d. *peaon*-class
Daughter of father's father's father's sister's daughter's daughter's daughter		Wote tang peaon chih (heung te) (man speaks)
Son of mother's mother's mother's brother's son's son's son............		Wote peaon chih neu (man speaks)
Daughter of mother's mother's mother's sister's daughter's daughter's daughter.		Wote peaon chih Wote epeaon chih neu (woman speaks)

LIST OF THE WORKS TO WHICH
REFERENCE IS MADE.

———◦◦◦———

Abhandlungen für die Kunde des Morgenlandes. Vols. 1-6. Leipzig, 1859-81.

Adair, J. The History of the American Indians. London, 1775.

Alberti, C. L. Die Kaffern auf der Südküste von Afrika. Gotha, 1815.

Amira, K. v. Erbenfolge und Verwandtschaftsgliederung nach den altniederdeutschen Rechten. München, 1874.

Andersson, C. Lake Ngami. 2nd ed. London, 1856.

Archiv für Anthropologie.

Asiatic Researches, or, Transactions of the Society instituted in Bengal.

Azara, F. de. Voyages dans l'Amérique Méridionale, 1781-1801, publ. par C. A. Walkenaer. 4 vols. Paris, 1809.

Bachofen, J. J. Das Mutterrecht. Stuttgart, 1861.

—— Antiquarische Briefe. Vols. 1, 2. Strassburg, 1880-86.

Baegert, J. Account of the Aboriginal Inhabitants of the Californian Peninsula. Smithsonian Institution's Annual Report, 1863-64.

Bagehot, W. Der Ursprung der Nationen. (Internat. wissenschaftl. Bibliothek, 4 vols.) Leipzig, 1874.

Baker, S. White. Albert Nyanza, the Great Basin of the Nile, and Explorations of the Nile Sources. 2 vols. London, 1866.

Barth, H. Reisen und Entdeckungen in Nord- und Central-Afrika. 5 vols. Gotha, 1857.

Bartram, J. Observations on the Inhabitants made in his Travels from Pensilvania to Onondago, etc. London, 1751.

Bartrams, J. Reisen durch Nord- und Süd-Carolina, Georgia und Ost-Florida. Aus d. Engl. von Zimmermann. Berlin, 1793.

Bastholm, C. Historiske Efterretninger til Kundskab om Mennesket i dets vilde og raa Tilstand. 4 vols. Kjöbenhavn, 1803.

Bastian, A. Die Völker des östlichen Asien. 6 vols. Leipzig und Jena, 1866-71.

Bastian, A. Ein Besuch in San-Salvador, der Hauptstadt des Königreichs Congo. Ein Beitrag zur Mythologie und Psychologie. Bremen, 1859.
—— Die heilige Sage der Polynesier. Leipzig, 1881.
Bickmore, A. S. Travels in the East Indian Archipelago. London, 1868.
Bodenstedt, F. Die Völker des Kaukasus. Frankfurt a. M., 1848.
Bolin, V. Familjen. Studier. Helsingfors, 1864.
Bonwick, J. Daily Life and Origin of the Tasmanians. London, 1870.
Bosman, G. Voyage de Guinée. Utrecht, 1705.
Brett, W. H. The Indian Tribes of Guinea, their Condition and Habits. London, 1868.
Brown. Die Eingeborenen Australiens. Petermann's Mittheilungen, 1856.
Brown, W. New Zealand and its Aborigines. London, 1845.
Bruce, J. v. Kinnaird. Reise zur Entdeckung der Quellen des Nils. 1768-73. Uebers. von Volkmann, mit Vorr. u. Anm. von Fr. Blumenbach. 5 vols. Leipzig, 1790-91.
Buchanan, F. A Journey from Madras through the Countries of Mysore, Canara, and Malabar. 3 vols. 1807.
Buller, J. Forty Years in New Zealand. London, 1878.
Bulletin de la Société de Géographie.
Burchell, W. J. Travels in the Interior of Southern Africa. 2 vols. London, 1822.
Burkhardt, J. L. Notes on the Bedouins and Wahabys. 2 vols. London, 1831.
Burnes, A. Travels into Bokhara. 3 vols. London, 1834.
Burton, Sir R. F. Personal Narrative of a Pilgrimage to El-Medineh and Meccah. 3 vols. London, 1856.
—— First Footsteps in East Africa; or, An Exploration of Harar. London, 1855.
—— Zanzibar, City, Island, and Coast. 2 vols. London, 1872.
Butler, J. Travels and Adventures in the Province of Assam. London, 1855.
Byron, J. Narrative of the Great Distresses suffered by Himself and his Companions on the Coast of Patagonia. 1740-1746. London, 1768.

Caillié, R. Journal d'un voyage à Tembucto et à Jenné. 1824-28. 3 vols. Paris, 1830.
Cameron, V. L. Across Africa. 2 vols. London, 1877.
Caro, J. Geschichte Polens. Vols. 2-4. Gotha, 1863-75.
Carver, J. Reisen durch die inneren Gegenden von Nord-Amerika in den Jahren 1766-68. Aus d. Engl. Hamburg, 1780.
Casalis, E. Études sur la langue Séchuana. Paris, 1841.
Chamisso, A. v. Reise um die Welt mit der Romanzoft'schen Entdeckungsexpedition. 2 vols. 2nd ed. Leipzig, 1842.
Charlevoix, F. X. Histoire et description de la nouvelle France. 6 vols. Paris, 1744.
—— Histoire du Paraguay. 6 vols. Paris, 1757.
Chasseaud, G. W. The Druses of the Lebanon. London, 1855.
Chiruël. Dictionnaire historique des institutions, mœurs et coûtumes de la France. 2 vols. Paris, 1855.

Cook, J. A Voyage to the Pacific Ocean. J. King. 2nd ed. London, 1785.

Cooper, T. The Mishmee Hills. London, 1873.

Crawfurd, J. History of the Indian Archipelago. 3 vols. Edinburgh, 1820.

—— Journal of an Embassy from the Governor-General of India to the Court of Ava. London, 1829.

Cruz, L. de la. Descripcion de la naturaleza de los Terrenos. P. de Angelis' Coleccion de Obras y Documentos relatives a la historia antiqua y moderna de las Provincias del Rio de la Plata. Vol. I. Buenos-Ayres, 1836.

Cuhn. Sammlung von merkwürdigen Reisen in das Innere von Afrika. 3 vols. Leipzig, 1790.

Curious Observations upon the Manners, Customs, etc., of Several Nations of Asia, Africa, and America, translated from the French of Lambert. London.

Dan, P. Histoire de Barbarie et des Corsaires. 2nd ed. Paris, 1649.

Dargun, L. Mutterrecht und Raubehe und ihre Reste im Germanischen Recht und Leben. Gierke, vol. XVI. Breslau, 1883.

Darwin, C. Descent of Man. 2 vols. London, 1871.

—— Reise omkring Jorden, overs. af Hansen og Jörgensen. Kjöbenhavn, 1876.

Decken, C. C. von der. Reisen in Ost-Afrika, 1859-61, bearb. von Kersten. 4 vols. Leipzig, 1869-73 (79).

Degrandpré, L. Voyage à la côte occidentale d'Afrique. 1786-87. 2 vols. Paris, IX. (1801).

—— Voyage dans l'Inde et au Bengale. 2 vols. Paris, 1801.

Denham, Clapperton, and Oudney. Narrative of Travels and Discoveries in Northern and Central Africa. London, 1826.

Dieffenbach, E. Travels in New Zealand. 2 vols. London, 1843.

Diez, H. F. Denkwürdigkeiten von Asien. 2 vols. Berlin u. Halle, 1811-15.

Dobrizhoffer, M. Geschichte der Abiponer. Aus d. Lat. von Kreil. 3 vols. Wien, 1783.

Dubois, J. A. Mœurs, institutions, et cérémonies des peuples de l'Inde. 2 vols. Paris, 1825.

Du Chaillu, P. A Journey to Ashango-Land. London, 1867.

—— Rejse i mellem Afriku. 2 vols Kjöbenhavn, 1862.

Dujlos de Mofras. Exploration du territoire de l'Oregon, etc. 2 vols. Paris, 1844.

Du Halde. Description de la Chine et de la Tartarie Chin. 4 vols. La Haye, 1736.

Duveyrier, H. Les Touaregs du Nord. Paris, 1864.

Earl, G. W. The Eastern Seas. London, 1837.

Ellis, W. Polynesian Researches. 4 vols. London, 1831.

Elphinstone, M. The History of India. 2 vols. London, 1841.

Engelmann, J. Die Leibeigenschaft in Russland. Leipzig, 1884.

d'Envieu, F. Les origines de la terre et de l'homme après la Bible et après la science. Paris, 1873.

Es, van den. De jure familiarum apud Athenienses. Leyden, 1864.

Ewers, J. Das älteste Recht der Russen in seiner geschichtl. Entwickelung. Dorpat, 1826.

Eyre, E. J. Journals of Expeditions of Discovery into Central Australia, and Overland from Adelaide to King George's Sound in 1840–1. 2 vols. London, 1845.

Falkner, T. Beschreibung von Patagonien. Aus d. Engl. Gotha, 1775.

Fison, L., and *A. W. Howitt.* Kamilaroi and Kurnai. Melbourne and Sydney, 1880.

Forbes, F. E. Dahomey and the Dahomans. 2 vols. London, 1851.

—— Eleven Years in Ceylon. 2 vols. 2nd ed. London, 1841.

—— Five Years in China, 1842–1847. London, 1848.

Forster, G. Reise um die Welt.

Forster und *Sprengel.* Beiträge zur Länder- und Völkerkunde. 14 vols. Leipzig, 1782–90.

—— Neue Beiträge. 13 vols. Leipzig, 1790–93.

Fortnightly Review. 1877.

Freeman, E. A. Comparative Politics. London, 1873.

Freycinet, L. de. Voyage autour du monde. Historique. 2 vols. Paris, 1827–39.

Garcilasso de la Vega. Histoire des Yncas, rois du Perou. Trad. de l'Espagnol. Amsterdam, 1737.

Gibelin. Études sur le droit civil des Hindous. 2 vols. Paris, 1846.

Gili, P. S. Nachrichten vom Lande Guiana. Uebers. von Sprengel. Hamburg, 1785.

Gill, W. W. Myths and Songs from the Southern Pacific. London, 1876.

Giraud-Teulon, A. Les origines du mariage et de la famille. Genève et Paris, 1884.

Gönner, N. T. Ueber die Succession in successiven Weiberlehen nach erloschenem Mannsstamme. Landshut, 1808.

Gray, J. H. China. A History of the Laws, Manners, and Customs of the People. 2 vols. London, 1878.

Grey, Sir G. Journals of Two Expeditions of Discovery in North-West and West Australia during the Years 1837–39. 2 vols. London, 1841.

Grimm, J. Deutsche Rechtsalterthümer. 3 vols. Göttingen, 1881.

Grose, J. H. A Voyage to the East-Indies. 2 vols. 2nd ed. London, 1766.

Grote, G. Geschichte Griechenlands. 6 vols. 2nd ed. Berlin, 1880.

Guinnard, A. Trois ans d'esclavage chez les Patagons. 2nd ed. Paris, 1864.

Guizot, M. Cours d'histoire moderne. Histoire de la civilisation en France. 5 vols. Paris, 1829–32.

Gumilla, J. Histoire naturelle, civile et géogr. de l'Orénoque. Trad. par Eidous. 3 vols. Avignon, 1758.

Hallam, H. View on the State of Europe during the Middle Ages. 4th ed. 3 vols. London, 1878.

Hawkesworth, J. An Account of the Voyages undertaken by the Order of His Majesty for making Discoveries in the Southern Hemisphere, and successively performed by Byron, Carteret, Wallis, and Cook. 3 vols. London, 1773.

Haxthausen, A. v. Transkaukasia. Leipzig, 1856.

Hearn, W. E. The Aryan Household. London, 1879.

Hehn, v. Culturpflanzen und Hausthiere in ihrem Uebergang aus Asien. 2 umgearb. Aufl. Berlin, 1874.

Hermann, K. F. Lehrbuch der griechischen Antiquitäten. 4 vols. Heidelberg, 1875-84.

Herodotus. History.

d'Herrera, A. Histoire générale des voyages et conquestes des Castillans, dans les isles et terre firme des Indes Occidentales. Trad. de l'Esp. de la Coste. 2 vols. Paris, 1671.

Heuglin, M. Th. v. Reise nach Abessinien, den Gala-Ländern, Ost-Sudan und Chartum, 1861-62. Jena, 1868.

—— Reise in Nordost-Afrika. Tagebuch eiuer Reise von Chartum nach Abessinien. 1852-53. Gotha, 1857.

—— Reise in Nordost-Afrika. Schilderungen aus der Beni-Amer und Habab. 2 vols. Braunschweig, 1877.

Hodges, W. Travels in India. 1793.

Hornemann, F. Voyage dans l'Afrique Septentrionale. Trad. de l'Anglais par Langles. 2 vols. Paris, 1803.

Huc, M. Souvenirs d'un Voyage dans la Tartarie, le Tibet, et la Chine, 1844-46. 2 vols. Paris, 1850.

Humboldt, A. v., und *Bonpland.* Reise in die Aequinoctialgegenden des Neuen Continents. 6 vols. Stuttgart u. Tübingen, 1815-32.

Hunter, J. D. Manners and Customs of several Indian Tribes located west of the Mississippi. Philadelphia, 1823.

Isert, P. E. Reise nach Guinea. Kopenhagen, 1788.

Johnston. The River Congo. London, 1884.

Jones, C. C. Antiquities of the Southern Indians, particularly of the Georgia Tribes. New York, 1873.

Journal of the Asiatic Society of Bengal.

Journal of the Royal Geographical Society. London.

Kane, P. Wanderings of an Artist among the Indians of North America. London, 1859.

Klaproth. Magasin Asiatique. 2 vols. Paris, 1826.

Klemm, G. Allgemeine Culturgeschichte der Menschheit. 10 vols. Leipzig, 1843-52.

—— Die Frauen. 6 vols. Dresden, 1854.

Knox, R. An Historical Relation of the Island Ceylon. London, 1681.

Kolben, M. P. Beschreibung des Vorgebirges der Guten Hoffnung und derer darauf wohnenden Hottentotten. Frankfurt u. Leipzig, 1745.

Krapf, J. L. Travels, Researches, and Missionary Labours during an Eighteen Years' Residence in Eastern Africa. London, 1860.

Labat. Nouveau voyage aux Isles de l'Amérique. 2 vols. La Haye, 1724.

Lafitau, J. F. Mœurs des·sauvages Amériquains. 2 vols. Paris, 1724.

Latham, R. G. Descriptive Ethnology. 2 vols. London, 1859.

—— Russian and Turk. London, 1878.

Laval, F. P. de. Voyage aux Indes Orientales, Maldives, etc., éd. Duval. Paris, 1679.

Laveleye, E. de. De la propriété et de ses formes primitives. Paris, 1874.

Lecky, W. History of European Morals from Augustus to Charlemagne. 2 vols. 6th ed. London, 1884.

Lejean, G. Voyage eu Abyssinie, exéc. de 1862-64. Paris.

Lenormant, F. Manuel d'histoire ancienne de l'Orient. 3 vols. Paris, 1869.

Lepsius, R. Briefe aus Aegypten, Aethiopien, und der Halbinsel Sinai. Berlin, 1852.

Lery, J. de. Histoire d'un voyage fait en la terre de Brésil. 4th éd. 1600.

Lesson, P. A. Les Polynésiens. 4 vols. Paris, 1880-84.

Le Vaillant. Voyage dans l'intérieur de l'Afrique, 1780-85. Nouv. éd. 2 vols. Lausanne, 1790.

—— Second voyage dans l'intérieur de l'Afrique, 1783-1785. 3 vols. Paris, an III.

Lippert, J. Die Geschichte der Familie. Stuttgart, 1884.

Livingstone, D. Missionary Travels and Researches in South Africa. London, 1857.

—— Narrative of an Expedition to the Zambesi and its Tributaries, 1858-64. London, 1865.

—— The Last Journals. 2 vols. London, 1874.

Lobo, J. Voyage hist. d'Abissinie. Trad. du Portug. par Le Grand. Paris, 1728.

Loebel, J. W. Gregor von Tours und seine Zeit. Leipzig, 1839.

Lubbock, Sir J. The Origin of Civilisation. London, 1882.

—— Prehistoric Times. London, 1872.

Lyall, A. C. Asiatic Studies, Religious and Social. London, 1884.

M'Cann, W. Two Thousand Miles' Ride through the Argentine Provinces. 2 vols. London, 1853.

Maciejowski, W. A. Slawische Rechtsgeschichte. Uebers. von Buss und Naurocki. 4 vols. Stuttgart, 1835-39.

Mackenzie, A. Voyages from Montreal on the River St. Lawrence, through the Continent of North America, to the Frozen and Pacific Oceans, 1789-93. London, 1801.

Mackenzie-Wallace, D. Russia. 2 vols. 3rd ed. London, 1877.

McLennan, D. Studies in Ancient History. London, 1876.

—— The Patriarchal Theory. London, 1885.

Madvig, J. Den romerske Stats Forfatning og Forvaltning. 2 vols. Kjöbenhavn, 1881-82.

Magyar, L. Reisen in Süd-Afrika, 1849-57. Aus d. Ungar. von J. Hunfalvy. Leipzig, 1859.

Maine, H. S. Ancient Law. London, 1861.
—— Early History of Institutions. 4th ed. London, 1885.
—— Early Law and Custom. London, 1883.
—— Village Communities in the East and West. London, 1871.
Manu. Institutes of Hindu Law, or the Ordinances of Manu. Translated by Sir W. Jones, 1869.
Marno, E. Reisen im Gebiete des Blauen und Weissen Nil im ägyptischen Sudan. Wien, 1874.
Marsden, W. The History of Sumatra. 3rd ed. London, 1811.
Martin. An Account of the Natives of the Tonga Islands. 2 vols. London, 1818.
Martius, C. v. Beiträge zur Ethnographie und Sprachenkunde Amerikas, zumal Brasiliens. 2 vols. Leipzig, 1867.
Maurer, G. L. v. Einleitung zur Geschichte der Mark-, Hof-, Dorf-, und Stadt-Verfassung und der öffentlichen Gewalt. München, 1854.
—— Geschichte der Fronhöfe, der Bauernhöfe und der Hofverfassung in Deutschland. 4 vols. Erlangen, 1862-63.
Maximilian, Prinz zu Wied-Neu-Wied. Reise nach Brasilien in den Jahren 1815-17. 2 vols. Frankfurt a. M., 1820.
Mayne, J. D. A Treatise on Hindu Law and Usage. 3rd ed. London, 1883.
Mayne, R. C. Four Years in British Columbia and Vancouver Island. London, 1862.
Meinicke. Die Inseln des Stillen Oceans. 2 vols. Leipzig, 1875-76.
Melville. Typee and Omoo; the Marquesas Islands. London, 1851.
Michaelis, J. D. Mosaisches Recht. 6 vols. Frankfurt a. M., 1776.
Mielziner, B. The Jewish Law of Marriage and Divorce. Cincinnati, 1884.
Mittheilungen der k. k. geogr. Gesellschaft. Wien.
Monatsberichte der Gesellschaft für Erdkunde. Berlin.
Moorcroft and *Trebek.* Travels in the Himalayan Provinces of Hindustan and the Punjab. 2 vols. London, 1841.
Morgan, L. H. Proceedings of the American Academy of Arts and Sciences, Vol. VII. 1865-68.
—— Systems of Consanguinity and Affinity of the Human Family. Smithsonian Contributions to Knowledge, Vol. XVII.
—— Ancient Society. London, 1877.
Müller, Max. Chips from a German Workshop. 4 vols. London, 1867.
—— Lectures on the Origin of Religion. N. ed. London, 1882.
—— Introduction to the Science of Religion. N. ed. London, 1882.
Mungo Park. Travels in the Interior Districts of Africa, 1795-97. London, 1799.
Munzinger, W. Ostafrikanische Studien. Schaffhausen, 1864.
Murray. Forty Years' Mission Work in Polynesia and New Guinea. London, 1876.
Musters, G. C. At Home with the Patagonians. London, 1871.

Nasse, E. Ueber die mittelalterliche Feldgemeinschaft und die Einhegungen d. 16. Jahrh. in England. Bonn, 1869.

Newbold, F. I. Political and Statistical Account of the British Settlements in the Straits of Malacca. 2 vols. London, 1839.

Nind, Scott. Journal of Royal Geographical Society, vol. i. 1832. " Description of the Natives of King George's Sound."

d'Orbigny, A. Voyage dans l'Amérique Méridionale. 6 vols. Paris, 1839.

Pallme, J. Travels in Kordofan. London, 1844.

Paus, H. Samling af gamle norske Love. 3 vols. Kjöbenhavn, 1751.

Percival, R. An Account of the Island of Ceylon. London, 1803.

Perrin, M. Reise durch Hindostan. Uebers. von T. Hell. 2 vols. Leipzig, 1810.

Peschel, O. F. Völkerkunde. 5 ed. Leipzig, 1881.

Petermann's Mittheilungen.

Pinto, Serpa. How I crossed Africa. Translated by Elwes. 2 vols. London, 1881.

Ploss, H. Das Weib in der Natur- u. Völkerkunde. 2 vols. Leipzig, 1885.

—— Das Kind in Brauch u. Sitte der Völker. 2 vols. 2 ed. Leipzig, 1884.

Plutarch. Lives. A. H. Clough. Boston, 1864.

Poiret. Reise in die Barbarey, oder Briefe aus Alt-Numidien, geschr. in d. Jahren 1785-86. 2 vols. Strassburg, 1789.

Poole, F. Queen Charlotte Islands. London, 1872.

Post, A. H. Die Geschlechtsgenossenschaft der Urzeit und die Entstehung der Ehe. Oldenburg, 1875.

Prschwewalski, N. v. Reisen in der Mongolei. Aus d. Russ. von Kohn. Jena, 1877.

Quatrefages, A. de. Hommes fossiles et hommes sauvages. Paris, 1884.

Raffenel, A. Voyage dans l'Afrique Occidentale. Paris, 1846.

Rienzi, D. de. Océanie. 3 vols. Paris, 1837.

Rochefort. Histoire naturelle et morale des Isles Antilles de l'Amérique. 2nd éd. Rotterdam, 1665.

Roepell, R. Geschichte Polens. Hamburg, 1840.

Ross, J. Entdeckungsreise um Baffins-Bay. Ausg. Nemnich. Leipzig, 1820.

—— Narrative of a Second Voyage in search of a North-West Passage. London, 1835.

Rusden, G. W. History of Australia. 3 vols. London, 1883.

Russell, J. Journal of a Tour in Ceylon and India. London, 1852.

Sandys, E. Consuetudines Kanciae: a History of Gavelkind. London, 1851.

Schirren, C. Die Wandersagen der Neu-Seeländer und der Maui-Mythos. Riga, 1856.

Schmidt, K. Jus Primae Noctis. Freiburg, 1881.

Schomburgk, R. Reisen in Britisch-Guiana, 1840-44. 2 vols. Leipzig, 1847-48.

Schoolcraft, H. R. History, Condition, and Prospects of the Indian Tribes of the United States. 6 vols.

Schrader, O. Sprachvergleichung und Urgeschichte. Jena, 1883.

Schweinfurth, G. Im Herzen von Afrika. Reisen und Entdeckungen. 2 vols. Leipzig, 1874.

Selden. De jure naturali et gentium. 1665.

Shaw, T. Voyages dans plusieurs provinces de la Barbarie et du Levant. Trad. de l'Angl. 2 vols. La Haye, 1743.

Sirr, H. C. China and the Chinese: their Religion, Character, Customs, and Manufactures. 2 vols. London, 1849.

Skene, W. F. The Highlanders of Scotland. 2 vols. London, 1837.

Smith, E. R. The Araucanians. New York, 1855.

Smith, T. Narrative of a Five Years' Residence at Nepaul. 2 vols. London, 1852.

Snow, W. Parker. A Two Years' Cruise off Tierra del Fuego, the Falkland Islands. Patagonia, and in the River Plata. 2 vols. London, 1857.

Sonnerat. Voyage aux Indes Orientales et à la Chine. 2 vols. Paris, 1782.

Spencer, H. The Principles of Sociology, 5th ed. London, 1876.

—— Descriptive Sociology.

Spiegel, F. Eranische Alterthumskunde. 3 vols. Leipzig, 1871.

Spix, J. B. v., und C. F. P. v. Martius. Reise in Brasilien, 1817-20. 3 vols. München, 1823.

Sprengel, M. C. Auswahl der besten Nachrichten zur Länder und Völkerkunde. 14 vols. Halle, 1794-1800.

Stemann, C. L. E. Den danske Retshistorie indtil Christian d. 5tes Lov. Kjöbenhavn, 1871.

Strabo. The Geography of Strabo. Translated by H. C. Hamilton and Rev. W. Falconer. 1854.

Tacitus. Germany and its Tribes. Translated by A. J. Church. 1868.

Terry, E. A Voyage to East India. 1777.

Tertre, Du. Histoire generale des Antilles habitées par les Français. 4 vols. Paris, 1667-69.

Thompson. The Story of New Zealand. 2 vols. London, 1859.

Turner, S. An Account of an Embassy to the Court of the Teshoo Lama, in Tibet. London, 1800.

Tylor, E. B. Anthropology. London, 1881.

—— Primitive Culture. 2 vols. London, 1871.

—— Researches into the Early History of Mankind, and the Development of Civilization. London, 1878.

Unger, J. Die Ehe in ihrer welthistorischen Entwickelung. Wien, 1850.

Vámbéry, H. Geschichte Bocharas od. Transoxaniens. 2 vols. Stuttgart, 1872.

Varigny. Quatorze ans aux Îles Sandwich. Paris, 1874.

Venegas, M. A Natural and Civil History of California. Translated from the Spanish. 2 vols. London, 1759.

Vogel, J. W. Zehnjährige Ost-Indianische Reise-Beschreibung. Altenburg, 1704.

Waitz, T. Anthropologie der Naturvölker. 6 vols. Leipzig.
Wallace. Malayan Archipelago. 2 vols. London, 1869.
—— Travels on the Amazon. London.
Weinhold, K. Die deutschen Frauen in dem Mittelalter. Wien, 1851.
Wilken, G. A. Das Matriarchat bei den alten Arabern. Aus d. Holl. Leipzig. 1884.
Wilkes, C. Narrative of the United States' Exploring Expedition, 1838–42. 5 vols. Philadelphia, 1849.
Wilks, Mark. Historical Sketches of the South of India. 3 vols. London, 1810.
Williams, T., and *Calvert, J.* Fiji and the Fijians. Ed. Rowe. London, 1870.
Winterbottom, T. An Account of the Native Africans in the Neighbourhood of Sierra Leone. 2 vols. London, 1803.
Wood, J. A Personal Narrative of a Journey to the Source of the River Oxus. London, 1841.

Zeitschrift für Völkerpsychologie und Sprachwissenschaft.
Zimmer, H. Altindisches Leben. Berlin, 1879.

INDEX.

www.ingramcontent.com/pod-product-compliance
Lightning Source LLC
Chambersburg PA
CBHW021125270326

41929CB00009B/1043